Diversification to a degree

European University Studies
Europäische Hochschulschriften
Publications Universitaires Européennes

Series XI
Education

Reihe XI Série XI
Pädagogik
Pédagogie

Vol./Band 994

PETER LANG
Bern · Berlin · Bruxelles · Frankfurt am Main · New York · Oxford · Wien

Kai Yu

Diversification to a degree

An exploratory study of students' experience at four higher education institutions in China

PETER LANG
Bern · Berlin · Bruxelles · Frankfurt am Main · New York · Oxford · Wien

Bibliographic information published by Die Deutsche Nationalbibliothek
Die Deutsche Nationalbibliothek lists this publication in the Deutsche Nationalbibliografie; detailed bibliographic data is available on the Internet at ‹http://dnb.d-nb.de›.

British Library and Library of Congress Cataloguing-in-Publication Data:
A catalogue record for this book is available from *The British Library*, Great Britain

Library of Congress Cataloging-in-Publication Data

Yu, Kai.
Diversification to a degree : an exploratory study of students' experience at four higher education institutions in China / Kai Yu.
p. cm. -- (European university studies. Series XI, Education, ISSN 0531-7398 ; v. 994 = Europäische Hochschulschriften. Reihe XI, Pädagogik ; Bd. 994)
Includes bibliographical references.
ISBN 978-3-0343-0365-1 (alk. paper)
1. College students--China--Case studies.
2. Education, Higher--China--Case studies. I. Title.
LA1133.7.Y83 2010
378.1'980951--dc22
2010001810

ISSN 0531-7398
ISBN 978-3-0343-0365-1

Printed in Switzerland

Preface

This research is an exploratory study of students' experience at four higher education institutions (HEIs) in a city in southeast China, conducted during 2006–2009. The four institutions differ from each other in their history, structure, size, type and location of campus, student intake and programme provision. They are referred to in the study as: Public University, Private College, Independent College and Public College. The study explores differences and similarities between these higher education institutions and offers potential explanations for them.

The study employs a mixed-method approach, and the data sources consist of a survey, focus group meetings with students, interviews with senior managers at the HEIs and field experts and analysis of public and institutional documents. The data were collected with a sample of students: namely, those in their third year (of four-year courses), and those studying in two *Benke* (broadly equivalent to BA degrees) undergraduate disciplines, namely Engineering and Languages. All of the students in the sample were school leavers who had taken the standard route of national admissions examinations into higher education study, or so-called *Tongzhao Benke* students.

The study found that certain types of diversification, namely institutional diversification (in terms of institutional type, ownership and programmes offered) and constituential diversification (in terms of the characteristics of the students, such as prior attainment and socio-economic background), were confirmed. However, the empirical data revealed that the diversity of the student experience of higher education was minimal, as the students' reported student experience was similar across the four institutions. Indeed, the more significant differences were found between disciplines in the same institution rather than between institutions.

The study explores potential reasons for this, including the patterns of institutional convergence, driven in part by the governmental regulatory framework; the forces of competition, driven in part by the perceived hierarchy of reputation of institutions, which may lead to new institutions imitating more established institutions; the use of retired teaching staff from older institutions at the newly-created institutions; and the arguably conservative and tradition-oriented nature of Chinese society in general, and attitudes to education in particular.

The study contributes to the field by providing data on the student experience in higher education in China (an under-researched perspective in the Chinese context), and also by offering an examination of the usefulness and limitations of student experience surveys. The study concludes with a discussion of its implications for policy, and suggestions for future research.

With deepest regard, I would like to thank many people who were instrumental in making this study a reality. I am extremely grateful to Dr. Hubert Ertl, for his many years of mentoring and serving as my adviser, and for his invaluable inspiration and guidance in making this research possible. I have been very fortunate to have such an outstanding mentor and friend.

I am also indebted to many people who have given their time and assistance. At the Department of Education, University of Oxford, Professor Ingrid Lunt, Dr. Geoff Hayward, Dr. Colin Brock and Dr. David Mills all made time in their busy schedules to provide helpful insight into the planning, implementation, and completion of this research. A special note of thanks goes to Dr. Stephanie Wilde for reading of this study and for her invaluable comments. During my stay as a visiting doctoral student at the Institute of Education, Xiamen University, Professor Wu Daguang, Professor Pan Maoyuan, Professor Shi Qiuheng and Professor Fan Yihong provided tremendous support and shared with me their invaluable expertise on the higher education issues addressed in this study.

I would like to thank the four institutions in this study which gave me the wonderful opportunity to conduct research. I would like to express my gratitude to the students, teachers, administrators, and topic experts, who must remain nameless, but who gave time out of their busy schedules to participate in the survey, focus groups, and interviews. I am extremely grateful for the generosity of these people in sharing their perspectives; I could not have asked for a better group of subjects. I am grateful to the contacts at the four institutions for their assistance in preparing the sample of people for research, in arranging the survey and interviews, and for their advice generally. However, the responsibility for the study, and for any errors in the text, remains with the author.

Kai Yu

Table of Contents

List of Tables

List of Figures

Glossary

Banzhuren	Class director. A pastoral advisor to the students in higher education.
Benke	The academic track in undergraduate education, usually leading to the Bachelor's degree qualification.
Chengren Gaokao	National admissions examinations for adult learners entering adult higher education institutions.
Duli Xueyuan	Independent college, a joint venture institution established by a public university or college and a private investor.
Gaokao	National admissions examinations for higher education. There are two main types (*Putong* and *Chengren Gaokao*), but this term usually refers to *Putong Gaokao*, which is the type of *Gaokao* that leads to admission to *Putong*, or regular, higher education institutions. See also *Chengren Gaokao*, *Putong Gaokao* and *Gaokao Yimin*.
Gaokao Yimin	Examination migration: people moving to regions with lower admission requirements to take *Gaokao* examination in order to improve their chances of access to higher education.
Gongban Daxue	Public university.
Gongban Xueyuan	Public college.
Keju	Imperial Examinations.
Like	Science track in the high school curriculum.
Minban	Private institutions, literally meaning "run by the people".
Muxiao	Literally "mother institution". For independent colleges, this refers to the public university or college under the auspices of which they have been established.
Minban Xueyuan	Private college.
Putong	Literally "regular". It refers to institutions offering full-time, on-campus, state-recognised undergraduate programmes. This excludes distance learning, adult education, and some special institutions.
Putong Gaokao	National Examinations for Admission to Regular Higher Education Institutions. The standard route to higher education for traditional students.

Shijian Ke	Practical classes. It refers to modules or classes with significant practical elements.
Sili	Refers to private institutions, literally meaning "privately established".
Tongzhao	The national admission process for higher education.
Tongzhao Benke	*Benke* programmes that admit students through the national admission process for higher education.
Wanzixi	Evening self-study sessions.
Wenke	Arts track in the high school curriculum.
Wenpin Kaoshi	Diploma tests.
Xuanxiu Ke	Optional modules. These are usually not directly relevant to the academic knowledge of the specific subject, but carry some credits that can be counted towards the total credits required for the subject programme.
Zhuanke	The vocational track in undergraduate education, usually leading to the Vocational Diploma qualification.
Zixue Kaoshi	National Self-Study Examinations for Higher Education, leading to *Benke* or *Zhuanke* qualifications; the entry and learning process are more flexible than *Tongzhao Benke* or *Zhuanke*, but are in general less recognised.

Note: All translations from the Chinese in this study have been undertaken by the researcher.

Chapter One

Introduction

Introduction

The Chinese higher education system has experienced a dramatic expansion in student numbers since 1998 and has seen the mushrooming of several new types of degree-granting institutions. In a very short period of time, these new institutions have developed into a primary provider of higher education in China. However, there has been very little empirical research into their students' experiences or the similarities and differences among different types of institutions.

The experiences of students in higher education have become an area of rapidly growing interest for higher education stakeholders internationally. In recent decades, many universities have become more attentive to students' experiences. This has happened against the backdrop of an explosion of interested stakeholders, including policymakers, who need to allocate funds efficiently; the general public, which is increasingly interested in higher education's accountability; students and their parents who want to make informed choices regarding institutions; and university administrators, who need to monitor institutional performance.

This study is located within the Chinese context of a fast-growing and increasingly diverse higher education system that has recently gone through, and is still experiencing, profound changes in institutional patterns, as well as the largest expansion in terms of absolute student numbers ever seen in the international higher education community (Zhou, 2006).

The Chinese system of higher education has experienced unprecedented expansion since 1998. The number of student entrants to

Putong (Regular) higher education institutions in China increased from one million in 1998 to six million in 2008, and this is anticipated to rise further. In order to accommodate the increasing demand for higher education, several new types of degree-granting institutions have been created. For instance, since 2000 over three hundred new independent institutions have been created, 172 existing public and private vocational colleges have been promoted to the *Benke* level (the Bachelor's level, see the chapter on *Higher Education in China* for further explanation), and dozens of existing public *Benke* colleges have been granted university status (Ministry of Education, 1978–2009).

The rapid enrolment expansion in China was not accompanied by an increase in governmental contributions to individual higher education institutions (HEIs). Since 1997, the financial burden has shifted increasingly from the government to the institutions themselves and, ultimately, to students. Further, with China's aspirations to achieve world-class status in higher education, most of the government's quality enhancement projects and funding since 1997 have not been targeted at teaching, but at research in key universities and key disciplines (Hong, 2007; Min, 2004; OECD, 2003b). Therefore, the question arises of how the unprecedented increase of students, combined with the decline in funding, will affect the Chinese higher education system.

Trow (2005) points out, with reference to other countries, that the expansion of student numbers always leads to the diversification of the higher education sector, in which students from a broad range of educational and social backgrounds undertake diverse kinds of study in diverse institutions. He also suggests that diversification leads to more variation in terms of teaching approaches, curricula modes and staff-student interactions. However, there is very little empirical research, in the Chinese context, on how far these dimensions of diversity have affected the higher education sector, or to what degree they have resulted in a diverse student experience.

In terms of diversity of study routes in undergraduate education, there are two distinct tracks to *Putong* higher education in China, namely, the *Benke* track (for the Bachelor's degree) and the *Zhuanke* track (for the vocational diploma). Furthermore, as a result of the expansion, the Chinese higher education system has become a complex enterprise comprising various different types of institutions which offer these study tracks. The university status – college status distinction is long established, but the distinction according to ownership is a much more recent phenomenon. In China, higher education institutions that can enrol *Benke* students can be categorised into four groups by status and ownership: *Gongban Daxue* (Public University), *Gongban Xueyuan* (Public College), *Minban Xueyuan* (Private College), and *Duli Xueyuan* (Independent College, i.e., privately funded college under the umbrella of a public institution). The four purposefully selected institutions in this study differ in terms of ownership and status.

Analysis of the mission statements and enrolment catalogues of the *Benke* institutions in this study reveals that, although *Benke* is designed to be the academic segment of higher education, in contrast to the vocational *Zhuanke* segment, the *Benke* segment is becoming more diverse. The new *Benke* institutions tend to aim to provide a more vocationally-oriented education that emphasises the practicality and application of what is taught, whereas the more-established and more prestigious institutions emphasise the cultivation of academic ability and pay more attention to research.

However, evidence collected for this study through focus groups with students and teachers, and interviews with institutional managers and researchers, indicated two contradictory trends. On the one hand, the creation of new institutions and the introduction of new institutional types provide diversity at the system level. On the other hand, diversity at the system level is threatened by so-called "academic drift" and "vocational drift" (see the chapter on *Diversity in Higher Education* for explanation). The data collected for this study show that the anecdotal and informal association of quality and excellence with public ownership and prestige reinforces the superior status of public research-intensive universities. As a result there is an inevitable temptation for the less prestigious institutions to seek to raise their standing by copying prestigious institutions – for example, for newer institutions to imitate traditional institutions, and for private institutions to imitate public institutions. At the same time, traditional institutions are also likely to come under pressure to become more concerned with the demands of students and industry (Codling & Meek, 2006; Huisman, 1995; Marginson & Considine, 2000; Meek et al., 1996; Perellon, 2003).

By examining students' backgrounds and their perceptions of their learning environment, it is possible to discover whether the diversification of institutional types has resulted in the diversification of the student population and their experiences. Understanding students' experiences in higher education is essential for developing the educational system. With its educational, social, and political implications, research on student experiences has increased (Ertl et al., 2008).

This study assesses the diversity in Chinese higher education. Does the systematic and structural diversity of higher education institutions affect the composition of the student body and the experience of students? Put another way, this study is not only interested in the diversity created by different types of institutions at the systemic level, but in what this systemic and structural diversity means for the students. The main research theme of this study is to gain insight into the student experience in Chinese higher education, which has not yet been the subject of empirical research studies.

This study aims to answer these questions through a study of four institutions located in a city in southeast China. This research chooses to use a mixed-methods approach (Axinn & Pearce, 2006; Bryman, 2004, 2006; Tashakkori & Teddlie, 1998), and specifically, a qualitative-quantitative-qualitative design, which utilises documentary analysis, focus groups with students, interviews with senior managers, and a large-scale survey as data sources, to contribute to a deeper understanding of the research problem.

Statement of the Problem

Across China, the quality of the student experience in higher education has become an area of growing concern. An Asia Times news article, entitled *Chinese Higher Education Fails the Test*, reported that the results of an opinion poll listed higher education as one of the three major targets of growing public discontent, the other two being health care and housing (Hartmann, 2006). Further, an Internet poll of the general public reported a remarkable 68.9% dissatisfaction rate concerning the quality of higher education, with only 4.3% people reporting high satisfaction. The most important reasons for this dissatisfaction were "decline in quality" and "graduates' lack of employability" (21st Century Education Development Research Institute, 2005). Headlines similar to this abound in the popular press, suggesting that the Chinese public is experiencing a crisis of confidence in higher education.

Researchers in the field argue that developing future quality assurance in higher education must involve students in the process (Donald & Denison, 2001; Ginns, Prosser, & Barrie, 2007; Ramsden, 1986). As higher education's principal stakeholders and direct participants, students' opinions should be given considerable weight in the new quality assurance process. They were not given input in the more traditional quality assurance methods (Harvey, 2003; Harvey & Green, 1993). Professor Pan, a respected Chinese higher education expert who established the first higher education research institute in China in 1978, argues that assessment of students' opinions toward their experience and expectations in higher education in the country is needed in the context of the huge increase in students and institutions, and the introduction and then increase of tuition fees in China (Hong, 2007). Despite the fact that student experience studies have been conducted in the US and Australia for many years, it is a subject that has been remarkably under-researched in China.

The practice of student evaluations started in American universities in the 1920s (Centra, 1973). Evaluating the much respected teacher, however, is not common practice in China (Yang, 2005; Zhao & Zhu, 2007), as teachers are traditionally regarded as the authorities on the subject of teaching, and students are expected to respect and follow their teachers rather than challenge or comment on them. Studies on student evaluations only began to appear in China from the 1990s, and there are even fewer studies that attempt to collect and analyse data about the student experience nationally.

In addition to *Gongban* (Public) higher education institutions, two other types of institutions, namely *Minban* (Private) and *Duli* (Independent) emerged as a phenomenon in the 1980s and 2000, respectively, and are developing rapidly. As teaching and learning occur in the institutional context, the differing cultures of public, private and independent institutions in institutional administration and institutional climate may influence students' learning experience. Despite the private and independent institutions now taking a large stake in higher education in China, very little is known about their students and how they experience the educational process. It is of interest, therefore, to compare the different types of institutions in terms of their students' experience.

In China, there is currently no significant national database of student experience. In fact, a search for studies using the key words "student experience" and "higher education" and "university" found no exact matches in the China National Knowledge Infrastructure (CNKI) indices of journals and dissertations. Most of the descriptions of students' experiences in higher education in China come from journalistic sources, which usually present an outsider's point of view and are based on partial and limited information. The absence of systematic research data does not allow the research community to comprehensively analyse student experience and perspectives in higher education.

Research Questions

In this context, the current study aims to answer the following overarching research question:

> What is the impact of the diversification of higher education institutions on students and their experiences in China?

More specifically, this study is guided by the following subsidiary questions:

1. Who studies at which type of higher education institution? What are students' social, economic, and academic backgrounds?
2. What are students' motivations for higher education study at different institutions?
3. What are students' experiences of the learning environment at different institutions? What can the institutions do to improve students' learning experiences?
4. How can the similarities and differences found in the students' experiences at different institutions be explained?

The notion of a learning environment is broad and complex, and there is no simple definition of the term. As will be discussed in the chapter on *Student Experience in Higher Education*, attempts to articulate a definition have been made by various authors, but these have not proven to be adequate. Specifically, this study is interested in the following elements of the students' experiences in the learning environment (Q3):

- The students' perceptions of their programme's structure and organisation
- The students' perceptions of teaching in their programme
- The students' perceptions of the available learning resources
- The students' perceptions of the areas of educational emphasis
- The students' self-evaluation and approaches to learning
- The students' overall experience with their programme and institution

Significance and Contribution of the Study

The fact that the number of *Benke* institutions and students is increasing, and the *Benke* sector is diversifying, highlights the significance of investigating and comparing *Benke* education offered at different institutions in China. Levy (1999) argues that a key question to ask when observing rapid change in institutional configuration is what difference it makes. The changes in the Chinese higher education system are so rapid that few pieces of research have been able to track them, let alone understand the difference the changes have made. A review of the literature shows that, up to this point, hardly anything has been written on the students' experiences of teaching and learning in different types of institutions in China.

Without a robust and up-to-date picture of the similarities and differences between students and their experiences at *Benke* institutions, extensive studies cannot be conducted to understand even the basic differences between institutions, let alone to identify ways of strengthening the present provision of education. Therefore, it is essential to collect and compare such data.

One of the fundamental difficulties in empirically measuring institutional diversity lies in the selection of variables, as diversity means different things to different interest groups and therefore can be measured from many different perspectives (Codling & Meek, 2006). In both Western and Chinese literature, most of what has been written about institutional diversity is based on broad and highly visible institutional parameters, such as programme level, institutional missions, research intensity, or sources of income. These variables may be meaningful and appropriate for the government perspective, as governments are mainly interested in the higher education system as a whole, and are concerned with varieties of institutional types within the system (Codling & Meek, 2006). This study's methodology makes an original contribution to the literature in that it looks at the students' actual experiences in order to examine the diversity of institutions.

Students offer a particular insight into the higher education system. However, students as primary stakeholders in higher education are often under-represented and their viewpoints appear to be lost or undervalued. There is a lack of systematic knowledge on almost every dimension of student experience at Chinese higher education institutions. Giving attention to students' experiences is valuable not only because students are direct participants in education, but also because focusing on the student experience provides a unique way to explore the diversification of higher education, and focusing on the student experience has many advantages over other perspectives. For example, institutional statements about programme aims and objectives are often merely written prescriptions of what should happen rather than accurate representations of what actually happens (Stenhouse, 1975). Therefore, examining the direct participants' experiences allows the study to investigate to what extent diversity at the system and institutional levels has resulted in pragmatic differences for students.

Limitations

The findings and conclusions of this study are limited to selected aspects of the overall student experience, since it is hardly possible to gain a sense of the totality of the student experience. However, the qualitative, open-ended questions provide an opportunity for the participants to further discuss their opinions.

This research was conducted with a sample of students in four institutions in one single province. Although the four institutions chosen are fairly representative in their categories, and the generalisability of this study is expected to be much greater than that of the single-case studies or reports in the existing literature in China, care should be taken not to over-generalise the findings from the study. It should be emphasised that China is a large and diverse country, and there are large variations in economic and educational capacity across provinces (Aguignier, 1988; Li, 1991).

In spite of the limitations of this study, it captures the views of those who responded and represents the largest survey of its kind to be conducted with Chinese students. It provides a more comprehensive and complete report of the student experience than is currently available.

Outline Structure of the Study

Chapter Two, *Higher Education in China*, outlines the background and the context of the study. This chapter provides a brief history of higher education in China and introduces the educational values that people in China hold. It then explores the diversities in the higher education system in China, including the diversities in higher education qualifications, institutional ownership, jurisdiction and prestige. It also introduces certain characteristics of the system, including national examinations, enrolment quotas, tuition fees, which are relevant to the analysis of results in later chapters.

Chapters Three and Four, *Diversity in Higher Education* and *Student Experience in Higher Education*, discuss the notions of diversity and student experience, and critically review the relevant literature. The *Diversity in Higher Education* chapter discusses the concept of higher education diversification, reviews and compares the rationales for and against diversity in higher education, examines binary and unitary higher education systems in operation in certain countries, explores the reasons for institutional convergence and academic and vocational drift, and discusses the relationship between diversity and quality. It also looks at the international literature that compares the characteristics of public and private higher education institutions. Finally, it reviews the literature on the effects of diversity on students.

The *Student Experience in Higher Education* chapter looks at the research on students' experiences. First, the chapter identifies the scope and definition of student experience, and then it examines the relevant theories. The purpose, methodology, and results of several large-scale and influential student experience studies, including the National Student Survey, the Course Experience Questionnaire, and the National Survey of Student Engagement are reviewed. It also reviews the literature that examines the learning characteristics of Chinese students, including the literature on the "Paradox of the Chinese Learner." Based on a critical review of existing studies and knowledge of the context of this study, a conceptual framework for the investigation of this study's research problem is developed.

Chapter Five, *Methodology*, presents the methodology employed to implement this research. It outlines the research framework and the rationales behind it (the qualitative-quantitative-qualitative strategy). The chapter also justifies the sampling of institutional and student samples, and compares the four selected institutions in terms of their mission, student number, campus size and age, tuition fees, and history. It then describes the design and the development of the survey and interview instruments in detail. The chapter also gives an account of ethical considerations, data collection method, analysis, and reporting.

Chapter Six, *Findings*, presents the findings from the data sources, including the student survey; interviews with students, teachers and managerial personnel; official statements and statistics, and then triangulates the data from different sources for analysis.

The *Conclusions* chapter first summarises the findings of this research and provides answers to the research questions. It then discusses the implications of the findings for diversity and student experience, both in China and internationally. Many of the results found have significance for the development of higher education in China, including diversity and equity of access, diversity and educational quality, the merits and the limitations of student experience as a tool for measuring and improving teaching quality, and approaches for improving the student experience. The study ends with recommendations for practice and future research. Recommendations for higher education institutions, government authorities, researchers and students are discussed.

Chapter Two

Higher Education in China

Introduction

This chapter describes the higher education context of this research. It provides an overview of the social and economic context in China and of the fieldwork base of the city. After briefly reviewing the social and economic changes in China since 1978 that have helped to shape the higher education system in China, it examines the higher education system, including its traditional values, its structure and its developments. This research is embedded within the discussions and information in this chapter, and they are crucial in informing the interpretation, analysis, and implications of the findings.

In constitutional terms, the political state of the People's Republic of China (PRC) comprises under its jurisdiction mainland China, self-governed Hong Kong and Macau Special Administrative Regions (SARs) and Taiwan. Because each of the aforementioned regions in China operates an independent system of higher education, for ease of expression, unless otherwise specified, the term "China" throughout this study refers specifically to mainland China.

A Brief History: Pre-1978

China's education system dates back some 3,000 years. The traditional educational system went through an uninterrupted course of development, despite numerous upheavals, during its imperial history. The contemporary Chinese higher education system is, however, based on the Western model that was first brought to China in the late 19th century (Zhou, 2006).

China's education system can be traced back to the Zhou Dynasty (1046–256BC), when the education system comprised both governmental and private colleges and schools. Many eminent thinkers established private schools during this period, most notably Confucius, who formulated comprehensive theories on politics, philosophy, ethics and education. His teachings, known collectively as Confucianism, have charted the course for the development of Chinese culture, and continue to have a profound impact on China and many other Asian countries today (Zhou, 2006).

The purpose of higher education in imperial China was primarily for producing civil servants and senior scholars. The imperial civil examination system *(Keju)*, which had a major influence on China's way of cultivating and selecting governors, was founded in 587 in the Sui Dynasty (581–618AD), and lasted for more than 1,300 years, until its demise during the last feudal dynasty of China.

Teachings based on Confucianism were the core of the curricula and syllabi of almost all schools. Confucianism attaches major importance to moral education and maintains that the fundamental purpose of education is to equip people with moral integrity and enhance people's sense of benevolence. At the same time, education in science and technology as a whole was weak and often neglected.

After consecutive defeats in the Opium Wars (1839–42 and 1856–60) and the Sino-Japanese War (1894–95), China was humiliated by the ensuing invasions by Western and Japanese powers, and the country was gradually reduced to a semi-colonial and semi-feudal society. The consecutive defeats delivered a fatal blow to the imperial Qing Dynasty and the Chinese classical tradition; they also demonstrated China's backwardness in terms of its science and technology development and the country's traditional higher education system (Fairbank & Reischauer, 1978).

In an attempt to strengthen the country, highly placed bureaucrats and scholarly officials advocated assimilating Western experiences, including learning Western military technologies, launching modern industry and Western-style schools, and sending students to study abroad. The first government-run modern college, the Metropolitan University of the Capital City (the predecessor of Peking University), was established in 1898 and sowed the seeds for China's contemporary higher education system (Zhou, 2006). The thirteen-centuries-old imperial civil examination system was also abolished by the Qing Dynasty in 1905 (Miyazaki, 1976), when the last Chinese empire was in its final throes, prior to its end in 1912.

Although the country suffered greatly as it went through periods of civil war and conflict with foreign powers and warlords, in the late 19th century and the early 20th century a new higher education system was developed under the influence of Western educational philosophies (Bastid, 1987; Ministry of Education, 2004). By 1947, China had established 207 universities. These included 107 governmental institutions, 79 private institutions, and 21 missionary institutions. The size of the student body was about 150,000 (Zhou, 2006).

The victory of Communists in the civil war and the ensuing founding of the People's Republic of China (PRC) in 1949 marked a turning point for the nation and its higher education system. In December 1949, the PRC central government convened the First National Work Conference on Education to discuss how to reform the educational system and develop a new one. The conference stated clearly that the country would be "drawing upon the experience of the Soviet Union to develop education" (Zhou, 2006, p. 6).

The new regime followed the philosophy and practices of the Soviet Union in many respects. Bian (1994) and Luo et al. (2001) summarise a number of the essential elements of China's Soviet-style management system at that time, all of which were applicable to the higher education system.

First, there was the predominance of public ownership. During the first decade of the PRC, private ownership was largely eliminated; all essential firms in the private sector were turned over to the state. The PRC government rejected the previous ownership system of higher education, and gained control over all the higher education institutions left by the previous government, and by private and missionary bodies.

Second, there was the central planning system. The essential feature of this system was the centralisation of economic decision-making. Organisations were to follow the state's unified plans strictly. Managers were deprived of autonomy. The prices of their products were determined by pricing authorities and the circulation of the products was controlled by governmental agencies. Every function of higher education, from admission of students to curriculum and instruction to the allocation of jobs to students, were all determined according to the central plan, as demonstrated in the following figure:

Figure 1. The central planning process

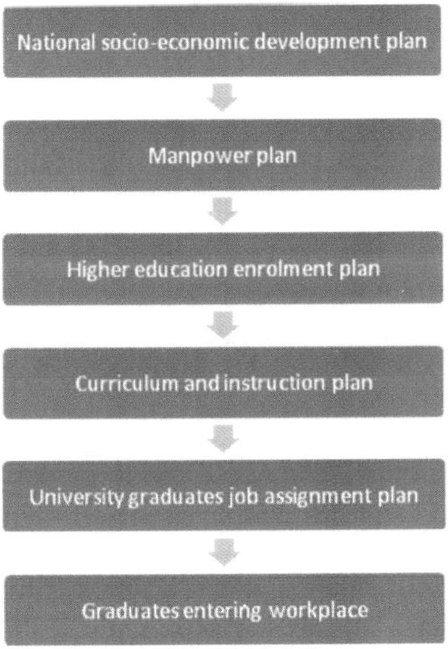

Source: Adapted from Min (2002, p. 6).

Third, there was the vertical command hierarchy. The centrally planned economy was controlled by a vertical or ministerial authority line. Organisations at all levels of the hierarchy were assigned bureaucratic ranks, which defined their power and authority within and across administrative boundaries, and consequently the power and authority of the individuals who headed them. Leaders of higher education institutions were governmental bureaucrats appointed by the relevant authority and assigned bureaucratic ranks. Government ministries responsible for such functions as transport, agriculture, and health created their own specialised universities for the manpower needs of their sector, and provinces operated institutions for their local needs.

Finally, there was the politicisation of management. The Communist Party had a parallel hierarchy structure within each organisation, centrally and locally. The Party leader of an organisation was considered to be superior to the executive leader of that organisation, and it was not unusual for that the two positions to be held by the same person. Higher education institutions were also led by the Party.

Also at this time, the *Gaokao* (National Examinations for Admission to Higher Education Institutions) system was introduced, faculty pay scales were fixed, jobs were directly assigned by the institutions to specific industries, and higher education was offered free to students.

The higher education system at this time could be characterised as an integral part of the highly centralised planned economy. Central ministries and local governments each ran their own universities under a unified central plan; therefore, higher education institutions became departmentalised, segmented and specialised (Bai, 2006). By 1957, there were 229 institutions of higher education, including 17 multi-disciplinary (comprehensive) universities, 44 industrial institutions, 58 normal institutions, 37 medical institutions, 31 institutes of agronomy and forestry, 8 institutes of languages, 5 institutions of finance and economics, 5 institutions of political science and law, 6 sports institutes, 17 arts institutions, and one special-purpose college (Zhou, 2006).

The development of the Chinese economy and higher education system was severely disrupted by the Cultural Revolution (1966-1976). During that decade, teaching and schooling were interrupted, and higher education enrolment was suspended for a number of years.

When enrolment was restored in 1972, the *Gaokao* was not resumed at the same time. During this period students were enrolled based on their family background, political loyalty and work performance. As a result, many people who could not even read a word became university students (Deng & Treiman, 1997; L. Li, 2004; Qing, 2005).

A Brief History: Post-1978

After the end of the Cultural Revolution, the reformist wing of the Party led by Deng Xiaoping launched the so-called "Reform and Open-door" policy, which was another turning point for the nation and its higher education system. At the macro-level, the reform was intended to replace direct control by the government with indirect control through the introduction of market mechanisms, while the open-door policy was to open China to the outside world in order to enable participation in the international economy.

The policy started a new phase in the development of higher education in China. The *Gaokao* was restored in the same year, marking the return from political criteria to academic criteria for admission to higher education. The policies of earlier years resumed – students were assigned to specific higher education institutions and programmes by the government, based on *Gaokao* scores; graduates were assigned by government to lifetime jobs based on performance and social and economic needs; and the specialised nature of higher education continued (Mohrman, 2003).

In the 1980s, China moved toward a "market economy with socialist characteristics" (Zhou, 2006). This dramatic reorientation led to reforms in many different segments of society, and higher education was no exception. The government showed its intention to reduce state control of higher education: existing institutions were allowed independent governance to some degree, and non-state-run higher education institutions have since emerged (Chan & Mok, 2001; Mok, 2001).

The higher education reforms in the 1990s could be characterised as similar to those in other parts of the world, that is, the marketisation of higher education, and greater emphasis on efficiency, competition and accountability (Bai, 2006). Notably, a number of educational reforms focused on the fourth of Deng Xiaoping's Four Modernisations – the advancement of science and technology, a priority that continues to the present day (Mohrman, 2003).

In 1993 the Chinese Communist Party Central Committee and the State Council's *Mission Outline for Education Reform and Development in China* reaffirmed decentralisation and encouraged social organisations and citizens to establish schools. The document called for less administrative interference, termination the allocation of jobs to graduates and the growth of private institutions. A "user-pays" system was also implemented (Bai, 1998; Chenery & Company, 2006).

In 1995, the government initiated the "211" plan, aimed at strengthening 100 of the most prestigious institutions in China and certain key fields of study. Extra funds (in addition to the normal funding given by the governing ministries and provinces) were provided to these institutions through the project. In 1998, the "985" plan was introduced as a further expansion of the "211" plan, with the aim of building a number of "world-class" and "world-renowned" universities. These two projects have given the universities involved a high status nationally, and the funds provided have helped improve their quality and reputation. The much-debated World University Rankings 2005, published by the *Times Higher Education Supplement*, placed Peking University 15th in the table, the highest ranked Asian institution (Ince, 2005). However, due to lack of confidence in Chinese institutions, the public in China in fact viewed Peking University's highly placed position in the ranking quite negatively, with many people suspecting that the university received the position through bribes and even regarded this as a "shame" for the country (Xinhuanet, 2005). Unlike institutions in other countries which usually publicise their high-ranking positions, Peking University kept a very low profile on this matter and did not comment on or even mention this ranking publicly. The university has slid down the rankings since 2005 and was placed 50th globally in 2008 (Times Higher Education, 2008).

Meanwhile, in the late 1990s, the government also ordered the merger of single-discipline institutions to form large and multi-discipline universities. This reversal of re-organisation implied the abandonment of the Soviet specialisation model (Duan, 2003). There has also been a trend to transfer the institutions that were previously administered by specific ministries to provincial administration, leaving only the top universities under the direct administration of the Ministry of Education. A large number of institutions have been relegated to provincial administration. It is notable that, although the mergers offered the institutions economies of scale, most mergers were "shotgun weddings" at the behest of government rather than initiated by institutions themselves (Mohrman, 2003).

In China, higher education had long been a privilege for the elite. Therefore the opportunity to receive higher education was considered a route to upward mobility. Although the government initiated a series of higher education reforms in the 1980s and early 90s, the fundamental change in the system's scale only started in the late 90s. However, it is important to note that the agenda for enrolment expansion in China appears to focus on increasing higher education enrolment only, and does not specifically address the equity issue, or the "expand access for whom" question. In contrast, the "widening participation" agenda in the UK specifically addresses the large discrepancies in the take-up of higher education opportunities between different social groups, and aims to improve access by the under-represented student populations (HEFCE, 2008).

Trow's definition of "mass higher education" – when over 15 percent of the age cohort have access to higher education (Trow, 1973) – helped the Chinese government set up its national goal (Bai, 2006): in 1999, in order to "improve the entire country's level of education, hasten the cultivation of a large contingent of high-caliber professionals, and meet the people's desire for higher education" (Zhou, 2006, p. 9), the central government decided to massively increase university enrolment: "by the year 2010, the higher education enrolment rate shall increase from the present 9 percent to around 15 percent" (Ministry of Education, 1999).

However, the expansion of enrolment that subsequently happened was unprecedented: new enrolments in higher education institutions rose from 1.08 million in 1998 to 1.59 million in 1999. By 2002, the state's goal of 15 percent participation had already been accomplished, eight years ahead of original schedule.

In 2004 the number of students studying in higher education reached 20 million, representing a 19 percent participation rate. As illustrated in the figure below, the Chinese system of higher education has experienced unprecedented expansion and has undergone dramatic change in the past decade. In quantitative terms, the country experienced a dramatic shift from "elite" to "mass" higher education during this period (Trow, 1973), and an unprecedented expansion of opportunities for people to participate in higher education. With this student population, China has become the world's largest provider of higher education (Ministry of Education, 1978–2004; OECD, 2007).

Figure 2. New student entrants to undergraduate programmes in China

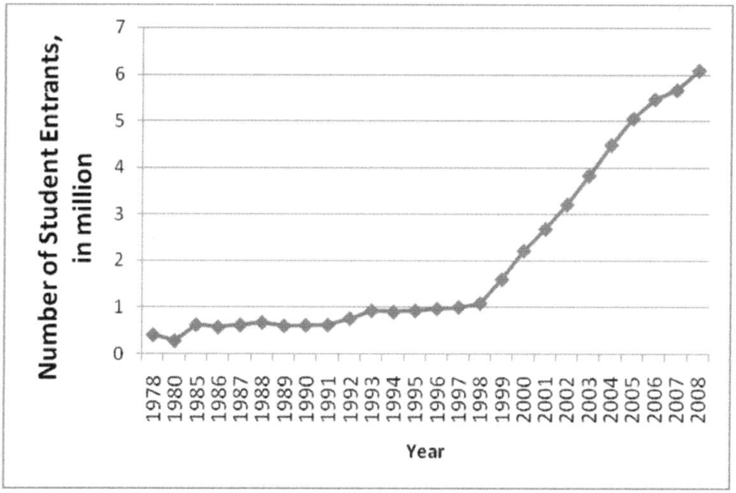

Source: Compiled with data from Ministry of Education (1978–2009).

However, the massive scale of expansion has been the subject of heated debate. Critics have questioned the real rationale behind this expansion. It has been argued that the immediate motivation for this expansion was, in fact, to boost domestic consumption which, since the 1997 Asia Financial Crisis, had been sluggish. The decision was partly based on the assumption that an expansion of higher education would stimulate China's economy effectively through increasing consumer demand and domestic spending (Bai, 2006).

In 1998, Tang Min, an economist at the Asian Development Bank, submitted a proposal to the State Council advocating the use of higher education to stimulate the economy (Tang, 1999; Tang & Zuo, 1998, 1999). Other economists had made similar proposals during the same period (Hu & Shi, 1999a, 1999b). Tang argued that Chinese parents had always been willing to spend a large portion of their income on their children's education, so the potential for educational spending was great, and such spending would make a positive and immediate impact on the economy. By expanding higher education enrolment, the government would be able to increase domestic consumption and promote the development of corporations that offer services relating to education. Furthermore, enrolling young people in higher education would delay their entry to the labour market for three to four years, and Tang predicted that by that time, the Asia Financial Crisis would be over and the employment issue would be easier to deal with. These ideas were very attractive to policy-makers, and were implemented as part of economic policy (Bai, 2006; Kang, 2000).

The economic reform initiated in 1978 allowed the nation's economic potential to begin to be more fully realised. Particularly since the 1990s, the educational system has been further challenged to adapt to the dynamic demands of a market-oriented economy. Coupled with structural reforms, national policies regarding higher education have gone through a major re-orientation, shifting away from an elite-based education system to a mass-oriented education system (OECD, 2003b).

An Organisation for Economic Co-operation and Development (OECD) report concluded that, along with the fast development of higher education in China since 1978 have come some major questions of policy and practice, such as 1) how to balance quantity and quality, 2) how to properly share administrative authority, 3) how to regulate private initiatives, and 4) what is fair and feasible in the sharing of financial cost between central government, local government, institutions, individuals and other organisations (OECD, 2003b).

Changes in Society

The economic reforms started in 1978 have brought about remarkable economic growth and have deeply affected the lives of the Chinese people. The reforms have lifted many Chinese out of poverty and made many far better off materially. It has also set in motion vast social changes, generated diversified values and brought increased choices and opportunities for people.

With China's increasingly market-oriented economy, many aspects of Chinese society have become far more liberalised. The guaranteed lifetime employment system for everyone, so-called the "iron rice bowl" *(tie fan wan)*, has disappeared. Increasing reliance on economic incentives and market forces has created autonomous interests and diversified values. The vigorous growth of the non-state sector has provided new ways to circumvent administrative restrictions, and China's exposure to the outside world has brought in new ideas and cultures (W. Zhang, 2000).

All these have combined to pave the way for a vast shift in values. During the first decades of the People's Republic, pursuing money and leisure were condemned as decadent. People were urged to devote their life to the Party and revolution, material motivation was denounced and spiritual reward was glorified. However, changes in social and economic reality have turned these values upside down. Today secularism and consumerism have become significant trends. Pursuing personal wealth, as exemplified by Deng Xiaoping's saying "getting rich is glorious" *(zhifu guangrong)*, has become accepted (W. Zhang, 2000).

Educational Values

Education has always played an important part in Chinese tradition, and learning has always been highly valued and respected in China (Zhong, 2005, 2006). Education can be characterised as "the true religion of the people" (Smith, 1991, p. 9).

Confucianism mandated that learning can develop and perfect an individual's morality and serve as the basis of an ideal society. It has also been argued that the Chinese enjoyed learning because of its intrinsic value (Lee, 2000).

Meanwhile, the utilitarian and extrinsic value of learning for social and economic mobility was also an essential element in the Chinese tradition (Liu, 1998). Learning and passing the civil examinations was regarded as a glorified, for most people the only, way to attain fame and wealth. Emperor Zhenzong (968–1022) of the Song Dynasty promoted learning in the *Urge to Study Poem (Quan Xue Shi)*:

> To be wealthy you need not purchase fertile fields,
> Thousands of tons of corn are to be found in the books.
> To build a house you need not set up high beams,
> Golden mansions are to be found in the books.
> To find a wife you need not worry about not having good matchmakers,
> Maidens as beautiful as jade are to be found in the books.
> To travel you need not worry about not having servants and attendants,
> Large entourages of horses and carriages are to be found in the books.
> When a man wishes to fulfill the ambition of his life,
> He only needs to diligently study the six classics by the window. (Guo, 1994)

In today's China, just as in past centuries, the idea of "all pursuits are of low value; only studying books is high" *(wan ban jie xia ping, wei you du shu gao)* may still be regarded as the dominant view of education (He, 2000). This is reflected in the significant investment in education by Chinese families. According to the *China Education and Human Resource Report*, in 2003 family expenditure on education amounted to 12.6% of the family budget and surpassed both housing and clothing to become, after food, the second highest expenditure in Chinese families (Yu & Suen, 2005).

These cultural values that promote educational endeavours are not limited to Chinese people living on the mainland; they are also shared by people of other Asian countries and Asian people living overseas. Research has found that in the US, children of Asian descent, especially those of Chinese, Korean and Japanese descent, spend more time studying than people of other ethnic backgrounds, due to the high value placed on education by their families (Sue & Okazaki, 1990; Xie & Goyette, 2003). In analysing the characteristics of Hong Kong students, Cheng (1998) points out that the aspiration for education is internalised in most people's minds and often requires no concrete economic justification.

The Structure of the Chinese Education System

The current Chinese education system basically adopts a "6-3-3-4" structure, that is, six years of primary school education, three years of junior secondary school, three years of senior secondary school education, and four years of undergraduate degree education. The first nine years, i. e. the primary schooling and junior secondary schooling, are compulsory and largely free. Junior secondary school graduates have the option either to enter the labour market, or to go to senior secondary schools or senior secondary vocational institutes to continue their studies (Ministry of Education, 2004).

Figure 3. The basic structure of the education system of China

Age	Academic year			
27	22	Doctoral education		
26	21			
25	20			
24	19	Master's education		
23	18			
22	17			
21	16	Bachelor's education *(Benke)*		
20	15		Terterity vocational education *(Zhuanke)*	
19	14			
18	13			*Gaokao*
17	12	Senior secondary education		
16	11			
15	10			
14	9	Junior secondary education		Nine-year compulosry education
13	8			
12	7			
11	6	Primary education		
10	5			
9	4			
8	3			
7	2			
6	1			
5		Preschool education		
4				
3				

Source: Adapted from Zhou (2006, Figure 1.2)

According to the *Higher Education Law of 1998*, higher education in China is defined as "education which is carried out on the basis of completion of senior secondary education" (Article 2, *Higher Education Law 1998*). To access higher education, the standard route is to take the *Gaokao*, which usually refers to *Tongzhao Putong Gaokao*, which is short for *Quanguo Putong Gaodeng Xuexiao Tongyi Zhaosheng Ruxue Kaoshi*, or National Unified Examinations for Admission to Regular Higher Education Institutions, at the end of senior secondary school study.

The above mentioned *Putong Gaokao* is for entry into *Putong Gaodeng Yuanxiao*, or Regular Higher Education Institutions only. "Regular" refers to institutions offering full-time, on-campus, state-recognised undergraduate programmes. This excludes distance learning, adult education, and some special institutions which have other recruiting channels. The *Putong Gaokao* is intended only for those leaving secondary education; adults or people who have already left school and wish to attend higher education have to take other routes – for example, *Chengren Gaokao* (National Examinations for Admission to Adult Higher Education Institutions), *Zixue Kaoshi* (National Self-Study Examinations for Higher Education), or *Wenpin Kaoshi* (Diploma Tests) (Ministry of Education, 2004). According to the 2004 statistics, two-thirds of the higher education student population in China are studying in "Regular" institutions, while the other third are studying in adult, distance, military, Party, or other special institutions (Ministry of Education, 1978–2009).

Benke and *Zhuanke* Qualifications

According to the *Higher Education Law of 1998*, China's higher education consists of *Zhuanke* education, *Benke* education and postgraduate education. *Zhuanke* and *Benke* are both considered to be undergraduate education, and the dual structure of *Zhuanke* and *Benke* is a distinctive feature of Chinese higher education.

The law specifically defines the content of the two tracks of higher education; for *Zhuanke* education, it is:

> To equip students with the essential principles and specialised knowledge of the subject area and the basic skills and elementary ability to conduct practical work within the subject area.
>
> (Article 16, *Higher Education Law of 1998*)

The requirements for *Benke* education are that it:

> Shall equip students with the essential principles and general knowledge of the discipline and subject area in a relatively systematic way, and the essential basic skills and methods and relevant knowledge of the subject area, and the elementary ability to conduct practical work and research work within the subject area.
>
> (Article 16, *Higher Education Law of 1998*)

It can be seen from the definitions that the major differences between *Zhuanke* and *Benke* are:

1) *Benke* teaches a broader scope of knowledge than *Zhuanke*, as *Zhuanke* teaches "specialised knowledge of the subject area", while *Benke* teaches "general knowledge of the discipline and subject area in a relatively systematic way".
2) Both tracks stress the ability to conduct practical work, but in addition to practical abilities, *Benke* cultivates the ability to do "research work".

According to the Education Minister Zhou Ji, *Zhuanke* education is designed mainly to produce senior engineers and technicians for the production, construction, management and service fields and therefore has a strong vocational orientation, and "can thrive only by adapting itself to the demands of society to fill large numbers of jobs with skilled and educated professionals" (Zhou, 2006, p. 31). Therefore, put simply, *Zhuanke* is the more vocational route within undergraduate education and *Benke* is the more academic route.

Zhuanke education usually takes three years, while *Benke* education usually takes four years, with the exception of a small number of subjects such as Medicine. Both *Zhuanke* and *Benke* are taught at the undergraduate level, immediately after secondary schooling. However, it has become possible for *Zhuanke* graduates to "upgrade" to a *Benke* qualification after further studies and passing required examinations.

Figure 4. Students in higher education, 1991–2004

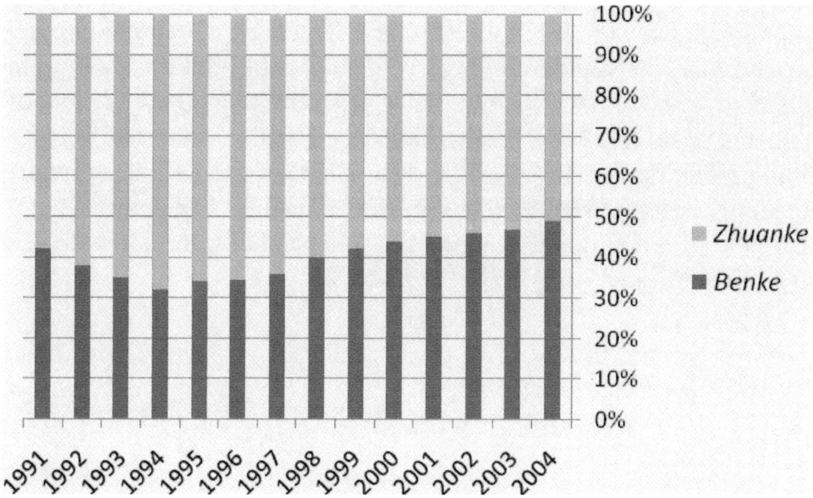

Source: Adapted from Zhou (2006, Figure 1.5)

The above figure shows the patterns of *Zhuanke* and *Benke* students from 1991 to 2004. It can be seen from the figure that, since 1994, more and more students have opted to take *Benke* study rather than *Zhuanke* study.

This study is restricted to *Benke* institutions and students, since its focus is on a comparison of students and their experiences across institutions, rather than between the two tracks. The study also examines weather the *Benke* education at all of the four institutions is identical in their orientation towards academic cultivation and vocational training.

There are also certain international programmes in China that are provided by a partnership between a Chinese institution and a foreign educational provider, such as Zhejiang Wanli College (Private) in China and Nottingham University in the UK, and Nanjing University (Public) in China and Edith Cowan University in Australia. These programmes usually adopt the curriculum of the foreign partner, but with the students and teaching based in the Chinese institution (some programmes send students to the foreign institution for part of the study period), and confer degrees, diplomas, certificates, or other kinds of credentials by the foreign institution. However, these international programmes constitute only a very small part of higher education in China in terms of both the number of programmes and the number of students pursuing them. This study is specifically interested in institutional diversity, defined as the difference between public, private, and independent ownership, and university and college status. Therefore, these international co-operation programmes are not reflected in the institutional sample of this study.

Diversity: Ownership

Higher education institutions in China can also be classified by the level of the qualification they are authorised to confer.

Figure 5. *Tongzhao Putong* higher education institutions in China, 2005

<table>
<tr><td></td><td colspan="4">Benke Track
for
Bachelor's Degree
(4 years)</td><td>Zhuanke Track
for
Vocational Diploma
(3 years)</td></tr>
<tr><td>Enrolment Tier</td><td>First</td><td colspan="2">Second</td><td>Third</td><td>Fourth</td></tr>
<tr><td>Official Title of Institution</td><td colspan="2">"University"</td><td colspan="2">"College"</td><td>"Vocational College"</td></tr>
<tr><td>Type of Institution (Number)</td><td colspan="2">Public (323)</td><td colspan="2">Public (353)
Private (25)
Independent (259)</td><td>Public (853)
Private (225)</td></tr>
</table>

Source: Compiled with data from Ministry of Education (1978–2004).

For the purpose of this study, "Universities" refer to institutions that officially bear the University title and are accredited to accept *Tongzhao* (students admitted through the National Unified Admission Process) *Benke* and postgraduate degree students; the term "Colleges" refers to institutions that officially bear the College title and are accredited to accept *Tongzhao Benke* students. "Vocational Colleges" are institutions offering education to *Tongzhao Zhuanke* students. In 2005, there were 323 Universities (all are public) and 353 public, 25 private, and 259 independent Colleges that can take *Tongzhao Benke* students in China.

The University group represents institutions that usually emphasise discovering new knowledge through research as a key element of their institutional mission. These institutions usually have a longer history and have a large number of students, campuses and disciplines.

The College group represents institutions that traditionally have fewer disciplines and are less focused on research; however, many of them have expanded in recent years to become more comprehensive in terms of the disciplines they offer. In addition, they may undertake advanced research in a small number of narrowly focused disciplines.

The *Provisions on the Establishment of Higher Education Institutions* (State Education Commission, 1986) outline the requirements that higher education institutions must meet before they can be established or upgraded; these include disciplines, characteristics of teaching and research, campus size, qualifications of faculty, number of full-time students, and so forth. All applications are subject to the approval of the Ministry of Education and of local authorities. A number of public and private institutions in China call themselves "universities", when they do not, in fact, meet the legal and formal requirements for using the title.

Private Colleges

After a 30-year hiatus following the founding of the People's Republic of China, private colleges returned in the 1980s. In the transition from central planning to a market-oriented economy, the Chinese government has gradually established a framework in which the governments at various levels continue to run most of the educational institutions, but it has also encouraged participation by the private sector (Zhou, 2006).

Private education in China is usually referred to as *Minban*, literally "run by the people". Although the Chinese phrase *Sili* represents "privately established" more precisely, it has not often been used to refer to private higher educational institutions in China (but it is frequently used to refer to private institutions in other countries), probably because it implies "for profit" and "capitalism" (although the word does not contain these meanings directly), which seem incompatible with the so-called socialist society. Although *Minban* institutions receive no state subsidies, non-profit institutions are tax-exempt according to the law.

Figure 6. Number of private institutions and registered students, 1996–2004

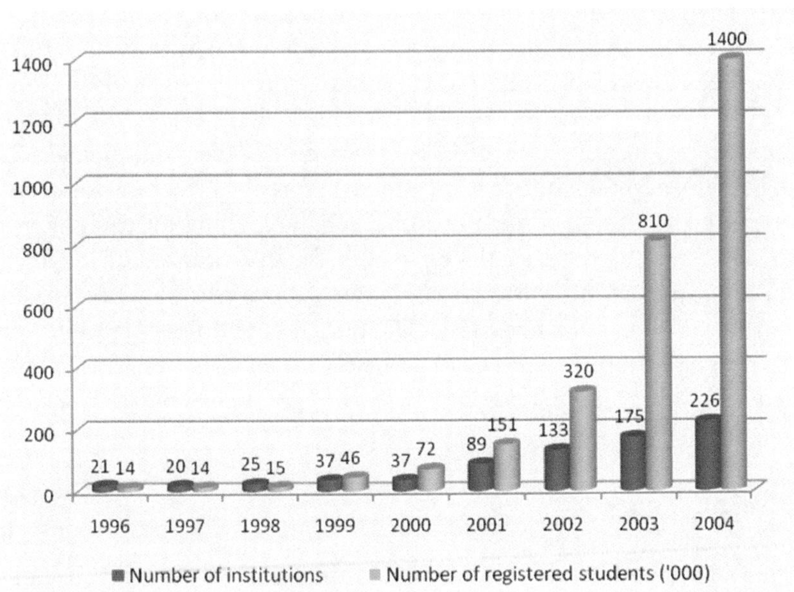

Source: Adapted from Zhou (2006, Figure 2.3)

The number of *Tongzhao Zhuanke* and *Tongzhao Benke* private higher education institutions was 250 in 2004 and reached 278 in 2006 (Ministry of Education, 1978–2009), accounting for 13% of the country's total number of higher education institutions. There are also thousands of private institutions offering remedial courses at post-secondary level.

Most private colleges started as a "School" or "Vocational School", and then gradually upgraded to "Vocational College", and then to "College". By 2008, the state had approved a total of 25 private Bachelor's degree-conferring Colleges. This is the private institutions group with which this study is concerned.

Although the *Education Law of 1995* states clearly that "any organisation or individual cannot operate schools and other educational institutions to generate profit" (Article 25), the *Minban Education Promotion Law of 2003* at the same time allowed and legitimised "reasonable economic returns to investors". However, what counts as "reasonable" is not outlined, and, to date, few additional regulations or policies have been promulgated by the relevant authorities in this regard. For the *Benke* programmes, the private colleges are generally allowed to set fee levels, but the fee levels usually have to be reported to, and officially approved by, the educational and price authorities.

In the US, for example, private universities are a strong force competing with traditional public institutions, and usually stand for educational excellence. Many for-profit higher education providers have also emerged. Supporters argue that private institutions increase educational opportunities at little or no additional public cost, and respond to changing demands more efficiently and flexibly (Zemsky, Wegner, & Innozzi, 1997).

However, private colleges in China are still relatively new. As private colleges initially served as a "supplement" to public institutions to satisfy the demand for higher education, and to enrol those who failed to gain entrance to the public institutions, the public recognition of private colleges is low. "*Minban* colleges are not as good as public ones, they don't have the reputation", is a commonly-held view (Hu, 2003).

Independent Colleges

Duli Xueyuan, literally "Independent Colleges", were introduced in the year 2000 as a measure to increase the supply of higher education places quickly. The underpinning philosophy is that, by combining the prestige and faculty of public institutions and the investment of private enterprises, large numbers of high-quality institutions could be established in a very short period. These colleges are established under the name of a prestigious *Muxiao*, or (public) mother institution, but with private funding; the *Muxiao* may share its teachers and equipments with its Independent Colleges to enhance the Independent College's academic competence. Since all initial investments and everyday running costs come from private sources, rather than public expenditure, Independent Colleges can be considered quasi-private, and can charge variable tuition fees, not limited by the restrictions applicable to public institutions. Independent Colleges pay the *Muxiao* and the investors a pre-agreed amount, or percentage from the tuition fees income or operating surplus to make financial returns to the *Muxiao* and investors.

Within just six years, 2000 to 2006, 318 Independent Colleges were established (Ministry of Education, 1978–2009). Unlike the private institutions which must develop for many years before they can be approved to open *Benke* courses and confer degrees, Independent Colleges usually become degree-conferring institutions upon establishment. Since they enjoy the prestige of their *Muxiao*, but with significantly lower admission requirements, their places are in great demand, even though their tuition charges are two or three times higher than those of their *Muxiao* (Ministry of Education, 2005; Zhou, 2003).

In 2003, the Ministry of Education placed many new restrictions on Independent Colleges; a crucial one being that, from that year on, newly-enrolled Independent College students' degrees would be conferred by the Independent Colleges themselves, rather than by the *Muxiao*. This reduces the attractiveness of the degrees to a certain extent, as the full institutional title indicates that it is an Independent

College, which imposes lower admission requirements. However, the *Muxiaos*' names are still included in the Independent Colleges' names, for example, *Zhejiang University City College* (Jin, 2003). Therefore, in general they may still be considered to have a superior reputation to private institutions (The Economist, 2006).

Diversity: Jurisdiction

The higher education administrative system in China currently operates at two levels, in three sequences (see Figure 7).

Figure 7. China's higher education administrative system

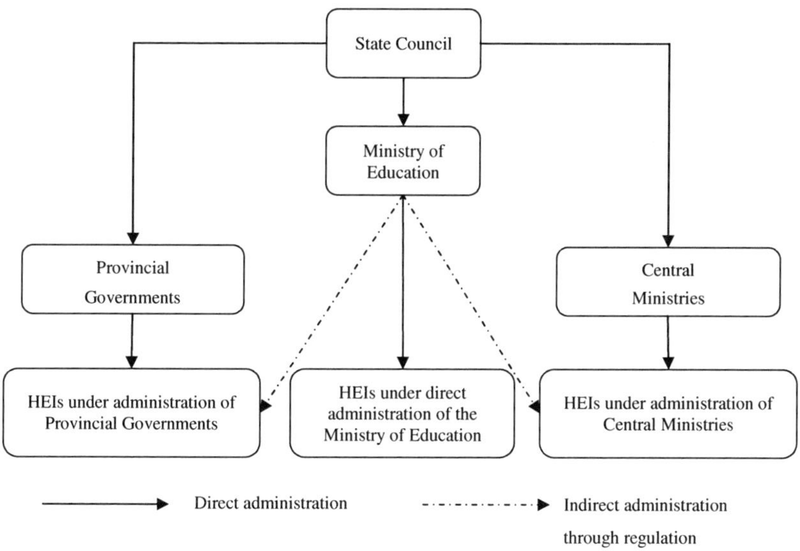

Source: Adapted from Zhou (2006, Figure 2.1).

The vertical *sequence* refers to the institution's affiliation, which determines the ownership, administration and funding of the institution. An institution can have one of three kinds of affiliation. The first possibility is affiliation with the provincial government; this indicates that the institution is more local than national, and the funding of a public university is in this case largely the responsibility of the provincial government. Most institutions belong to this group. Although private and independent institutions are not owned by the provincial governments – they are administered by provincial governments as the local institutions in this category.

The second possibility is affiliation with the Ministry of Education. Universities in this type are more national than local, and this affiliation usually implies that the institution is more prestigious. The third possibility is affiliation with other central ministries, such as the Ministry of Commerce or the Ministry of Mining. Institutions in this group receive funding from the governing Ministries and train relevant personnel for the Ministries.

The horizontal *level* is about the administration and governance of higher education institutions. At the first level, the State Council and the Ministry of Education are responsible for the central administration and overall guidance of the provincial governments and relevant central ministries with regard to the national principle of education and its related policies, funding, and planning – for example, the implementation of the *Gaokao* and the assignment of enrolment quotas. At the second level, the provincial governments and central ministries including the Ministry of Education included are responsible for the direct administration of the institutions of higher education affiliated to them.

The Ministry of Education is the State Council's executive body in charge of education nationally. It is responsible for planning the nation's educational development, scrutinising the establishment of new institutions, determining relevant policies and regulations, and evaluating the quality of institutions. Provincial governments and relevant ministries run their own education departments and oversee the institutions affiliated to them.

Since 1998, a large number of institutions originally affiliated to the central ministries have been relegated to the provincial governments, and the total number of institutions affiliated to the central ministries has reduced substantially. From 1998 to 2001, the number of institutions affiliated to the central ministries' (including the Ministry of Education) decreased from 277 to 126, while the number of local institutions increased from 855 to 1467 (Yan, Zhuo, & Yu, 2006). The proportions of students and teachers also changed, as shown in the table below:

Table 1. Proportions of students and teachers at different types of institutions, 1998–2001

	Year (% of total)			
	1998	1999	2000	2001
Students				
Central Ministries' Institutions	33.76%	30.42%	19.88%	17.8%
Provincial Governments' Institutions	66.24%	69.58%	80.12%	82.2%
Teachers				
Central Ministries' Institutions	29.29%	27.67%	25.86%	22.97%
Provincial Governments' Institutions	70.71%	72.33%	74.14%	77.03%

Source: Compiled with data from Yan et al. (2006).

This change indicates that in the expansion of the higher education system in China, the structure of the educational system has also changed. The local institutions have enrolled more than 80% of the total student numbers and have become the major force in expanding the education system (Yan et al., 2006).

Diversity: Hierarchy of Prestige

So far a number of diversities in Chinese higher education have been introduced, these include:

1) Diversity in qualifications: The more academically-oriented *Benke* qualifications, and the more vocationally-oriented *Zhuanke* qualifications.
2) Diversity in ownership: Public, private and independent institutions.
3) Diversity in jurisdiction: Institutions governed directly by the Ministry of Education and other institutions governed by the provincial authority.

There also seems to have been an increase in the hierarchy of reputation and prestige of institutions. Most of the expansion within the higher education system has taken place in its lower echelons, in the lower level public institutions and the newly emerged private and independent institutions. The recent elite universities' schemes of the 985 and 211 projects have greatly strengthened the elite status of a relatively small number of public universities. Although these projects are primarily targeted at raising the research capacity of the listed universities, the listed institutions may also greatly benefit from their improved reputation, and as a result receive better applications from both prospective students and prospective staff.

The figure below, showing the hierarchy of higher education institutions in China, is adapted from a paper presented by Yu Lizhong, the President of East China Normal University.

Figure 8. Hierarchy of higher education institutions in China

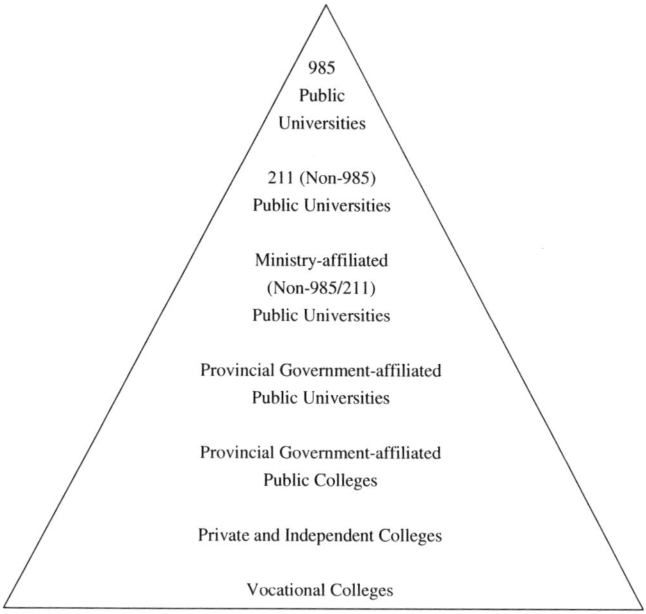

Source: Adapted from Yu (2008).

National Examinations

The imperial national examinations to select governmental officials *(Keju)* were traditionally an important part of China's culture. In fact, although the two exams of *Keju* and *Gaokao* focus on different content and serve different explicit purposes – civil service employment versus higher education entrance – a number of studies have argued that they share many similarities, including being extremely competitive, maintained by state systems, a critical step for upward mobility, and both have had a profound effect on society (Feng, 1994; Yu &

Suen, 2005). Lewin and Wang (1991) argue that: "For most of the existence of the People's Republic of China, university selection has been a prominent issue in education policy" (p. 231).

The *Gaokao* is the principal route for students to access regular higher education in China. It has been in operation since 1952 (it was interrupted during the Cultural Revolution) and is taken by final year secondary school students, typically over a period of three days in the June of their final academic year.

Until 1987, the exams were sat at the same time and used the same test papers across the whole country. The Ministry of Education later allowed many provincial authorities to determine their own textbooks and curricula for secondary school teaching and allowed some provinces to compile their own examination papers, based on a national syllabus framework (Sun, 2005). In 2005, 14 of the 31 provinces in China used their own examination papers. Different papers imply that examination marks cannot be directly compared across all provinces. Higher education institutions set enrolment benchmarks for each individual province from which they plan to enrol students.

In most provinces, students need to choose their track of study in senior secondary school (usually in the second year of senior secondary education, or two years before graduation and taking the *Gaokao*); most students choose between Science *(Like)* and Arts *(Wenke)* tracks. Students in different tracks take different classes and sit different test papers in *Gaokao*. In many provinces, Chinese, Mathematics, and English are compulsory elements in *Gaokao* for all students; Science students take Physics, Chemistry, and Biology in addition, while Arts students take Geography, History, and Politics in addition. Because the test papers are different for the two tracks, the *Gaokao* marks of students taking different tracks are not directly comparable. Higher education institutions can impose track requirements on admission standards. For example, an institution can stipulate that its computer science programme only enrol Science track applicants, while another higher education institution may welcome students from both tracks into the same programme, but sets different mark thresholds for the two tracks.

Although the higher education participation rate has increased substantially since 1998, secondary school graduates still compete fiercely for admission to higher education, or for admission to better institutions. It is not unusual for those who fail the first attempt at *Gaokao* to re-take another year in school and then to re-take the *Gaokao* the following year.

The *Keju* system has been praised by historians and psychometricians as reliable and sophisticated and was adopted in different forms by numerous other nations. Similarly, the *Gaokao* system is considered to be more reliable than subjective recommendations in selecting students for higher education (He, 2000; Yu & Suen, 2005).

One argument is that the *Gaokao* is fair across the country as it provides equal opportunities for students from different socio-economic backgrounds, since academic performance is generally the only standard for admission, and the test instrument is unified across the province, and to some extent, the whole country (K. Li, 2004). However, this argument is unconvincing, as the imbalance of educational development between cities and the countryside meant that in 2000, 70 percent of the university and college students came from urban families, while the overwhelming majority of the country's population resided in rural areas (K. Li, 2004).

There have been calls for the reform of the *Gaokao* system, and the Ministry of Education has altered the system in a number of ways over the years. Most recently a pilot project, initiated in 2004, allows a small number of top universities to enrol a small proportion of students, currently 5 percent of their total enrolment plan, at their own discretion. These institutions make enrolment decisions for this 5 percent of students based on school recommendations, interviews or separate examinations (China Education Online, 2005). However, the public's greatest concern is that admission by interviews might bias the result and become susceptible to corruption: for example, in Russia, standardised examination was re-implemented when it was found that some students entered higher education through bribes (MacWilliams, 2001). Meanwhile, the majority of enrolments in higher education in China are still made through the national *Gaokao* system.

National Enrolment Quotas

The quota system was inherited from the Soviet manpower planning system. The central government *used to set the* state's student enrolment plan every year according to the manpower needs of each industry. Although decentralisation has taken place in the central planning system, the quota system for higher education is still in operation (Long, 2003; Yin & Gordon, 1994).

Each year, the supply of available places in regular higher education institutions is pre-determined by the state, which also assigns an enrolment quota to each higher education institution (including private and independent institutions). In today's economic environment, however, it is unrealistic to try to predict accurately the specific manpower needs of each industry sector, and the quota system is now mainly used as a tool for controlling enrolment growth, promoting regional development and supporting equity of access (Ministry of Education, 2004).

Institutions have also shown their preference for local students. For example, Tsinghua University in Beijing enrolled 3,300 undergraduate students in 2005, of whom 350, or 10.6 percent, were from Beijing, though only 1 percent of the nation's population resides in Beijing (National Bureau of Statistics of China, 2005; Tsinghua Admission Office, 2005). In Shanghai, official statistics show that the higher education participation rate in the city had already reached 55 percent in 2004, much higher than the national average of 19 percent (Shanghai Education Commission, 2005). This regional imbalance has caused the phenomenon of *Gaokao Yimin*, or "examination migration": people move to regions with lower admission requirements to take the examination in order to improve chances of access to higher education (Lai & Wu, 2003). Since only relatively wealthy people have the opportunity to move to another area, this impedes equity of access.

The preference for local students through assigning a larger quota to local students is, in fact, imposed by the government, rather than simply by the institutions. For example, Shanghai Jiao Tong University currently recruits one-third of its students from Shanghai, but the institutional administration would actually prefer to lower the figure to 20% to 25% in order to be more selective in admissions. However, the University recognised the need to be sensitive to the demands of the Shanghai government, which provides substantial financial resources to the university in addition to the Ministry of Education's funding. As one administrator from the institution said, "Government money means government control" (Mohrman, 2003).

Some observers have questioned the Ministry-affiliated universities' preference for local students, as these universities are primarily funded by the central government rather than by local governments. The Ministry of Education has therefore proposed plans to restrict Ministry-affiliated universities' enrolment of local students to no more than 30% of the total enrolment (Guo, 2008).

Financing of Higher Education and Tuition Fees

The financing of higher education has also undergone a dramatic change during the reform and expansion of higher education in China. Chinese institutions only began to charge students tuition fees in the late 1990s. Before then, university and college students enjoyed free tuition, free accommodation, free or inexpensive food and textbooks, and the government even offered allowances to some students. At the beginning of the tuition fee reform in the 1990s, only a small number of students had to pay a nominal fee, but all students have paid tuition fees since 1997.

According to the OECD, between 1995 and 2000, although absolute government spending on higher education increased, the government share of higher education investment in public institutions declined from 70% to 56%, while the average tuition fees and other fees tripled to help offset the decrease of governmental contribution. In 2000, 22.2% of total expenditure and 27.7% of current expenditure per capita were financed by tuition fees and other fees, compared to 13.5% and 17% respectively in 1995 (OECD, 2003b).

Currently the tuition fees vary from place to place, from school to school, and from one field of study to another. Generally speaking, tuition fees are comparatively higher for engineering, medicine, fine art, and other much sought-after disciplines of learning, and are comparatively lower for such fields as agriculture, forestry, education, and history (Zhou, 2006).

Although it is now widely accepted in China that "those who benefit should pay", many have still accused the government of setting high tuition fees, and there have been many cases of students or parents who have committed suicide because they could not afford the tuition fees after receiving an offer from a university or college (Chen, 2005; Hai, 2005; Xu, 2004).

There are several empirical studies on the affordability of Chinese higher education, and their findings are contradictory. One study indicates that students and their families are very willing to pay for higher education, and the maximum amount of tuition they would be willing to pay is still higher than the fee they actually have to pay (Lu, 2003). However, another study that compared the tuition fees with Chinese families' disposable income concluded that the normal annual tuition for public institutions in China of 5,000–6,000 Chinese Yuan already exceeds the paying ability of most families (D. Zhang, 2000).

The Ministry of Education document, *Provisions on Higher Education Institution Charges of 1996*, which is still in effect, states that the "tuition fees a higher education institution charges shall not exceed 25 percent of the educational cost per capita of the institution", and that "all tuition fees charged have to be approved by the provincial authority". But, in practice, the concept of "educational cost per capita" is very ambiguous, as none of the current laws and regulations provides an official formula or guidelines for determining and auditing the "educational cost" of higher education institutions.

Moreover, for institutions that do not receive governmental subsidies, such as private and independent institutions, charging only 25 percent of the educational cost per capita is obviously unrealistic, given that most independent and private institutions rely on tuition fees as the main or even the sole source of income. Today many provincial governments have set their own guidelines on university and college charges. For instance, in Guangdong Province, higher education institutions are classified into four categories:

Table 2. Guangdong province higher education tuitions policy, 2003

Type of Institution	Range of tuition fees (Yuan/year)	Policy
Public Adult Institutions		
Part-time	2,000–3,900	Government sets a standard fee level, institutions are allowed to float upwards or downwards in a specific margin
Full-time	2,800–6,200	
Public Regular Institutions		
Universities and some Colleges	4,180–5,760	Determined by the government, the current level has been kept unchanged from the year 2000 level
Colleges	3,800–4,800	
Vocational Colleges	4,500–5,500	
Independent Colleges		
	Max. 13,000 to Max. 23,000 depending on institution	Only upper limits for Independent Colleges
Private Institutions		
	No Restriction	Private institutions can determine their tuition fees freely

Source: Compiled with data from Guangdong Prices Bureau (2003).

In practice, public institutions charge similar, relatively low tuition fees to students, while independent and private institutions charge much higher fees. The setting of fees at independent and private institutions is more market-driven than at public institutions; for example, independent and private institutions located in wealthier provinces charge higher fees than those in poorer provinces, and institutions with better reputations charge higher fees.

The financial costs of attending higher education are high, and the National Student Loans programme, which lends eligible students money to cover the tuition fees, is often criticised for its failure to meet many students' needs. The major problems of the programme include the inflexibility of repayment terms and the high default rates due to the lack of national credit recording and monitoring mechanisms (Likun Li, 2006; Su & Zhang, 2006). In practice, the programme has also imposed some restrictions on non-public institutions, for example, excluding these institutions or asking them to contribute a certain amount to the loans, and as a result many non-public institutions do not participate in the programme.

The higher education financial reforms have brought about a cultural shift in the relationship between the state and higher education. From a totally government-funded enterprise in the 1980s, higher education is now much more dependent on the funds raised by individual institutions. Chinese university leaders now spend much of their time dealing with financial matters. In the dynastic Chinese society, the scholar was at the top of the status hierarchy and the merchant near the bottom, although both groups were vilified during the Cultural Revolution. Today, scholars have to become merchants in order to support the academic enterprise (Mohrman, 2003).

Admission Procedures

Under the centralised admission system in China, the nationally unified higher education institutions' admission process is administered by the Ministry of Education. Each province has an admissions office responsible for maintaining candidate records, communicating with institutions, and sending enrolled student profiles to the institutions.

Currently, so-called "Admission Tiers" are in operation in the admission process. Most provinces have four tiers. Higher education institutions (and in some cases, subjects at the institutions) are categorised into these tiers. Each student is allowed to identify a number of institutional choices in each tier. Students need to identify the priority of their institutional choices – as first choice, second choice, and so on. For each institution, students are normally offered several choices of majors. In a single tier, a student's profile is firstly sent to the first choice institution; if rejected by that institution, the student's profile goes to the second institution, and so on. If no institution in this tier accepts the student, the student's application will be sent to his or her first choice in the next tier down.

The first tier in the order is called the "Priority Tier", which usually contains military, public security and judicial institutions. The second tier in the order is called the "First Tier", which usually contains institutions in the 985 or 211 projects. The "Second Tier" and sometimes the "Third Tier" are for other *Benke* institutions. The latter tiers are for *Zhuanke* institutions. In this study, of the four case study institutions, the Public University, as a 211 project university, is in the First tier, and the other three institutions are in the Second and Third tiers in the province.

Sometimes institutions give priority to students who indicated that institution as a higher priority in their application, even when there are other applicants with higher *Gaokao* scores. For example, if a student fails to get a place at their first choice institution, and as a result the application is sent to the second choice institution, they may be disadvantaged in the second choice institution because the institution may give priority to students who indicated that institution as their first choice.

If no institution in a student's choice set accepts the student, the student may be entered into the clearing process, in which the student's profile is sent to an institution that still has places available.

It is therefore notable that the Chinese admission system is devised and administered by the state. Higher education institutions are under close scrutiny of state authorities and generally do not have the freedom to admit students to regular *Benke* and *Zhuanke* courses.

The Labour Market

When higher education in China was free, Chinese university and college students accepted the jobs the state assigned to them upon graduation, as planned before their admission. Graduates normally had little control over their job and place of work. Today, however, the government no longer assigns jobs, and all graduates must find employment themselves.

Many critics have ascribed high levels of unemployment to the rapid enrolment expansion that started in 1999; they claim the labour market does not need so many graduates, and it was wrong to increase the supply of graduates at such a rapid pace. For example, the *2006 Survey on Employment of Graduates* indicated that nearly half of the graduates could not find employment upon graduation (Li Li, 2006). However, other observers argue that there is not an over-supply of graduates but rather that the reason some graduates cannot find work is that their expectations are too high (Yang, 2006).

Summary

This chapter has introduced the context of this study and laid the foundations for understanding the study's findings. It has clarified relevant concepts and shown that Chinese higher education has undergone an array of developments in recent decades, and that the successive reforms have changed the landscape of higher education in China substantially. The diversity of different aspects of higher education in China warrants an investigation of the impact of institutional diversity on the student learning experience. The concepts and practices introduced in this chapter, such as the change in cultural values, the hierarchy of higher education institutions, and the role of tuition fees, will be taken into consideration in the analysis of the study's results.

Chapter Three

Diversity in Higher Education

Concepts of Diversity

Diversity in higher education can mean many different things. On the one hand, diversity can imply a set of powerful social and political values, including social inclusion, anti-elitism, greater student choice, and access for non-traditional learners. This may be regarded as an ideological view of diversity (Huisman, 2000; Taylor, 2003). In the US in particular, the term "diversity" is most often applied to concerns about people within higher education, specifically regarding diversity among students or faculty members, especially in terms of gender and race (Hurtado & Dey, 1997). In the UK, the main concerns are to open higher education to people of different socio-economic groups and to students with a wider range of entrance qualifications. On the other hand, the term "diversity" has been used to refer to the variety in the structure or products of higher education in terms of differences between the types of institutions, or differences between the programmes or services provided by higher education institutions (Meek et al., 1996). Neave (1996) refers to this as the different levels of observation of diversity. He points out that it is important to define at what level questions of diversity and convergence are being investigated: the discipline, institution, or system level.

The Higher Education Funding Council for England (HEFCE) has defined a diverse higher education sector as "one with the capacity to meet the varying needs and aspirations of those it serves: students, employers, purchasers of HE services, and the wider community" (HEFCE, 2000, p. 4). HEFCE recognises that these needs and aspirations are becoming increasingly varied, most notably in regard to the expectations, abilities and circumstances of students, as participation in higher education grows progressively wider. In this sense, diversity means securing the best higher education fit for the needs of its various stakeholders, and HEFCE notes that diversity in higher education should "keep pace with changing circumstances, and should itself help to shape and raise aspirations and expectations" (HEFCE, 2000, p. 4). HEFCE also provides a more operational definition of diversity as an institution that is able to provide "… choices of curriculum offer; choices as to the mode, pace and place of delivery; choices regarding the physical and intellectual environment available; and choices between a range of different institutional forms and missions" (HEFCE, 2000, p. 4), which can be achieved through increasing the diversity of institutional types, the diversity between and within institutions, and the capacity for dynamism, responsiveness and change within the sector.

The well-known distinction made between elite, mass, and universal systems by Trow (1973, 2005), often regarded as a model of system evolution characterising the different historical stages of higher education, is in fact also a model of system diversity, as it is perfectly possible for elite, mass, and universal systems to co-exist within Trow's conceptualisation. As noted by Teichler (2008), elite higher education is supplemented in the process of expansion by mass higher education and, later, by universal higher education.

Teichler (1998) found that there was a bewildering diversity of terms employed by researchers in the public debate on higher education diversity. The terms included "short-cycle higher education" or "non-university higher education"; "academic" versus "vocational" higher education; "unitary" systems; "binary" systems; and "hierarchical", "multipurpose" models; "specialised", "elitist" models or "comprehensive" higher education systems. These terms referred to different aspects of diversity in higher education. Diversity may be realised through different types of higher education institutions, curricular approaches, levels of programmes and degrees, programme lengths and their varied reputation and prestige among formally equal institutions and programmes. The detailed classification of diversity in higher education developed by Birn-baum (1983) lists seven types of diversity:

- systemic diversity: the different types of institutions to be found within a higher education system in terms of mission, size, and locus of control;
- structural diversity: institutional differences that exist due to the historical and legal foundations of institutions or differences in the division of authority within institutions;
- programmatic diversity: differences in the programmes (e.g., degree level, degree area, comprehensiveness, mission, and emphasis) and services provided by different institutions within a system;
- procedural diversity: differences in the ways that teaching, research, and/or services are provided by institutions;
- reputational diversity: differences perceived on the basis of status and prestige;
- constituential diversity: differences in the students and other constituents served within institutions (e.g., faculty or administration); and
- diversity of values and ethos: differences in social environment and culture.

Teichler (2008) has created a useful classification of different diversities based on the distinction between the "horizontal" and "vertical" forms of diversity, with the former emphasising functional differences (such as programme types, subjects covered, and links with industry) and the latter reputational and prestige differences (world-class, high-ranking and so on). In the UK higher education system, for example, there is considerable vertical diversity in terms of reputation, such as the self-classified groups of institutions (the Russell Group for the elite research universities and the Million+ for post-92 universities), and the results of various external assessments, including the Research Assessment Exercise (RAE), National Student Survey data and awarding of research grants. Examples of horizontal diversities include curriculum focus, the choice and flexibility offered by programmes of study and the character of the campus. Higher education institutions can also be classified according to other characteristics, such as the size of the institutions and the location of the campuses. These distinctions, however, are referred to less frequently in public debates on higher education diversity.

At the institutional and structural levels, diversity depends on highly complex interactions with the environment (Fulton, 1996) and, as a result, there is currently a rather limited understanding of the mechanisms and forces that lead to diversity or convergence (Teixeira & Amaral, 2001). Organisational, environmental and ecological theories sometimes lead to contradictory interpretations: either that, over time, organisational diversity will decrease due to the climination of weaker and less adaptable organisations (Hannan & Freeman, 1977); or, on the contrary, that organisational diversity will increase due to the creation of an increasing number of market niches (Aldrich, 1979). For similar reasons, literature on higher education diversity also presents similarly contradictory conclusions. A group of authors, including Riesman (1956), Birnbaum (1983), and Rhoades (1990), reaches the conclu-sion that, over time, diversity will decrease, while Parsons and Platt (1973) and Burton Clark (1978, 1983) assert that higher education systems have a tendency to diversify.

Arguments for and against Diversity

Diversity has been identified in the higher education literature as one of the major factors associated with the positive performance of higher education systems. Birnbaum (1983) presents a detailed discussion of the advantages of diversity in higher education. Thc arguments in favour of diversity include the following points.

First, increasing the diversity of a higher education system is an important strategy for meeting student needs. A more diversified system can better accommodate students with different educational backgrounds and with a variety of prior academic achievements. An increase in student numbers also implies an increase in diversity in terms of background, ability, and the motivations driving the labour market expectations of students, and this diversity should be accommodated by heterogeneous higher education providers (Clark, 1983; Trow, 1973, 2000).

Second, diversity can better meet the needs of the labour market. In modern society, economic and social development demand an increasing variety of specialisations. A diversified higher education system can better respond to the needs of the labour market than a non-diversified system.

Third, a diversified higher education system allows for the vital combination of elite and mass higher education. Trow (1979) indicates in his influential analysis of mass and elite systems that the survival of elite higher education depends on the existence of a comprehensive system of non-elite institutions.

Fourth, diversity also increases the level of effectiveness of higher education institutions. For example, the Carnegie Commission on Higher Education (1973) suggested that institutional specialisation in disciplines allows higher education institutions to focus their attention and energy, which helps them to achieve higher levels of effectiveness.

There is also an economic rationale for diversity, as it would be extremely expensive to expand research universities or create new universities based on the research university model in order to accommodate increased student demand.

However, diversification may also have adverse consequences. Skolnik (1986) argues that there are at least two potentially adverse effects of diversification of higher education. The first relates to inequality in a diversified higher education system. Students enrolled in different institutions and programmes may receive educations of different quality and, as a consequence, they may have different options for postgraduate education and employment. The second potentially adverse impact hinges on the tendency of the more specialised higher education institutions within a diversified system to have a rather narrow focus on specific disciplines and to cater for specific groups of students with specific groups of faculty, which can lead to reduced interaction between different disciplines, programmes and activities.

In practice, as van Vught has noted, there seems to be consensus in the academic community that diversity is assumed to have a broadly positive impact on higher education systems (van Vught, 2008). Diversified higher education systems are supposed to address the needs of students and the labour market more effectively, and have the potential to be more effective, flexible and innovative. Many governments have designed and implemented policies to increase the level of diversity in higher education systems. However, it is not always clear how an increase in diversity should be realised. According to van Vught, the many governmental policies that have been developed and implemented do not always lead to the desired results.

Furthermore, there is a lack of evidence in the literature in terms of informing the public debate and expert discourse on the issue of diversification. It has even been claimed that the diversity debate triggered by the US had a strong analytical and normative bias in favour of diversity from the outset, and this conscious or unconscious preference was not open to evidence-based discourse at all (Teichler, 2008). In addition, the arguments in favour of diversity tend to present increasing institutional diversity as the only reasonable way forward, without examining whether other moves could also take place, for example, through an emphasis on intra-institutional diversity rather than inter-institutional diversity. There is also little discussion of the danger of over-diversification (Teichler, 2007, 2008).

Binary and Unitary Systems

The structure of higher educational systems became a major issue in higher education policies in the 1960s. Two-type or multi-type structures emerged in many countries, including the establishment of polytechnics in the United Kingdom, and the *Fachhochschulen* in Germany, and the divisions between the University of California, California State University, and the California Community Colleges in California. The binary and unitary discourse on higher education in many countries is a topic of the past, but it shows how the diversity discourse has developed over time.

The binary or divisional higher education system, at least in theory, imposes some form of managed diversity on two or more distinct institutional groups. The idea behind the policy is based on a rigid division between "academic/scientific" and "professional/vocational" types of education. This division also implies the existence of two sharply segregated sectors of higher education, with their respective missions, students and delivery methods.

Other countries continued to rely on a unitary system, rather than introducing divisions. For example, Italy preserved a system of universities as the only institutional type. In other countries, such as France, diversified levels of programmes were more strongly advocated than the type of higher education institution (Guri-Rosenblit, Sebková, & Teichler, 2007).

In the late 1980s, reforming the formal structures of higher education systems was back on the agenda. The decision by the Council of the European Community in 1988 that three years of successful study is the regular entry qualification to high-level occupations implied that various types of programmes and institutions were no longer relevant for certain career opportunities. In addition, Australia and England abolished the binary division. In England, the former polytechnics were upgraded to full universities in 1992, and have since operated within a single system with the traditional universities and been governed and administered by the same rules. The former attempts to explicitly manage distinctions, such as access to research funds, disappeared. However, HEFCE has claimed that, since 1992, diversity has in fact been encouraged rather than discouraged. In England, higher education diversity was expected to be achieved through a market-based approach, in which each institution determines its own direction based on its own strengths, priorities, and philosophy. However, since the abolition of divisions, concerns have frequently been raised that institutional diversity is being lost and institutions are becoming more alike (Fulton, 1996; Kogan, 1993, 1997; Scott, 1996). In contrast, various other countries have established or reinforced a binary structure, for example the *Hogescholen* in the Netherlands, the *Ammattikorkeakoulu* in Finland, and the *Fachhochschulen* in Austria and Switzerland (Kyvik, 2004).

The *Dearing Report* (1997), formally known as the reports of the National Committee of Inquiry into Higher Education, a major review of higher education since Robbins, described the higher education system in England as follows, under the heading of *Diversity*:

> Institutions of higher education have different profiles of activity. At the risk of over-simplification, universities at one end of the spectrum can be char-acterised as more heavily engaged in research; having a higher proportion of postgraduate students, and more selective entry requirements for under-graduate students; and playing a predominantly national or international role. Those at the other end tend to concentrate on teaching activities; have a higher proportion of sub-degree students and promote the access of non-conventional students; and focus on serving the locality or region. There is a tendency for the pre-1992 and 1992 universities to be concentrated towards opposite ends of the spectrum but there is a great and increasing variation, not only between institutions but also between departments within one uni-versity. (Paragraph 3.90)

However, the report recognised that there were forces driving the institutions towards homogeneity, with the most obvious being the funding methodologies for research and teaching, and the convergence of institutional ambitions:

> All higher education institutions entered the last Research Assessment Exercise (1996), because it is one of the few opportunities for securing additional funding, but many received little or no financial return from it. There are few funding incentives to encourage teaching excellence or activities such as support for local economies. (Paragraph 3.92)

Furthermore, the RAE and Quality Assurance Agency for Higher Education (QAA) assessments, which judged all institutions by a single set of rules, also had an impact on the institutions (Brown, 1999). However, Dearing offered no detailed assessment of these issues and stopped short of any specific recommendations intended to implement diversity (Taylor, 2003).

The HEFCE policy statement on *Diversity in Higher Education* is considered to be a significant outline of strategies towards diversity in higher education, following the end of the binary system (Taylor, 2003). In the document, HEFCE identifies a number of ways in which it claims to be encouraging diversity (HEFCE, 2000):

- Institutional flexibility in the use of block grant funding, with freedom to determine resource allocation internally.
- Dual support for research, enabling universities to plan their own research profiles.
- Activity with business and the community. Based initially on the new Higher Education Reach-Out to Business and the Community Fund and, more recently, on the Higher Education Innovation Fund (HEIF), institutions are free to determine the form of such engagements and how they develop.
- Student premiums, which recognise differing costs between the levels and modes of study.
- Specialist institution premiums, especially for small and mono-subject institutions.
- Other institutional premiums to reflect particular institutional circumstances (e.g., specialist organisational structures or old and historic buildings).
- Special funding for minority subjects (especially languages).
- Additional student numbers, allocated by a bidding process that allows institutions to follow their own aspirations to grow by level, mode and subject area.
- Development of higher education in the further education sector (possible since 1999).
- Special funding incentives for particular purposes.
- An approach to strategic planning that aims to support institutions in developing their own missions and strategies, supported

by performance indicators that recognise the variety of institutional types and allow benchmark comparisons to be made.
– A Restructuring and Collaboration Fund that supports particular missions.

Although this may seem a substantial list, Taylor (2003) points out that this list in fact illustrates the *laissez-faire* approach to diversity that prevailed throughout the 1990s. As the HEFCE policy document went on to explain:

> There are many ways in which we can sustain and promote diversity, both within and between institutions ... But in general our function is to provide a supportive framework within which institutions can decide their own posi-tioning, rather than seeking to decide that positioning for them. Maintaining diversity sufficient to meet future as well as current needs requires constant adaptation. That is much more likely to happen if driven by the choice of individual institutions rather than by an attempt at central planning. (2000, Paragraph 19)

The Department for Education and Skills in the UK emphasised the importance of diversity in the White Paper on *The Future of Higher Education* (Department for Education and Skills, 2003). One of the key challenges identified was "… to recognise and encourage diversity of role, with universities and colleges proud to be different and to play to their individual strengths" (p. 92). The paper claims that the government seeks to encourage institutions to focus on what they do best and emphasises the "… need to move to a funding regime which enables each institution to choose its mission and the funding streams necessary to support it, and to make sure that our system recognises and celebrates different missions properly" (p. 20).

This English debate is important because it shows that there can be different approaches to encourage diversity. In England, although the state claims to be encouraging diversity, the emphasis is still on developing funding methods and programmes that reduce barriers to diversity, while stressing institutional self-determination in shaping contrasting missions. In Taylor's (2003) words, this gave the impression of "diversity by accident rather than diversity by design" (p. 271).

Institutional Convergence

This section discusses the theories of institutional convergence in higher education, it should be noted that interactions between higher education institutions and their environments are highly complex, and the Chinese higher education system is a large and complex one, this complexity does not allow for simplistic theoretical interpretations. Empirical evidence is necessary to assess the status of institutional diversification and convergence trends.

Institutional convergence and academic and vocational drift are not new concepts, as they have been the subject of research for many decades. These concepts refer to the tendency of diverse groups of institutions to grow more homogeneous over time, as institutions with contrasting missions and resources make efforts to adopt some of each other's paradigmatic foundations (Birnbaum, 1983; Huisman & Morphew, 1998; Neave, 1979).

Figure 9. The relationship between academic drift, vocational drift and university type

Source: Adapted from Codling & Meek (2006, p. 5)

As the figure above illustrates, the traditional universities and the newer universities symbolise the two "ideal types" of higher education institutions and are referred to for analytical purposes. The traditional universities have a positive attitude towards the value and significance of research and a somewhat ambivalent attitude towards vocationalism. By contrast, the newer universities have a positive attitude towards the value of vocational education and training, and a somewhat ambivalent attitude towards academic and research (Codling & Meek, 2006).

Academic drift represents the tendency of institutions to copy the role and mission of the prestigious institutions. It has often served to reinforce traditional universities as the "gold standard institutions" in higher education. As noted by Morphew (2000), Riesman's (1956) seminal research on academic drift painted a picture of imitation, where less prestigious colleges and universities followed the lead of the more successful and prestigious colleges and universities. Riesman's metaphor of a snake depicts the leadership position of the most prestigious universities at its head, modelled by the universities at its tail. In contrast, these traditional universities have nevertheless come under pressure to become more concerned with demands from industry and the students, and therefore experience vocational drift.

Researchers have frequently used environmental or biological concepts to discuss institutional diversity in higher education (1995). Using the biological analogy, since organisms will adjust to different local conditions, variation in species is more likely to occur in a heterogeneous ecological environment. In contrast, if organisms are subjected to the same environmental conditions, they will tend to evolve towards convergence (Codling & Meek, 2006). The ecological environment for higher education institutions includes conditions such as governmental regulations, student choice, stakeholder influence and funding. Variation in each environmental condition across the higher education system will promote variation in higher education institutions' responses and foster diversity. In contrast, uniform environmental conditions will promote similar responses from individual institutions and promote homogeneity across the system.

In England, for example, the former polytechnics are expanding their postgraduate segment and research profile and beginning to acquire an international presence. The old universities are continuing to broaden their teaching profiles with more professional and part-time studies. In most other parts of Europe, according to van Vught (1996), the national governments are very strong actors that opt mostly for homogeneous systems or types of higher education, and therefore contribute to a low degree of diversity among institutions. Institutional convergence is also evident in the recent history of Australian universities. According to Codling and Meek (2006), the distinctive types of the "university of technology" and the traditional "sandstone university" in Australia have shown clear signs of convergence. For example, the newer universities have exhibited academic drift by:

- appointing more traditional-university trained and experienced academic staff;
- adjusting their organisational cultures to be more academic;
- shifting enrolment patterns to include more school-leavers;
- increasing the emphasis on research and broadening the research focus; and
- adopting much of the symbolism and nomenclature of the traditional university.

At the same time, more traditional universities have exhibited vocational drift by:

- adopting more applied missions;
- developing active partnerships with industry and the new professions;
- offering more qualifications with overt vocational outcomes;
- generating more applied research funded by industry; and
- becoming more flexible with their admission policies to encourage non-traditional learners.

According to Codling and Meek (2006), the drivers of this institutional convergence and reduction in systemic diversity are two-fold. Firstly, institutional convergence is driven by a desire for status emulation on the part of less prestigious universities. Secondly, in Australia, it has been driven by a competitive spirit amongst universities in a deregulated market environment. In such a deregulated environment with a uniform funding regime, institutions inevitably tend to respond to similar stimuli in similar ways, and to become more and more alike.

Codling and Meek further argue that higher education financing policy was a powerful governmental tool for encouraging or discouraging differences between higher education institutions. In Australia, research funding is distributed to universities according to specific institutional research performance indicators; this leads to a hierarchy of universities, which has the inevitable consequence of encouraging poorly funded, low-ranked universities to emulate the research performance of those higher on the ranking list in order to maximise their income. Although this system raises the overall research performance, it also carries with it the unintended outcome of institutional convergence.

Research funding policy can also influence universities' research directions. Newer universities are seeking recognition for activities rendering research more practical and useful to industry and society, but if the research funding distribution criteria do not recognise these activities, there will be a tendency for the new universities to abandon their alternative and possibly innovative approaches to research in exchange for more research funding.

The ranking of institutions has similar effects on convergence. There seems to be a natural tendency for stakeholders to rank institutions. This ranking may be official in that it is conducted by the government or its agency, and is the product of assessing institutions based on a number of benchmarks or indicators, such as research performance and quality. Although these benchmarking practices are usually aimed at assuring the quality of higher education, through references to the top universities, they inevitably have the effect of encouraging lower-status institutions to imitate prestigious institutions, minimising their differences in the process. The ranking may also be unofficial, such as the ranking promoted by consumer commercial magazines. It may also be entirely informal and anecdotal, and based on factors related to institutional age, wealth and perceptions of prestige. In a slightly different way, the Carnegie Classification has resulted in the ranking of higher education US institutions as an unintended outcome. The doctoral and research-led universities tend to be the oldest and wealthiest and are acknowledged as the most prestigious, and are therefore perceived to be "the best," while the masters and baccalaureate colleges are ranked below them (Carey, 2006; Ye, Zhong, & Li, 2006).

A number of economists have offered an explanation for this phenomenon. Brewer, Gates, and Goldman (2002) argued that, because demonstrating performance is so difficult in the academic arena, the characteristics of a small number of highly visible institutions become the surrogates for quality. The other institutions then identify the traits and elements of these more visible institutions and seek to develop similar characteristics. In these circumstances, the prestige of institutions is therefore not about performance *per se*, but the appearance of doing what highly regarded institutions do and relative comparisons to the prestigious and visible institutions. The authors conclude that: "Customers develop images of the features of good service providers. Certain characteristics of a college or university become associated with good providers, even though these characteristics are not directly related to the quality of the output" (p. 28).

University rankings therefore provide a mechanism for making a number of institutions visible and affirming their prestige. Once a ranking system has been established for higher education institutions, there is an inevitable tendency for the lower ranked institutions to seek to raise their standing by copying the successful activities of those institutions that are ranked higher. The lower ranked institutions pursue this mimetic isomorphism voluntarily, and as a result, institutional convergence is promoted. This isomorphism is further accentuated if there is also a direct financial advantage to a higher ranking (Marginson & Considine, 2000).

Another source of convergence is derived from both the training and perspective of the faculty staff. Henderson and Kane (1991) point out that the increased professionalism in academia, reflected in "… the push by accreditation agencies for doctoral-level faculty" (p. 341), has increased the tension between teaching and research expectations of faculty, and as a result, new faculty members are less likely to see themselves as teachers and more likely to see themselves as scholars and researchers. Morphew (2000) notes that faculty members who have done their graduate work at traditional universities and then teach at new universities bring with them an image of what a university should look like. Because of this, they have the tendency to create and deliver programmes with the methods and structures adopted by more prestigious universities, which may not complement their university's mission and resources. Weathersby (1983), found that in the US, regional universities have given up their distinctiveness in order to accommodate the professional needs of faculty members focused on research. On the other hand, the institutional evaluation criteria that focus on research rather than teaching also shape the faculty's professional perspective (Rhoades, 1990), and in turn lead to convergence upon a single organisational form: one based on the model of the research university.

Studies on diversity in higher education often examine the role of the government in promoting diversity. There is disagreement within this body of literature. On one hand, researchers have suggested that government interventions are necessary to induce and protect institutional diversity (Huisman & Morphew, 1998; Meek, 1991; Skolnik, 1986). For example, Rhoades' (1990) discussion of political competition and diversification in higher education suggests that increased governmental control over mission and programme diversity in the US and Sweden has played a positive role in maintaining the diversity of these systems. On the other hand, researchers contend that government interventions are not necessarily effective in diversifying higher education institutions (Birnbaum, 1983; Geiger, 1996). For example, Birnbaum (1983) studied the diversification of institutions in eight US states and concluded that increased governmental control over the states' higher education systems had not produced greater institutional diversity. Jenniskens (1997) studied the relationship between governmental steering and curriculum innovations, and argued that there is no simple relationship between the activity or role of government and the relative rate of curricular innovation or drift; rather, other variables related to market demand and institutional life cycles may be more important.

There is a widespread conviction that market forces will be effective in promoting higher education diversity in terms of institutional types and programmes. Geiger (1996) formulated the hypothesis that, when resources are tight, the market is a much more powerful force for the diversification of higher education institutions, and functions more effectively, than centralised policy and control. Geiger argues that when resources are abundant, academic drift will prevail; institutions at the bottom of the spectrum will try to raise their institutional status in imitation of the more prestigious universities. However, when resources are scarce, institutions will fight for survival in the market by diversifying in search of market niches and new clientele. However, this view has been questioned by other researchers. For example, Meek et al. (1996) contend that when institutions need to compete for scarce resources, they can respond in one of two ways. The first is to diversify in an attempt to capture a specific market niche, while the other is to imitate the activities of successful competitors, which will result in institutional convergence.

Public and Private Higher Education

In many countries, the inter-relations between public and private higher education institutions highlight different missions and cultures and have an impact on the structure of higher education systems. In some countries, private higher education is almost non-existent. For example, in England, of more than one hundred universities, only one is considered private. In contrast, in the US, there has been a very strong private force in higher education, and many private research universities have established themselves as leading, world-class universities. There is also a significant sector of for-profit higher education institutions in the US that caters to various clienteles.

In a seminal study that analysed the structure, function, and changes of private higher education in eight countries, Geiger (1986) developed a taxonomic, analytic description of the functions of the private sector of higher education. He identified three roles for private higher education providers: providing more, different, or better higher education. For example, in the case of the US, Geiger groups these institutions into three categories: large urban universities that provide more higher education, liberal arts colleges that provide different education, and private research universities that fulfil the function of providing 'better' education.

The establishment of private higher education institutions in systems comprising only public institutions automatically creates a form of ownership diversity and this often, though not always, leads to the diversification of cultures and missions in higher education. For example, in the US, it has been observed that while the public institutions "educate", the for-profit private institutions "train" (Bailey, Badway, & Gumport, 2001). However, there are important limitations on the ability of private higher education to incorporate diversity. For example, the literature has pointed out that the rationales and functions of the private higher education sector are highly dependent on higher education policies (Levy, 1986; Zumeta, 1992). The diversification brought about by private institutions, then, can be interpreted as a direct function of the regulatory framework that governs the institutions. For instance, the state may require private providers to conform to the model of the public institution, an action Levy terms "coercive modelling", which serves as a significant source of homogeneity (Levy, 1999, p. 24). Levy suggests that private higher education is often, but not always, about something different and innovative; due to isomorphism, private higher education may closely resemble public higher education and fail to contribute diversity to the system.

As indicated in the earlier chapter on *Higher Education in China*, a number of non-public higher education institutions have been established since 1980s and they have increased the systematic institutional diversity in higher education. However, on closer scrutiny, coercive and non-coercive isomorphism forces can be identified. The state applies the same standards and requirements to the private and public sectors, and as the public sector maintains predominance, it is natural for the private sector to emulate its public counterpart.

Therefore, for this study, it is relevant to analyse the effects of non-public higher education institutions on diversity in China. Since diversification efforts are highly dependent on higher education policy, it is also important to look at the policies governing these institutions to examine whether non-public institutions are allowed to diversify themselves, to what degree they are given freedom, and whether they develop distinct features when they have the freedom to do so.

Summary

This chapter has discussed the different definitions and concepts of diversity in higher education, and presented the arguments for and against diversity. After reviewing the historic and current structure of a number of higher education systems, this chapter has discussed in detail the conflicting forces that drive institutions toward diversity and convergence. The chapter has also looked at the different control or ownership of higher education institutions, and discussed the differences made by private institutions.

Chapter Four

Student Experience in Higher Education

Background

In the 1980s, it was still relatively rare for institutions to obtain formal feedback from their students about their educational experiences. With the expansion of the higher education sector, as well as the need for accountability, concern with quality, and the growing "consumerism" of higher education, there has been significant growth and an increasing sophistication in processes designed to collect feedback from students (Harvey, 2003). The student learning experience has become a high priority on the political and policy agenda in many countries. In the UK, following the Cooke Committee's (Cooke, 2002) announcement on information requirements for quality assur-ance in higher education, student satisfaction feedback has become an important and official element of the higher education quality process (Harvey, 2001). The Higher Education Academy has also identified the student learning experience as a core component of its mission (Higher Education Academy, 2005). Australia and the US have similar national surveys aimed at gathering quality information on higher education from students (three such surveys are reviewed later in this chapter).

The concept of student experience is a broad one, as it encompasses a student's participation in the learning environment. Fraser (1998) defines a learning environment as follows:

> "Learning environment" refers to the social, psychological, and pedagogical contexts in which learning occurs and which affect student achievement and attitudes (p. 3).

Therefore the "student experience" refers to a wide range of aspects. In fact, although there has been a large body of literature on student experience and various agencies have identified student experience as a top priority, what is meant by "student learning experience" is not clearly defined. Some studies in this field, such as the student experience network of the Society of Research in Higher Education, aim "... to find out what ... students in UK higher education are learning in the widest sense of the word from their experiences within and outwith formally institutionalised study" (Society of Research in Higher Education, 2009, p. 1). However, most studies have confined their focus to the students' experience with the formal academic curriculum and classroom learning in higher education institutions.

Undoubtedly, teaching and learning are regarded as the most important aspects of a student's experience in higher education. Other aspects of the student experience can include experiences with recreational and sporting facilities, catering, accommodation, and so on. Many of these non-learning experiences are not directly relevant to the quality of teaching and learning, but, in some cases, the relationships can be complex. Using accommodation as an example, students' satisfaction with accommodation is usually influenced by the quality of the facilities, cost, availability, and proximity to classrooms and other academic and living facilities. However, the suitability of accommodation for study, such as quiet space and Internet access, can also have an impact on students' learning experience (Brennan et al., 2003).

Some surveys, such as the National Survey of Student Engagement (NSSE), measure a number of non-learning items, such as engagement in team sports or student organisations. The surveys justify the inclusion of these non-learning items by arguing that active engagement in these activities is positively correlated with better learning. Other surveys, such as UNITE's Student Experience Report (UNITE, 2005), attempt to capture the wider experience of students. This type of survey usually includes a substantial number of items that are not directly linked with the quality of teaching and learning, such as student finances and extra-curricular activities.

The learning experience, and especially the relationship between institutional diversification and students' learning experiences, is a field that has not been extensively researched in China. The current study is concerned not only with students' learning experiences, but also with the non-learning factors associated with institutional diversification that may have an impact on students' learning. These issues are reflected in the questionnaire design and data analysis presented in the study.

Level of Reporting and Analysis

One of the essential methodological issues of student feedback surveys is determining the appropriate level or unit of reporting and analysis. A review of current survey practices shows that student feedback can be collected at a number of different levels. The use of student feedback at different levels may reflect the different purposes of survey practices (HEFCE, 2003). These levels can include:

- an individual teacher or class
- a module or unit
- a semester or year of study
- a programme of study
- a discipline
- a department
- an institution

Many of the earlier student feedback practices focused on evaluations of individual teachers or module units, as they were usually developed by the individual teacher or course director to assess students' opinions on the course unit. This is because the module is where teaching and learning takes place; it is the most immediate area for the instructors and the closest to student experience. Feedback at this level, therefore, is appropriate to contribute effective, efficient improvements to the learning and teaching process.

While evaluation at the module level is common, evaluating teaching and learning at the programme level is less common, especially when the course has a modular structure, as students' frames of reference and experience are more easily related to the modules than the programme. Students need to generalise their experiences with modules to the higher programme level. If evaluation is confined to individual teachers or modules, however, it could be argued that important aspects of the wider teaching and learning environment become neglected as module-level questionnaires do not usually assess course and institutional level factors. It could also be argued that the course needs evaluation "… at least as much as the parts which make it up" (Kember & Leung, 2009, p. 3). Other researchers have focused on students' perceptions of the learning environment across their entire degree, and how these perceptions are related to approaches (Lizzio, Wilson, & Simons, 2002; Ramsden & Entwistle, 1981).

Lack of clarity regarding the unit of reporting or analysis may cause confusion. For example, in responding to the programme-level student experience survey at the Chinese University of Hong Kong, some students reported that because teachers performed differently, they felt it was difficult to assign single values to certain teaching quality items. Despite the difficulty in aggregating teachers' performances, however, analysis reveals that agreement across different students' ratings of the same course is very high (Kember & Leung, 2009).

From the perspective of a higher education institution seeking to maintain and improve teaching quality institution-wide, or from the perspective of a national government seeking to evaluate and assure higher education quality nation-wide, it can be argued that the appropriate focus of assessment is an entire degree programme or the entire institution (Richardson, 2005a), and this has become the dominant focus in higher education now.

The following examples from HEFCE show the different applications that student feedback might have at different levels (e.g. module, programme, support service) and those who might be interested in using it.

Figure 10. The uses and users of student feedback

Users of student feedback	Uses of student feedback	Level
A teacher	To improve teaching	Module
A programme team	To check that learning objectives have been met, to check coherence of a programme as a whole, and to improve the student learning experience in general	Programme, plus individual modules
A department or faculty	To help satisfy responsibilities for quality and standards and to help plan future provision	Programme
Institutional leadership and senior academic committees	To help satisfy responsibilities for quality and standards and to help plan future strategy	Programme, subject and institutional support services (i.e. institution-wide)
Current students	To inform module choices	Module
Prospective students	To inform choice within and between HEIs	Programme, subject

Source: HEFCE (2003, Figure 4.1)

The use to which students' experience will be put, and the level at which feedback is collected and/or analysed, has implications for the administration of this practice (HEFCE, 2003). For example, student experiences collected at the module level can be used by instructors to check the progress students are making and to enable relatively immediate changes to the module, if necessary. This suggests that the collection of student experiences at a mid-point of module delivery is desirable. However, the institution or department may also need data about the modules and courses to make comparison between modules and to inform discussions about longer-term developments and improvements. For these purposes, students' experiences are best collected at the end of the module, and indeed, the most common practice is to administer surveys at the end of the semester.

There is definitely potential for tension between the requirements of different users and different levels. Therefore, the unit selection should be directed by the purpose of the research, and the development and administration of a survey needs to clearly reflect the purpose, too. As stated, feedback at the module level is popular, as it has immediate relevance to the individual teacher and learner. Information at this level, however, is less useful in serving the needs of programme committees and external stakeholders. These groups need more holistic data on the student experience to enable them to judge the quality of a programme or institution (Brennan et al., 2003).

Conceptual Framework

In the 1980s and 1990s, several studies established that institutions of higher education have a profound impact on their students; the quality of teaching provided in higher education is a more powerful factor of student success than student demographics (Astin, 1993; Kuh, Pace, & Vesper, 1997; Pascarella, 1985; Pascarella & Terenzini, 1991, 2006; Tinto, 1993). The National Center for Educational Statistics (1991) therefore recommended that institutions of higher education assess the student learning experience to direct learning and teaching outcomes.

In order to understand the broad and complex notion of student experience, it is necessary to develop a conceptual framework. Three different student learning models have been employed to develop the framework for this study. The first model is the seminal 3P Model devised by Biggs, which was adapted by Trigwell and Ashwin (2003) to assess students' learning experience at the University of Oxford. The second model, developed by Kember and associates (Kember & Leung, 2009; McNaught, Leung, & Kember, 2006), was used to assess student experiences at the Chinese University of Hong Kong in the Student Engagement Project (SEP). The third model was developed by the Enhancing Teaching-Learning Environments in Undergraduate Courses (ETL) project team led by Hounsell and Entwistle at the University of Edinburgh. The ETL project is a part of the UK's nationwide Teaching and Learning Research Programme (TLRP), established by the UK Economic and Social Research Council (ESRC) (Entwistle, 2003a, 2003b). In this study, the three models are combined and adapted in a way that is suitable for an investigation within the context of the Chinese system.

The 3P Model of Learning

The 3P Model of learning (Biggs, 1987, 1993) clarifies the nature of learning in higher education. It describes how learning takes place by discussing the 3P factors: Presage, Process and Product. The model views students' perceptions of teaching and learning as the interaction between their characteristics, their previous experiences with teaching and learning, and the context of teaching and learning. More specifically, the model argues that all students come to a learning situation with beliefs, abilities, knowledge, and personal characteristics, and these personal characteristics then interact with the learning environment to enable the individual to develop concepts and motivations, as well as perceptions of the environment, in order to engage in the learning process (Biggs, 1987; Prosser & Trigwell, 1999). The student uses a particular learning approach to support the learning process in order to achieve the desired or required learning outcomes (Biggs, 1985). For example, if students are interested in and enjoy studying their subject, they will adopt a deep approach to learning to understand ideas and seek meanings; otherwise, students will adopt a surface approach to learning characterised by memorising information for assessment rather than for understanding. These inputs then result in outcomes of learning.

The 3P Model was first conceived in a sequential-causal way (Biggs, 1989). Later, the components of the model were considered to be engaging in dynamic relationships (Biggs, 1993). Each element interacts with and influences other components in the model.

The 3P Model is powerful in that it captures the essence of the learning process. It does not, however, provide details regarding the variables that may influence students' learning. The conceptual frameworks of the Chinese University of Hong Kong SEP project and the University of Edinburgh ETL project provide discussions of such variables.

Trigwell and Ashwin (2003) adapted the 3P Model, as shown in the figure below.

Figure 11. Trigwell and Ashwin's adapted version of 3P Model

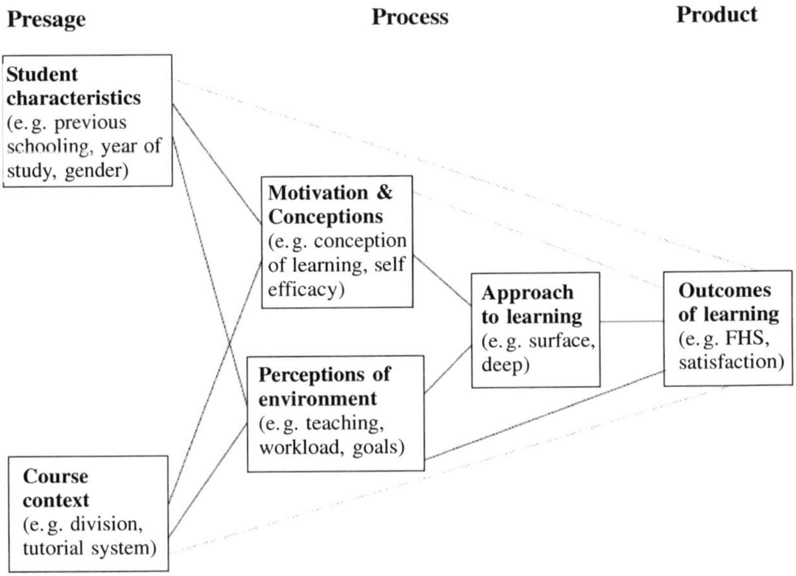

Source: Trigwell and Ashwin (2003)

Differences in students' personal characteristics, such as their gender or parents' education level, may cause differences in the quality of their learning. Similarly, differences in the course context, such as library resources or computer facilities, may directly influence the outcomes of learning. The links between student characteristics, the learning environment, and learning outcomes have been demonstrated in the literature (Crawford et al., 1998; Watkins, 2001). The literature also maintains that students who experience good teaching are more likely to adopt approaches aimed at developing meaning and understanding (Lizzio et al., 2002; Prosser & Trigwell, 1999; Ramsden, 2003).

The Student Engagement Project

The Chinese University of Hong Kong SEP project is designed to evaluate the teaching and learning environment at that specific institution. Its design is based on the hypothesis that the learning and teaching environment, as characterised by the variables included in the survey inventory, have a significant influence on the development of a set of generic competences selected by a number of stakeholders as important attributes for university graduates. The relationships in the model have been confirmed by Structural Equation Modelling (SEM). The conceptual framework of SEP is presented below:

Figure 12. Conceptual framework for the SEP Project

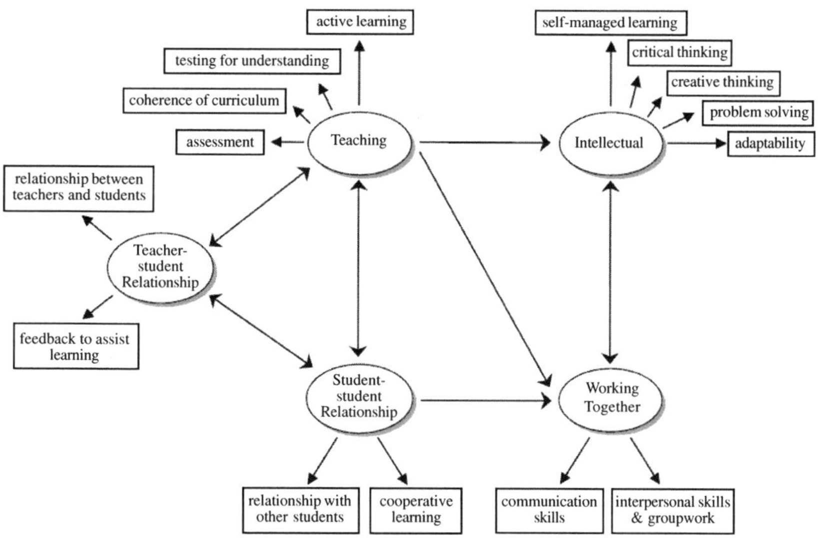

Source: McNaught, Leung, and Kember (2006, p. 9).

The most obvious difference between this model and the 3P Model is that this framework disregards student characteristics and the approach to learning, but it involves a large number of carefully selected course and outcome variables. The SEP model also places teaching in a more central position.

The ETL Project

The Enhancing Teaching-Learning Environments in Undergraduate Courses project (ETL) team at the University of Edinburgh led by Dai Hounsell and Noel Entwistle developed a conceptual framework to provide a more precise way to think about university teaching and learning. The framcwork is illustrated below:

Figure 13. Conceptual framework of the ETL project

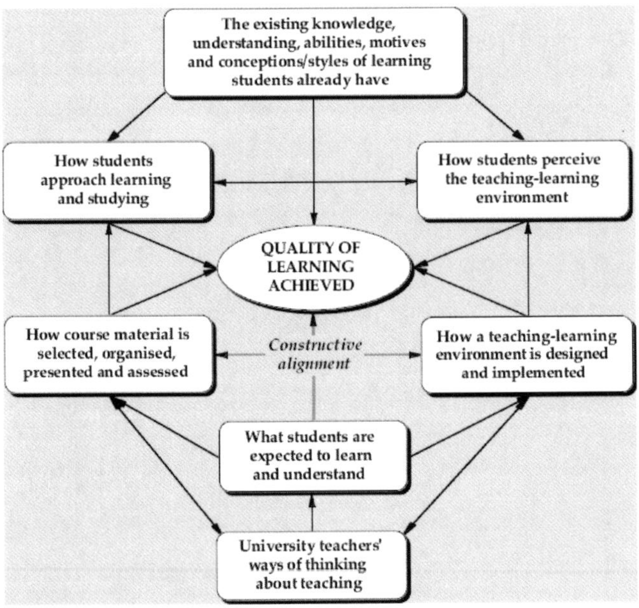

Source: Entwistle (2003a, p. 1)

The top half of the ETL framework includes components referring to the variations between students' characteristics, attitudes and perceptions, while the bottom half of the framework covers influences attributable to the instructors and the teaching and learning environment. The centre is the focal concept of the quality of the learning achieved. The framework is also built on the hypothesis that a series of factors, including students' perception of the learning environment, the design and implementation of the learning environment, students' learning approach, the learning materials, and so forth, influence the quality of students' learning.

Although presented quite differently, the three models have certain conceptual overlaps. The core elements in these three models have been selected to form a new framework that informs the design of this investigation.

The conceptual framework of students' higher education experiences for this study is presented below.

Similarly to the ETL model, the upper half of this model illustrates components referring to variations between students' characteristics, attitudes and perceptions, and the bottom half illustrates influences attributable to the teaching and learning environment, such as characteristics of the course, instructors and institutions. Rather than placing learning outcomes at the end of the model (as in the 3P Model), this model positions learning outcomes in the centre, and shows that a number of factors situated around the central concept can influence the quality of learning outcomes. The model also illustrates that, if institutions and educators can shape the teaching and learning environment, they can influence the student learning experience and induce better learning outcomes. The highlighted boxes form the focus of this study – that is, after accounting for the students' characteristics and the disciplinary differences, the effects of diversification of institutions on students, teaching and learning environment and the students' experience of learning and teaching.

Although presented quite differently, this model can actually be framed within the 3P framework. In considering learning outcomes as the *Product*, approaches to learning and perceptions of the course context and teaching and learning environment as the *Process*, and the remaining factors as the *Presage*, the current model therefore fits the 3P Model. However, the model presented here does not follow the sequential nature of the 3P Model.

Figure 14. Conceptual framework of higher education student experience

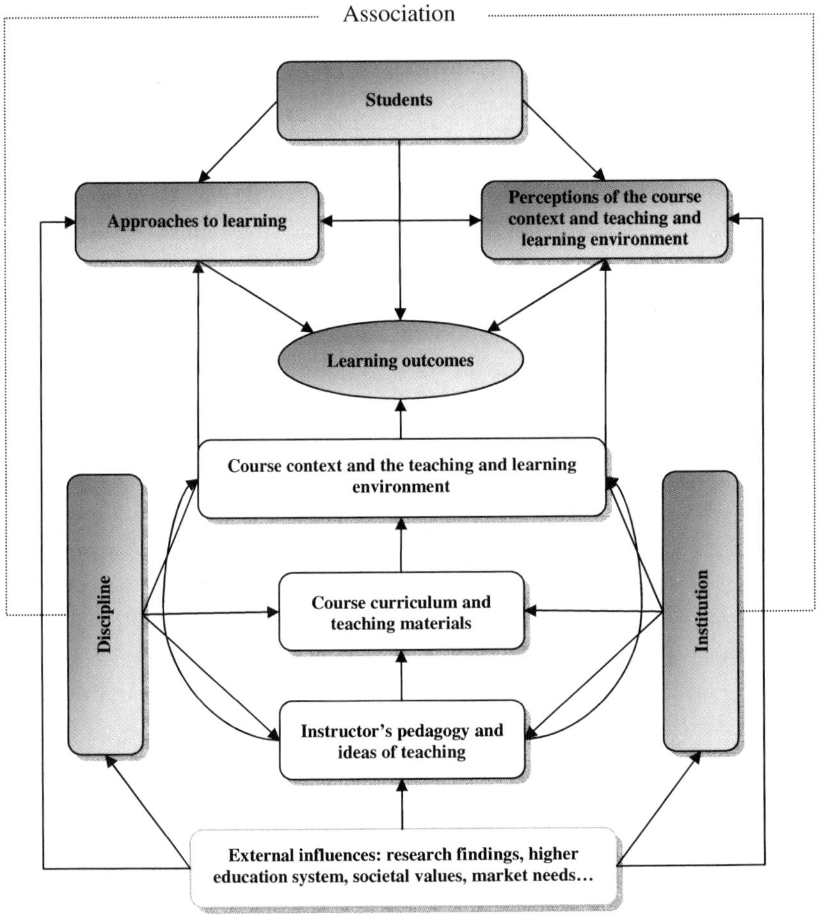

Constructs in the Conceptual Framework

The conceptual framework provides an illustration of the overarching model for understanding the higher education student experience. However, because this study is primarily interested in the key effects of the diversification of higher education institutions, it does not aim to examine every factor in the framework. The concepts that are the main focus of this study are introduced below.

Student's characteristics

The quality of learning outcomes may depend on students' abilities, motivations, attitudes towards learning and prior learning achievements. This component covers a variety of factors that indicate the influence of students' existing characteristics on approaches to learning, perceptions of the course context and the teaching and learning environment.

Approaches to learning

Approaches to learning are known to be related to the quality of learning outcomes (Prosser & Trigwell, 1999). The literature suggests that the approach to learning can be regarded as a partial proxy for the quality of learning outcomes. A number of questions will be selected from the Oxford Learning Context Questionnaire (Trigwell & Ashwin, 2003) and the Revised Two-Factor Study Process Questionnaire (Biggs, Kember, & Leung, 2001) to measure students' approaches to learning. A detailed discussion of the approaches to learning is presented in the next section.

Perceptions of the course context and the teaching and learning environment

The learning environment arguably has the greatest influence on students' learning, and is the element over which the institution has control. This construct needs to encompass measures that reflect numerous facets of the learning environment.

It has been argued that although existing student learning surveys have good psychometric properties, they provide only limited coverage of the broader student experience. For example, a wide range of student experience aspects, such as the quality of computer facilities and support services, is neglected (Yorke, 1996). This study assesses students' perceptions of the supporting services that are relevant to the study, such as the availability and quality of learning resources.

Although students' perceptions of their learning experience can be combined into an overall measure, this study emphasises the multi-dimensionality of students' perceptions about their learning experience. A single measure of the learning experience is too general to diagnose and inform any particular area that needs improvement.

Learning outcomes

Mastering disciplinary knowledge and skills are certainly the main purpose of receiving disciplinary education. The ability to gain new knowledge and transferable skills, however, including communication skills, teamwork, and the application of theoretical knowledge to the workplace, are also significant concepts for students to master. Within and beyond higher education, the need to produce graduates whose competencies are not restricted to their field of study has increased. Graduates, therefore, must also possess skills relevant to employability and lifelong learning. A number of items measuring learning outcomes will be selected from the institutional survey of Chinese University of Hong Kong; these items were identified by panels of academics and tested with graduates (Kember, Leung, & Ma, 2007).

Approaches to Learning

The approach to learning is a central element of Biggs' 3P Model, and this study accepts the fundamental principles of the deep and surface learning approaches laid out by Marton and Saljo in the mid-1970s.

The authors claimed that, depending on what they learn, the environment in which they learn and what they are used to learning, students adopt what they called “deep” or “surface” approaches to learning (Marton, Hounsell, & Entwistle, 1984; Marton & Saljo, 1976).

A surface approach is characterised by memorising superficial facts and an emphasis by the student on reproducing those facts. Prosser and Trigwell (1999) later characterised this approach as being “instrumentally or pragmatically motivated and seek[ing] to meet the demands of the task with minimum effort” (p. 91). A deep approach is characterised by students’ active engagement in the learning process. In following this approach, students seek real meaning and understanding and are interested in the subject matter. Students adopting a deep approach possess the ability to relate new information to old, generate high quality inferences, and retain the knowledge for problem solving or applying information to unfamiliar contexts.

Marton and Saljo’s (1976) seminal research showed that qualitative differences in learning outcomes were associated with qualitative differences in the students’ approaches to learning. This finding has been replicated and extended in many later studies (Entwistle & Ramsden, 1983; Prosser & Trigwell, 1999; Svensson, 1977). The literature (Biggs, 1987; Ramsden, 1991; Svensson, 1977) also shows that students with a surface approach are usually unsure about the value of their learning, while students with a deep learning approach typically report higher satisfaction with their performance (Biggs, 1987). The literature has further claimed that deep approaches to learning result in a higher quality of learning outcomes, while surface approaches result in little or no understanding and thus little or no “learning”. Based on this foundation, it has been suggested that a deep approach to learning is to be encouraged. Biggs (1999) added that the generic aim of good teaching is actually to encourage students to adopt a deep approach and to discourage the use of a surface approach. Therefore, the deep approach to learning can be regarded as a partial proxy for a good quality of learning. These findings are therefore significant for course designers and instructors, as they need to adapt the learning environment to induce changes in students' approaches to learning (Ramsden, 2003; Trigwell & Prosser, 1991).

However, in the Chinese context, a phenomenon called "The Paradox of the Chinese Learner" has questioned the validity and relevance of this learning approach theory. Marton et al. (1993) drew attention to two irreconcilable images of the Chinese learner. Observed from a Western perspective, Chinese classrooms are described as "... large classes, expository methods, relentless norm-referenced assessment, and harsh classroom climate" (Watkins & Biggs, 2001, p. 46). Chinese students are described as passive and uncritical, and inclined to adopt low-level learning approaches and rote memorisation by repetition (Bradley & Bradley, 1984; Hofstede, 1986; Salili, 1996; Samuelowicz, 1987). Referring to the surface approach and learning theories, it seems that these observations lead to the conclusion that Chinese students will have low academic achievement, yet a series of evaluations shows that the "Chinese learners" have consistently outperformed their Western counterparts. This therefore forms the "Paradox of the Chinese Learner". Of course, this "paradox" does not reflect the learning realities of all Chinese learners, and must be viewed as an over-simplification.

Kember (1996) argues that the binary separation of deep and surface approaches is too crude to explain the paradox of the Chinese learner. The Western perspective equates memorisation and rote learning, and it is commonly believed that rote learning does not lead to understanding. Kember points out that it is a myth that memorisation equals mechanical rote learning – in other words, learning without understanding. He argues that, in fact, memorisation, as practised by the Chinese learners, can actually lead to deep learning. However, in the original classification, an important element that determines the binary distinction between surface and deep learning is the learner's intention to understand or memorise. Kember claims that understanding and memorising are seen as almost mutually exclusive here, but it is actually possible that students who seek understanding may strategically use memorisation, and vice versa.

A number of later studies have found evidence that Chinese students use learning approaches featuring a combination of understanding and memorising. There are, however, variations in the form in which the approaches are described. The narrow approach of Kember and Gow (1990) ranks understanding before memorisation, while another study by Marton et al. (2005), citing the Chinese proverb "Read a hundred times and the meaning will appear", found that participants memorise the text first and, when in repeating the content, comprehend the same text from different perspectives or focus on different aspects each time through the repetition process.

Students aiming to understand material may strategically use memorisation, but without some understanding, they have a limited basis for determining what to memorise. Therefore, students who view memorisation as their primary objective may also try to reach some minimal level of understanding to aid the process of memorisation or make it more efficient (Kember, 1996). In line with Tang (1991), Marton et al. (1993) established a multi-layer relationship between memorisation and understanding by suggesting a dual categorisation for the concept of memorisation: mechanical memorisation and memorisation with understanding.

These studies show that Chinese students' practice of repetition or memorisation can have different purposes. On the one hand, memorisation can be related to mechanical rote learning. On the other hand, memorisation through repetition is part of the process of developing and deepening understanding. Given the nature of educational assessment, this combined approach to study is often regarded as successful. The use of a learning approach that combines understanding and memorising appears to provide part of the answer to the paradox of the Chinese learner (Marton et al., 1993). Watkins and Biggs (1996) argue that, as long as memorisation is used with the intent to understand, either as a pre-condition or an organic element, the approach should no longer be regarded as surface. Instead, in the Chinese context, it is culturally defined as a deep approach.

Watkins and Biggs believe that much of the so-called paradox was based upon the misconceptions of observers. Special care should be exercised in conducting cross-country comparative studies (Phillips & Zhong, 2006). Smith and Smith (1999) argue, that apart from resulting in illogical conclusions and potentially misleading course designers and teachers, the failure to consider cultural and environmental differences poses the danger of creating "new colonialism", which assumes that, without adaptation, the knowledge and belief structures that are developed in the West will transfer to another culture without any problems. The paradox also shows that the learning approach theory, which tries to use a few questions to categorise people, is too simplistic to capture the complexity of learning.

Review of Existing Surveys

National student surveys used in three different contexts, the United Kingdom, Australia, and the US, are described and reviewed in this section to provide background for the student survey conducted in this study. The first two surveys focus on students' perceptions of their learning experience, while the third investigates students' engagement with their higher education studies. The three different surveys show that there are different conceptualisations of the student learning experience (Hanbury, 2007). This section reviews the background of these different surveys, their purpose and rationale, development process and psychometric properties. The results of the surveys and how these results are used are also summarised here. The section ends with some recommendations on how to develop, analyse, and utilise student surveys.

A series of other instruments in the field, including The College Student Experiences Questionnaire (CSEQ), The Oxford Learning Context Questionnaire (OLCQ), The Sydney Student Course Experience Questionnaire (SSCEQ), and The Chinese University of Hong Kong Student Engagement Questionnaire (CUHKSEQ), have also been consulted to inform the design of this study and its survey instrument. Together with the three national surveys, these questionnaires are considered a strong basis for developing the questionnaire in this study because they have been subject to extensive testing and analysis by numerous researchers, and research evidence suggests that they provide valid indicators of the quality of modules, courses, and/or institutions. However, this section will focus only on the review of the three national surveys.

Course Experience Questionnaire

The Course Experience Questionnaire (CEQ) is a questionnaire instrument that collects students' and graduates' perceptions of their higher education experience. It was designed to provide a performance indicator of teaching quality between comparable academic organisational units at the entire programme level (Wilson, Lizzio, & Ramsden, 1997). In the Australian context, the CEQ is the major source of comparative data on student experience.

The current version of the CEQ asks students who have just completed their undergraduate study to give scores on five-point Likert scales on 25 statements related to their perceptions of the quality of their overall study course. The questionnaire items are grouped into four scales concerned with teaching (good teaching, clear goals, appropriate assessment, and appropriate workload), a scale concerning the acquisition of generic skills for the workplace, and a single item on satisfaction with the overall course quality.

The CEQ is included alongside the Graduate Destinations Survey (GDS) as part of the national survey of all university graduates in Australia conducted annually by the Graduate Careers Council of Australia (GCCA). Therefore, the CEQ is a national survey that all higher education institutions in Australia take part in, and it is sent annually to the previous year's graduating students (Australian Vice-Chancellors' Committee and Graduate Careers Council of Australia, 2005).

The CEQ was in fact an established instrument prior to its use in the GDS by the GCCA. It is based on the Course Perceptions Questionnaire (CPQ) designed in the 1980s in work carried out at Lancaster University in the UK (Entwistle & Ramsden, 1983; Ramsden & Entwistle, 1981). The developers devised the CPQ to identify the factors in the learning environment that influenced students' approaches to learning. The theory-base of CEQ was the Presage-Process-Product or 3P Model of student learning (Biggs, 1987). The developers found that students were likely to learn more effectively when these factors were provided by the academic departments; in other words, these factors are believed to lead to more effective learning. Further studies confirmed the importance of these factors in defining good teaching (Entwistle & Ramsden, 1983; Entwistle & Tait, 1990).

The CEQ is designed to capture these factors (Ramsden, 1991). It focuses on students' perceptions of their learning context, on whether the context provides these factors, as this is proposed in the model as being the mediator between teachers' approaches to teaching, and students' approaches to learning, with the hypothesis that this in turn influences students' learning outcomes. Put another way, students' perceptions of their learning context, collected through the questionnaire, can be indicative of students' future learning outcomes (Hanbury, 2007). Therefore, although the CEQ is often described as a "student satisfaction survey" in the literature, the developers argue that, while it provides a broad view of student and graduate satisfaction, it has the potential to accomplish much more than this.

According to the developers, the instrument does not aim to capture every aspect of teaching effectiveness; rather, it aims to gather reliable and valid data on those elements of teaching that students experience directly (Ramsden, 1991). One of the reasons is that students do not directly experience, and therefore cannot comment on, many aspects of teaching, such as the time and effort put into curriculum design, nor are they necessarily able to make valid comments on matters such as the relevance, quality and topicality of the content.

The CEQ was developed at a time of considerable reform in the higher education sector in Australia. Two 1980s discussion papers (Green and White Papers) on higher education demanded greater accountability for the public funds invested in the sector, and called for the development of appropriate indicators of institutional performance. In particular, student satisfaction was identified as a measure of institutional performance that should be considered (Byrne & Flood, 2003). The Australian government established the Performance Indicators Research Group (PIRG) to examine a number of quantitative indicators that could be used to evaluate the performance of individual institutions and of the university sector as a whole, and the group determined that the Graduate Careers Council of Australia (GCCA) should administer the CEQ on an annual basis to all new graduates through the Graduate Destination Survey. Subsequent surveys have covered all Australian universities, with overall response rates of around 60% (Ainley & Long, 1994; Johnson, 1997; Johnson, Ainley, & Long, 1996; Long & Hillman, 2000). Due to the needs of the GCCA, an additional Generic Skills scale was added to the original version of CEQ, with the aim of investigating "... the extent to which higher education contributes to the enhancement of skills relevant to employment" (Ainley & Long, 1994, p. xii). This scale covers items on problem solving, analytic skills, teamwork, communication and work planning.

Brevity is of great importance for a national survey like the CEQ, and GCCA has chosen to drop a number of items in the questionnaire. For example, the scale assessing the encouragement of independence in learning in the original version of CEQ was dropped in the GCCA version. The GCCA survey also does not attempt to measure the provision of resources, guidance, and pastoral, physical, or social support for students. The social dimensions of the student experience and the learning climate, such as students' attitudes, outlooks, and behaviours, which constitute a significant part of the total higher education experience for students, are also not considered in the questionnaire. Efforts to simplify the questionnaire have also attracted criticism (Byrne & Flood, 2003). An examination of the data from some Australian institutions that included extra items in the survey regarding administrative matters, student services and recreational facilities shows that students' satisfaction with their facilities was a much weaker prediction of their overall satisfaction than the original GCCA scales in the CEQ (Wilson et al., 1997). Therefore, the CEQ's intention to capture the most essential information about teaching and learning without being comprehensive is still valid here.

Another inevitable problem with the GCCA version of the CEQ is its study population. Since it collects teaching and learning information from graduates, not current students, its application in terms of helping to examine and improve current practices at institutions is therefore rather limited. However, it benefits from the graduates' ability to reflect on their course. There is also some debate as to whether students' perceptions of the value and quality of their higher education experience change following the completion of their studies and thus cannot be used to represent the perceptions of current students (Niland, 1999).

As stated, the Australian national trial has provided evidence concerning the psychometric properties of the CEQ. Various studies carried out by individual universities and departments in Australia and the UK have provided similar evidence (Ramsden, 1991; Richardson, 1994; Trigwell & Ashwin, 2003). Investigations at the Open University and Oxford University show that there is a connection between students' perceptions of their programmes and the approaches to learning that they adopted from those programmes, i.e., students who evaluate their course units more positively on the CEQ are more likely to adopt a deep approach to learning (Lawless & Richardson, 2002; Trigwell & Ashwin, 2003).

Studies have shown that there is also a connection between students' perceptions of their programmes and their achievements. Using cumulative grade point averages as a proxy for achievement, Wilson et al. (1997) found that the correlations were strongest for the good teaching scale and the clear goals and standards scale, and they were weakest for the generic skills and appropriate workload scales. As previously stated, it is hypothesised that students' satisfaction with receiving higher grades can result in positive student ratings (Marsh, 1987). Lizzio, Wilson, and Simons (2002) also found correlations between students' scores on the CEQ scales, their satisfaction, and their grade point averages. The authors conclude that students' perceptions of their academic environment, based on the CEQ, had a direct influence upon academic outcomes and an indirect influence that was mediated by changes in the students' approaches to studying. Furthermore, the authors argue that, students' academic achievement prior to their entry into higher education only had a weak influence on their achievement in terms of grade point average and no effect on their overall satisfaction at all.

In examining the CEQ data from GDS in Australia, Ramsden notes that, although the CEQ was intended to differentiate between students undertaking different programmes of study, the GCCA surveys have also identified apparent differences related to the demographic characteristics of the respondents, including gender, age, first language and ethnicity. Ramsden claims that these effects could simply reflect the enrolment of different kinds of student into programmes in different disciplines with different teaching practices and different assessment requirements at different institutions (Ramsden, 1999). In other words, observed variations in CEQ scores might arise from respondents taking different programmes, rather than from the inherent characteristics of the respondents themselves. This means that it may be necessary to study the characteristics of students in different programmes and the effects of these characteristics on students' experience.

The GCCA surveys provide a descriptive summary of the average scores obtained by students in each programme at each institution (Ramsden, 1991). Since this information is publicly available, it can be used by various readerships. The report by Hand et al. (1998) notes that CEQ data have come to be widely utilised by institutions in the form of performance indicators, and in light of pressure from the government and other stakeholders to hold universities accountable for the quality of their provision. The use of CEQ and local institutional surveys for enrolled students seems to have been accepted as a matter of routine in most Australian institutions. In some cases, the results of the surveys have implications for the allocation of funds to departments.

Although there has been no systematic research into the GDS' and the CEQ's influence on institutional policies and practices, Harris and James (2006) provide an account of their observations on the impacts of CEQ and GDS. First, the GDS and CEQ have drawn attention to the teaching function of higher education in a context in which teaching is usually neglected; most of the previous and commonly used quantitative performance indicators were focused on research. Management intervention into the evaluation of the quality of teaching and learning within units, subjects, and courses was stimulated. The authors argue that, to some extent, the evaluation of teaching and learning has become a top-down management requirement, rather than a bottom-up initiative from the academic community itself. Therefore, in some cases, the CEQ and its local institutional counterparts are viewed negatively by academics as "symptoms of managerialism" (Harris & James, 2006, p. 9).

Second, the GDS and CEQ data provide important information for prospective applicants to higher education institutions. Commercial publications, such as the *Good Universities Guide,* have utilised these data in presenting information about institutions. But the influence of the data on students' choice of institutions is not altogether clear since students usually follow well-established institutional reputation and patterns in the market. For Australia, the authors note, the dataset, and the system's willingness to collaboratively self-evaluate, have been valuable in promoting the Australian higher education system by assuring international markets of its quality.

Third, the structure and content of the CEQ have had a profound influence on conceptions of effective teaching. In their efforts to improve their CEQ scores, higher education institutions have tended to use the CEQ design as the dominant paradigm of effective teaching. On the one hand, this has positive benefits, as the CEQ contains items that indisputably relate to well-established good teaching practices. Equally significant, however, is that, as the authors put it, the CEQ is necessarily a broad, generic instrument that might be criticised for being "bland, superficial and unlikely to detect important nuances of the educational environment in specific contexts" (Harris & James, 2006, p. 9).

Although the GCCA in Australia is probably the largest single user of CEQ, the questionnaire itself and its adaptations have been employed in many other countries. Various adaptations have also been made to make the survey refer to particular study courses or programmes and compare different ways of teaching (Gibbs, 1996; Lucas et al., 1997; Prosser et al., 1994).

A number of recommendations can be found in the literature in terms of providing guidance on best practice for analysing and making use of CEQ data. The strongest cautionary note pertains to the comparison of institutions based on CEQ data. The Australian Vice-Chancellors' Committee suggested that it is "… critical that comparisons are made between like courses, in like institutions with similar survey response rates" (Australian Vice-Chancellors' Committee, 1995, p. 57). Hand et al. (1998) made a similar recommendation that CEQ data be designed to allow for comparisons within fields of study, and that they are not valid for comparing different subjects across institutions, and the results should be interpreted with reference to specific institutional, organisational, unit and course contexts.

It is also noted in the literature that CEQ data should be viewed as a starting point rather than an end point, in any evaluation process, and that survey results should be used "… to indicate productive directions for investigations into underlying factors affecting teaching quality" (Wilson et al., 1997, p. 48), and there is a much stronger basis for action if a set of performance indicators all point in the same direction (Hand et al., 1998).

National Student Survey

The National Student Survey (NSS) was established in the United Kingdom in 2005. The survey, described by HEFCE as an "… essential element of the revised quality assurance framework for higher education", is part of a package comprised of new public information on teaching quality in higher education (Surridge, 2006), and is intended to inform the public and, in particular, prospective students in choosing higher education institutions (HEFCE, 2007).

The NSS was firstly administered to all HEFCE funded students in 2005. Unlike the CEQ survey, the NSS is administered to students in their final year of undergraduate studies. The most recent NSS comprised 22 questions, grouped into six analytical scales and a measure of overall satisfaction. The scales measure Teaching and Learning, Assessment and Feedback, Academic Support, Organisation and Management, Learning Resources and Personal Development. In addition, similarly to the CEQ, an open response item is provided to ask students if there are any positive or negative aspects in their experience that they would like to highlight (Surridge, 2006). The NSS was developed based on the Australian CEQ, suggesting that the theory base of the NSS is the same as for the CEQ, i.e., it emphasises the importance of students' perceptions regarding their learning context and the impact of these perceptions upon their learning outcomes (Hanbury, 2007).

Based on the HEFCE report (Surridge, 2006), some of the key results from the 2005 administration of NSS include:

- Students' responses to all of the 22 questionnaire items were strongly positive. The percentage of students agreeing with the questionnaire statements ranged from 85.9% on "Staff are good at explaining things", to 53.0% for "Feedback on my work has been prompt", with no element of teaching quality being evaluated negatively.
- Over 170,000 students responded to the survey, of whom 81.4% agreed that "Overall, I am satisfied with my course". Thus, students viewed higher education courses in the UK very positively.
- Multivariate analysis showed a significant relationship between student responses and age, ethnicity, subject of study, qualification aim, the size of the institution and the Research Assessment Exercise (RAE) score for the subject of study.
- Students from Asian ethnic backgrounds were less positive about their courses than those from white ethnic backgrounds.
- Students' prior attainment (as measured by A-level scores) was positively correlated with responses for teaching and learning, those with high A-level scores being more positive regarding Teaching and Learning. Prior attainment had no significant impact on the remaining scales or on overall satisfaction.

- Students at departments that achieved RAE scores of 5 or 5* were more positive about all aspects of their courses.
- The six analytical scales had differential impacts on overall satisfaction. Teaching and Learning had by far the greatest impact, followed by Personal Development. The weakest relationship was found to exist between Learning Resources and overall satisfaction, but Assessment and Feedback also had a relatively weak relationship with overall satisfaction (i.e., around 25% of the impact of Teaching and Learning).

As NSS is intended to inform prospective higher education applicants, HEFCE makes the NSS data publicly available on a dedicated website – the Teaching Quality Information (TQI) website. Users can access the NSS results on specific criteria. Website users can also view institutional data on students' entry qualifications, the continuation rate of their studies, awards achieved, and the types of jobs obtained after graduation. HEFCE and the British government highly praised the quality of higher education in the UK based on the NSS findings, notably HEFCE-issued press releases with titles such as "Students Continue to be Very Satisfied with Teaching and Give Higher Ratings to Learning Resources". According to HEFCE, the use and quality of NSS is very well-received by the organisation, the government and students (HEFCE, 2006).

The Higher Education Academy in the UK, headed by Paul Ramsden, who developed the CEQ survey, has developed two initiatives to encourage institutions to share ideas and good practice in using NSS data to inform teaching enhancement activities (Hanbury, 2007). It formed a working group comprised of individuals from a sample of institutions who work with NSS data as part of their job assignment, especially those working in the fields of quality assurance in teaching and learning. The group meets to discuss and share their ideas and experiences of analysing, disseminating, and encouraging others within the institution to use NSS data to enhance the students' learning experience. The group has highlighted the need for more guidance on how to analyse the data, particularly in terms of how to make the statistics meaningful and useful to institutional administrators seeking to improve teaching and learning. The group has suggested that institutions triangulate and align international institutional surveys with NSS data, ask departments for more contextual information on the data in order to interpret and NSS data, and provide feedback to students on the actions taken as a result of the survey in order to increase response rates in the future. A number of examples of how institutions utilise NSS data were published by the Academy (Higher Education Academy, 2007). The Academy's second initiative is to set up a National Student Survey Conference to allow participants to discuss their experiences in using the NSS to improve teaching and learning.

On the institutional side, in addition to the efforts made to improve teaching and learning, a number of institutions have used the positive findings of the NSS regarding their institution for promotional marketing. Institutions that achieved relatively high overall scores or high scores on the teaching and learning scale on the survey quickly publicised these achievements on their website and brochures. It is also interesting to observe that many institutions that received less strong scores on the NSS were able to find ways to interpret the results in a positive manner – for example, by showing that students' scores for one specific scale were high, despite low scores for other scales, and showing that students' experiences are "positive", despite the scores being relatively low compared to those of other institutions.

Prosser (2005), the former Director of Research and Evaluation at the Higher Education Academy, recommended that, rather than interpreting NSS data as student satisfaction scores, the focus should be on understanding *why* students respond the way they do, on regarding their responses as perceptions of the learning context, and on seeking further data through, for example, focus groups designed to uncover where problems may lie and to find ways to improve teaching and students' learning experiences.

Perhaps in direct opposition to what the developers of the NSS recommend, NSS data has quickly become a tool used to rank universities. Although the TQI website does not rank universities, rankings based on the NSS data can easily be complied by other organisations since the data is publicly available. For example, the *Times Higher Education Supplement* publishes a ranking table of universities based on their scores on the overall satisfaction question and the table is publicly accessible on their website. Many other university rankings that previously used traditional indicators, such as research capacity, student-staff ratio, entry grades, and so on, have quickly embedded the NSS data into their ranking methodology.

Since its position in university rankings can have a huge impact on an institution's reputation, and therefore its attractiveness to students and faculty and, in some cases the funding an institution receives, institutions may have great incentives to improve their position in the ranking tables and performance in the evaluation. Therefore, there are legitimate concerns that, if used to rank institutions, student experience surveys may face the serious threat of manipulation. In England, there have already been public reports of institutions trying to manipulate the NSS to improve the standing of the institution, mostly by encouraging students to give more positive responses. For example, it has been reported that at London Metropolitan University, staff were asked to tell students to "seriously reflect" on their response "as it impacts on the reputation of your university, your teaching department and your award" (Attwood, 2008, p. 1); at Kingston University, a lecturer suggested that students should inflate Kingston's scores because they were in competition for jobs with peers studying at other institutions: "If you think something is a four (out of five), give it a five because that's what everybody else is doing" (Newman, 2008b, p. 1). Commenting on these fraudulent actions, the former Director of Research and Evaluation at the UK's Higher Education Academy said that they were "just a rather unsubtle form of a widespread practice", and it was a "testament to the fraudulent nature of the NSS" (Harvey, 2008, p. 1).

National Survey of Student Engagement

The National Survey of Student Engagement (NSSE) was established in 1998 in the US as a tool to survey undergraduate students' engagement in the academic and social activities in higher education institutions, and the results are perceived as an indicator of the quality of the education offered at these institutions (Ertl et al., 2008).

The development of the National NSSE as a means of assessing quality in higher education also coincided with the emergence of accountability as the central issue in US higher education policy. A pilot was conducted in 1999, in which 75 selected higher education institutions were involved, with approximately 275 universities and colleges participating in the inaugural launch in the spring of 2000. In 2005, more than one million undergraduate students at 557 four-year degree granting institutions in the US and Canada were sent the NSSE survey (NSSE, 2006).

The survey is comprised of 42 questions organised in five benchmark scales; each scale correlates to one empirically confirmed "good practice" in undergraduate education: level of academic challenge, active and collaborative learning, student–faculty interaction, enriching educational experiences, and supportive campus environment (Kuh, 2002). Students are asked to rate the frequency with which they engage in various activities that represent good educational practices. However, unlike the NSS and CEQ, the questionnaire does not ask students to provide more detailed feedback on open-ended questions.

The evidence base for the questionnaire instrument is built on a body of literature that argues that student engagement can result in positive educational outcomes. Astin's (1985) theory of involvement defines student learning as a function of a student's level of academic and social involvement with the institutional learning environment. Pace's (1984) theory maintains that quality of learning depends on the learning opportunities that an institution offers and on the extent to which students utilise those opportunities in their academic as well as personal experiences. Tinto's (1993) theory suggests that students' retention in higher education depends on the extent to which students share the values and norms of other individuals in the institution. Although the theories are significantly different from each other, they all point to the conclusion that student engagement plays a critical role in higher education. There is also a large body of literature on the empirical effects of student engagement on learning. The most illustrative examples of involvement theories include Terenzini, Springer, Pascarella, and Nora's (1995) study demonstrating that academic and out-of-class experiences contribute to gains in intellectual orientation and curiosity; Braxton, Milem, and Sullivan's (2000) study shows that active learning activities, such as class discussions, have a positive relationship with student retention; Chaney, Muraskin, Cahalan and Goodwin's (1998) research illustrates that the use of student support services, such as peer counselling, has a positive impact on student retention; and Thomas' (2000) demonstrates that student retention in higher education is a result of academic integration in the institutional environment, which is defined as satisfaction with intellectual development, the academic experience, and its impact on personal growth and interest in ideas.

Chickering and Gamson's (1987) *Seven Principles for Good Practice in Undergraduate Education*, derived from decades of research into students' learning in higher education, were also influential in the design of the NSSE questionnaire. The seven principles suggest that higher education institutions should 1) encourage contact between students and faculty, 2) develop reciprocity and co-operation among students, 3) use active learning techniques, 4) give prompt feedback, 5) emphasise the time spent on tasks, 6) communicate high expectations, and 7) respect diverse talents and ways of learning.

As noted earlier, the pilot studies of the NSSE were conducted in 1999. The developers examined the psychometric properties of the survey in the pilot study. The alpha coefficient was 0.85 for items measuring higher education institutional activities, 0.80 for items measuring reading and writing, 0.52 for items measuring educational programme experiences, 0.90 for items measuring educational and personal growth, and 0.84 for items measuring opinions about the school. Except for a relatively low alpha coefficient for items measuring educational programme experiences, the field test shows that the NSSE has satisfactory reliability levels. A number of findings have supported the validity of the survey, including evidence of senior students reporting greater overall gains in educational and personal growth than first-year students, and positive correlations between students' grade point averages and their scores on the five benchmarks (Kuh, 2007).

Furthermore, a number of tests have been conducted to assess the test-retest reliability of the NSSE. In 2002, the developers conducted a test-retest analysis using 1,226 respondents who completed the same form of the paper survey twice over a period of several months. The reliability coefficients of the students' responses to the five benchmarks were all between 0.74 and 0.78, suggesting little variation in students' responses from one testing period to the next. In 2003, the developers conducted a stability analysis to measure the associations between scores for the 214 institutions that participated in the 2002 and 2003 administrations of the survey and the values of the Spearman's rho correlations, with the scores ranging from 0.81 to 0.93. The same test was conducted at the 236 institutions that participated in 2004 and 2005 administration, and Spearmen's rho correlations ranged from 0.78 to 0.92. These findings suggest that the NSSE data are stable at the institutional level from year to year, assuming no major changes in the institutional learning environment (Center for Postsecondary Research at Indiana University Bloomington, 2007; Kuh, 2007).

The NSSE covers public and private four-year higher education institutions. It is administered annually to different levels of students at participating institutions. Unlike the NSS and CEQ, the NSSE is conducted by an independent organisation (Indiana University Centre for Postsecondary Research) that has no government support. The use of NSSE is voluntary for higher education institutions, and it requires a financial commitment of between \$3,375 and \$7,500 from an institution, depending on the size of the student sample (Hanbury, 2007). Institutions are asked to provide support in survey administration, including identifying students, providing incentives for their participation, and reminding them to complete and return the surveys.

The NSSE team provides an institutional data report to every participating institution, including a description of the benchmark scores, means comparisons, and frequency distributions. (Kuh, 2001). The participating institutions decide how to use the survey data. Some higher education institutions have developed or changed strategies based on their NSSE data by, for example, expanding course-based halls of residence and encouraging faculty-student collaboration on research (Center for Postsecondary Research at Indiana University Bloomington, 2007).

The NSSE team conceived several initiatives to help institutions utilise the survey data. For example, in collaborating with the American Association for Higher Education, it started the *Documenting Effective Educational Practice* project, which used case study methods to explore the everyday working of approximately 20 institutions with higher-than-predicted graduation rates and high scores on the five benchmarks of the NSSE. The project also incorporated national roundtables and campus consortia work to develop action plans for improving students' engagement in higher education institutions (Hanbury, 2007). Kuh et al.'s (2005) book, *Student Success in College: Creating the Conditions that Matter*, documented suggestions from the project to higher education institutions for achieving high student engagement, which included creating: 1) a living mission and a lived educational philosophy, 2) an unshakeable focus on student learning, 3) clearly marked pathways to student success, 4) environments adapted for educational enrichment, 5) an improvement-oriented campus culture, and 6) shared responsibility for educational quality and success.

The NSSE team also reported more frequent use of their survey data in accreditation matters. The NSSE team found that the accreditation agencies have given more weight to evidence of student learning and, at the same time, reduced the weight on the traditional indicators that represent institutional resources. The NSSE team devised toolkits for the accreditation agencies that comprise and suggestions for incorporating NSSE data into regional accreditation processes and standards (NSSE Institute, 2009). One of the intentions of developing NSSE was to shift the nature of the public debate about higher education quality, as well as to shift the current focus on institutions' resources and reputation to a factor the developers believe is far more important to student learning: student feedback on how they actually use the resources for learning that their school provides (Kuh, 2001).

Potential Problems with Student Experience Research

In general, the research literature argues that student evaluation is a more valid and reliable indicator than evaluations from other sources (Marsh & Roche, 1997). Students experience the teaching and learning fully and are able to judge the delivery of teaching, assessment, feedback, communication with students, and departmental and institutional resources (Cashin, 1995). However, in the literature, there are also concerns with the potential biases in student evaluation, such as those caused by gender and grade awarded.

Numerous studies have examined potential biases. After controlling for other factors, research shows that both the teacher's and the student's gender have little overall impact on student evaluation (Basow, 1996; Basow & Silberg, 1987). Some other teacher qualities, however, especially the use of humour, have been found to influence teaching evaluations (Adamson, O'Kane, & Shevlin, 2005; Liu, 1998). Arguably, such factors make the course interesting and can positively influence students' learning and should therefore justifiably be included in the evaluation. Another primary concern for the validity of student evaluation is "grading leniency". It is argued that teachers who give inflated grades to students will receive inflated student evaluations. This may become a serious threat to the validity of student evaluation, as teachers may intentionally give higher grades in the hope of receiving higher evaluations. By analysing experimental studies, however, Marsh (1984, 2007) concluded that support for this argument is weak, and such a effect is likely to be insignificant in the actual use of student evaluations. The grading leniency effects can also be minimised by conducting evaluations prior to assessments or before grades are published.

A large volume of the related research has investigated the validity and reliability of students' assessment of teaching (Prebble et al., 2005). Most formal surveys of students' experiences are theory-based, and they typically contain groups of items measuring different concepts, referred to as "scales" (Hanbury, 2007). Tests of reliability and validity are performed on these scales, and, as such, establish the robustness of the psychometric properties of these instruments.

The reliability of student evaluations refers to the consistency and stability of the measurement. Consistency is defined as agreement between different students judging the same thing, while stability refers to the extent to which the indicators are rated similarly by the same students at different times (Braskamp & Ory, 1994; Cohen, 1990).

Numerous studies report that student evaluations are reliable. With well-designed instruments and a sufficient number of students, agreement on the ratings given by different students within the same class is consistently high (Marsh, 1987; Marsh & Roche, 1993). Remmers (1963) tested the correlations of student ratings taken two weeks apart and obtained a very high correlation of .90. Overall and Marsh (1980) tested the correlation between mid-term and end-of-term ratings, confirming the stability with a .83 correlation. Drucker and Remmers (1951) compared ratings from alumni and students and also reported a high correlation, demonstrating that elapsed time since the learning experience does not alter graduates' course ratings.

Murray et al. (1990) summarised the literature on the reliability of student evaluations and concluded that "... the weight of the evidence suggests that student ratings of a given instructor are stable across items, raters, and time periods" (p. 250). Theall and Franklin (1990a) offer the same conclusion: "Whether reliability is measured within classes, across classes, over time, or in other ways, student ratings are remarkably consistent" (p. 50).

Validity refers to the extent to which the results of student evaluations actually represent teaching and learning quality. This measure is more difficult to prove, as debate continues regarding what constitutes teaching and learning quality (Cashin, 1988; Feldman, 1988; Marsh, 1987; Marsh & Overall, 1980). Teaching and learning quality is a hypothesised concept that cannot be directly measured. The validity of student evaluations, therefore, has to be demonstrated through a construct validation approach. According to Marsh (1987), a construct validation approach requires student evaluation to be "… substantially correlated with a variety of other indicators of effective teaching" (p. 8).

One of the most commonly used indicators of teaching effectiveness is student learning. According to Theall and Franklin, the correlations between students' evaluations and the knowledge they gained in the course are high (Theall & Franklin, 1990b). Student evaluations have also been found to correlate with teachers' self-evaluation. It has been argued that teachers' self-evaluations demonstrate very similar factor structures to their students' evaluations (Marsh, 1987).

The research literature has also argued that the teaching effectiveness construct is much broader than the learning outcomes that can be measured objectively by student examinations. Marsh and Roche (1999) argues that teaching quality includes other indicators, such as "different aspects of learning, competency, and understanding; professional growth; appropriate attitudes; a sense of mastery; plans to pursue the subject; future coursework selection" (p. 517), none of which can be adequately measured merely by examination scores.

Kuh (2007) summarises the factors that may compromise the validity of student evaluations. He suggests that the most important factor is students' inability to provide accurate responses to evaluation questions. For example, students may not have enough experience with the teacher to judge teaching quality precisely, or they may not understand the question. The second factor is students' potential unwillingness to provide accurate and truthful information. In this instance, students may intentionally give untruthful responses to sensitive questions because they may feel that accurately reporting the information may put them in an awkward or embarrassing position. Kuh also suggests that students' self-reports may be subject to the halo effect; that is, students may slightly inflate some aspects of their behaviour or performance. Kuh clarifies that inflations appear to be consistent across different types of students and schools. This means that, although what students report and what they actually do may differ slightly, this does not advantage or disadvantage one institution or student group compared with another.

Citing various studies (Bradburn & Sudman, 1988; Brandt, 1958; Pace, 1985; Pike, 1995), Kuh (2007) argues that student self-reports are more likely to be valid under five conditions:

- When the information requested is known to the respondents;
- The questions are phrased clearly and unambiguously;
- The questions refer to recent activities;
- The respondents think the questions merit a serious and thoughtful response; and
- Answering the questions does not threaten, embarrass, or violate the privacy of the respondent or encourage the respondent to respond in socially desirable ways.

As will be detailed in the chapter on *Methodology*, the survey for the current investigation is designed to satisfy all of Kuh's conditions.

Marsh (1987) summarised the research on the validity of student evaluations by stating: "… student ratings are significantly and consistently related to a number of varied criteria … this provides support of the construct validity of the ratings" (p. 11). In fact, given that students are the most direct recipients of teaching and experience teaching, it can be argued that students are best qualified to provide accurate and valid evaluations of teaching and learning.

Although some methodological problems are evident, both the validity and reliability of properly designed student evaluations can be attested. The consensus of the research literature is that, if properly designed and administered, student evaluations can be a valuable source of information. However, the confirmed reliability and validity of student experience data do not, in and of themselves, lead to useful data or improved teaching quality (Theall & Franklin, 1990a). The literature suggests that whether the data is useful and helpful depends on whether students and faculty members take the evaluation seriously and have the will to make changes (Brennan et al., 2003; Kember, Leung, & Kwan, 2002).

The literature also points out that students, for the most part, do not know why their institutions collect feedback or what happens to the collected data. Students value having their opinions solicited, and want to be empowered in the quality enhancement process (CHERI, 2004). It is necessary, therefore, to convince students that their opinions matter. Richardson (2005a), referring to the work of Spencer and Schmelkin (2002), suggests that institutions and faculty keep students informed of how the collected information will be used to improve teaching and learning; otherwise, students may feel reluctant to spend time completing the survey.

This scenario also applies to teachers. Kember et al. (2002) argue that teachers may perceive that institutions attach more importance to research than to teaching. In addition, teachers may lack the ability to analyse and interpret the potentially valuable data of student experience, which is critical in utilising the data to improve teaching effectiveness. It is crucial, therefore, to guide teachers and administrators on how student evaluation information can be interpreted. Empirical research has shown that, when accompanied with professional consultation, student experience data can greatly improve the quality of teaching and learning (Marsh & Overall, 1979).

Summary

From the initial investigations conducted by Remmers in the late 1920s to the present, the student experience has been the most researched method of teaching evaluation. The literature review has outlined some of the issues and open questions that are of immediate relevance to this study. The current controversy about the use of student evaluations revolves mainly around the issue of validity. The literature review shows that extensive work has been completed by researchers in the field to provide empirical support to the validity and reliability of student evaluation as a means of evaluating teaching. It is maintained in the literature that a high level of validity can be achieved when instruments and procedures are properly designed and tested.

Researchers also argue that there is not a perfect instrument appropriate for all teaching situations and advise caution about possible misuse of student evaluations. Student evaluations of teaching should not be used as the only source of data to make judgments about an instructor or an institution's performance. Nevertheless, the literature suggests that student evaluations can and should be used as a valuable source of data to support the academic evaluation and decision-making process.

This chapter has also reviewed three national surveys. The three surveys share many commonalities, including that are all theory and evidence-based, all have proven and satisfactory reliability and validity, all have the intention to improve the student learning experience, all have been developed in a context that stressed quality assurance and the accountability of higher education institutions, and, in practice, all have been used as performance indicators to benchmark institutions or academic departments.

All three surveys recognise that a barrier to the effective use of student survey data is the lack of understanding and guidance on how to use and interpret the data. If used appropriately, the data can be valuable in identifying particular areas for improvement, and in promoting further research to explore areas where problems have been identified. However, if used incorrectly, the findings can be biased and misleading. Therefore, the three surveys have conducted various initiatives aiming at informing the participating institutions and making the best use of the survey findings.

The findings of these surveys have profound implications for this study. The CEQ and NSS suggested that, when making comparisons, the comparing units should themselves be comparable in that they, for example, compare the same subjects across institutions. The surveys' findings also cautioned that some personal characteristics, including gender, prior achievement and socio-economic status, may have an impact on students' scores, and the composition of students at different institutions and in different disciplines can be different. It is therefore necessary to take into account the student composition of both institutions and subject areas when comparing survey scores in order to avoid bias in reporting.

The three surveys and the subsequent analysis all suggest that other institutional data should be considered or even triangulated when reporting the survey results. The survey data should not be relied on as the sole source of information. Attention should be given to the institutional and subject context of the data, as well as factors that may have had an impact on the results, but are not considered in the survey.

Another potential problem with the use of student experience data is the possibility of manipulation. Although so far there have not been any systematic studies of the likelihood or effects of institutional manipulation of studies of the student experience or how the survey mechanisms can be improved to avoid manipulation, the nature of student experience surveys, has made the surveys a "simplistic device that is easy to outmanoeuvre" (Harvey, 2008, p. 1).

This aspect is especially relevant in China, where there has been a tradition of manipulation and corruption in audits, and this practice can also be found in academia. For example, the official *Benke* evaluation programme has been widely criticised for introducing a heavy burden on institutions and inducing institutions to manipulate.

For this study, because the administrators of the institutions surveyed have been informed that the institution's privacy will be protected as its name will not be disclosed to other institutions or to the public, and the survey results will be used solely for research and improvement purposes, rather than compiling ranking tables, there are fewer incentives for institutions to systematically manipulate the data. In addition, conducting the survey in class environment allowed the researcher to talk to respondents face-to-face and explain the importance of the accuracy of the data to further reduce the chance of manipulation.

Any attempts to manipulate the student experience information not only have a negative effect on the attempt to compare institutions, but, they also undermine the genuine efforts made by institutions to listen to students and to use the results to improve their learning experience. Using student experience to rank and determine the standing and welfare of faculty and institutions will certainly offer them the incentives for manipulation. It may be a debatable question whether student experience should be used for this comparison purpose at all. But if it is to be used in such way, there is the question of how manipulation can be avoided to ensure the credibility and use of student experience information. These two questions certainly warrant further studies, but are out of the scope of this study.

Chapter Five

Research Design and Methodology

Research Design

This chapter presents the methodology employed by this research. It discusses the methods for the literature review, instrument development, the population and sample, the survey administration procedures, and the methods used to analyse the data.

A review of the student learning experience literature (Ertl et al., 2008) concludes that the findings of many studies on this topic are not convincing, as these studies rely on only one source of data, and the methodological framework is too narrow to capture the mediated and contextualised nature of learning. This is particularly and often the case in studies that are heavily reliant on the use of student experience inventories.

For this study, the research purposes require the study to provide not only facts, but also meanings and social constructions. A high level of interpretation is needed to understand the facts of students' characteristics and experiences. Therefore, in order to produce robust, comprehensive and relevant research findings, this research chooses to use a mixed-methods approach (Axinn & Pearce, 2006; Bryman, 2004, 2006; Tashakkori & Teddlie, 1998), and specifically, a qualitative-quantitative-qualitative design, to overcome the inefficacy of many studies in the existing literature and to contribute to a deeper understanding of the research problem.

Research Framework

Phase 1: Qualitative

In order to enhance the knowledge and understanding of the relatively unexplored topic of students' experience within the Chinese context, and to inform the design of the research, this study first conducted focus groups with students, and interviews with teachers, senior managers and researchers, to explore the topic of students' experiences of higher education generally, and, specifically, what the diversification of higher education institutions means for students' experience in China. Furthermore, the participants were also asked to critique the draft questionnaire for face validity and to discuss their problems or concerns regarding the questionnaire.

The findings that emerged from these explorative field consultations suggested the main areas of interest and informed the design of the next stage of the investigation. The fieldwork consultations conducted in November 2007 provided key data for carrying out the next phase of the research.

Phase 2: Quantitative

To answer the research questions, a large-scale survey was conducted because this allowed both factual and perceptual, or attitudinal, data to be gathered from a large sample of *Benke* students. The survey collected around 1,200 responses from students. The large sample size allowed the study to document the student experience and background patterns at the institutions. The quantitative results from the survey allowed statistical analyses to be performed in order to compare and contrast the student characteristics and their actual experiences at the selected institutions.

Using a formal student survey has three key advantages. The first two benefits are methodologically grounded, in that a formal survey can provide an opportunity to collect students' opinions from a large population, and that a formal survey can document the experiences of the student population in a systematic way. These two benefits are delivered because the survey instrument is standardised, with the associated psychometric properties of reliability and validity, enabling comparisons across institutions and programmes. The other benefit of the use of a formal student survey is that it can be developed based on learning theories. That is, the survey can measure aspects of the student learning experience that have an influence on students' learning outcomes (Hanbury, 2007).

There is a large body of literature on the use of quantitative instruments in assessing students' learning experience (see, for example, Ertl et al., 2008; Richardson, 2000). The questionnaire used in this study represents a further development of the relevant inventories in the literature. As none of these questionnaires were specifically designed for this study's research purposes and none of them had been thoroughly tested in the Chinese context, it was necessary to adapt them to the needs of this study, and to test the new questionnaire in the Chinese context. Therefore the field consultations were vital, and a critical and systematic review of the existing student survey literature was needed.

The survey instrument developed for this study collected student background information which was used in two ways. Firstly, the data reveal the demographic patterns of the student intake at the selected institutions, allowing the study to establish differences in students' prior educational and socio-economic backgrounds. Secondly, it provides the opportunity to examine – if applicable – differences in students' learning experiences in the light of differences in students' backgrounds.

The face validity of the questionnaire was improved in the field consultation in the qualitative Phase 1, and was further improved by a pilot. The construct validity could only be seriously tested after the formal administration of the survey because a large sample is needed to do this. The development of the instrument itself is a contribution of this research to the field.

Phase 3: Qualitative

The aim of the third phase was to develop deeper insights into the findings from the survey instrument. The qualitative elements in this phase generated rich data from students and staff on how learning processes are conducted in different higher education settings in China.

Following Hammersley's (1996, p. 167) concepts of "facilitation" and "triangulation", in this phase qualitative investigations based on document analysis, focus groups with students, and interviews with senior managers were conducted to follow up, supplement and complement the findings from the large-scale survey. The survey results produced a number of specific and relevant questions for more in-depth investigations, and the findings from the two phases were used to check against each other to increase the validity of the framework.

Focus groups with students at the institutions were conducted to give students the opportunity to describe their learning experiences in greater depth, and to discuss the reasons that caused the similarities and differences in their experiences that emerged in the analysis of the survey. Semi-structured interviews were conducted with a small number of Presidents, Vice-Presidents in charge of teaching, Directors of Studies or Directors of Higher Education Research, and others holding relevant posts, who are well-informed on the institutional diversity and student experience matters in the four institutions. Questions were asked in order to ascertain how the institutions perceive the students' experiences, what is the underpinning philosophy and rationale of their education, and what is the institution's position on the diversification of higher education. The focus groups and interviews offered the researcher an opportunity to uncover complex interconnections and meanings that could not be deduced from describing the students' experiences. Finally, an expert panel of higher education researchers was formed to discuss the findings of the study in order to enhance the quality and impact of the research.

Selection of Institutions, Disciplines and Students

In order to ensure that the focus of the research was not excessively broad and the fieldwork did not become unmanageable, it was necessary to make key decisions to focus the study appropriately. These decisions referred to the student sample (year of study and programme of study) and the institutional sample. In summary, this research involved a study of third-year students studying Arts and Engineering *Tongzhao Benke* programmes at four selected institutions by means of questionnaires, interviews, focus groups and document analysis.

In China there are other forms of undergraduate study, including *Benke* students admitted through channels other than the unified national admission process and the *Zhuanke* track (described in chapter on *Higher Education in China*). *Tongzhao Benke* was chosen as the research focus because it is the primary and the most established form of undergraduate education in China. Indeed, a large part of the expansion in institutional and student numbers since 1998 was targeted at *Tongzhao Benke* education. This study focuses on *Tongzhao Benke* education only.

Another decision was to focus on third-year *Benke* students to participate in the survey. First year students were excluded from the sample, because they have not been fully exposed to teaching and learning at their institution at the time of investigation. Furthermore, in Chinese higher education institutions, students in their first and second years receive a relatively general education, and have not been fully exposed to specific subject education. Final (fourth) year students were excluded as their focus is on their final examinations and internship activities, which meant also that they were difficult to contact.

In terms of disciplines, students studying Arts and Engineering programmes were chosen because fieldwork consultations showed that the programmes in these two fields have different course organisation patterns, and students' experiences appeared to be different to some extent. This diversity therefore offered the study the opportunity to explore and control for the programme effects, while investigating institutional effects on students' experiences. One reason for choosing these two specific programmes was that these are the programmes in which the institutions concerned, and in fact most institutions in China, had a relatively large population of students.

The four institutions are all relatively engineering-oriented in that they have a stronger focus on the engineering discipline. This focus has implications for interpreting the findings of the investigation. For example, some institutions' engineering programmes received significantly higher ratings than their languages programmes. This finding does not necessarily suggest that there is a difference between the two disciplines *per se*, but it may reflect the fact that the institutions give priority to the engineering programmes. Because the four institutions selected are all relatively engineering-oriented, they are more comparable in this sense, and this also reflects the fact, as will be discussed in the findings chapter, that engineering is the largest and most popular discipline in Chinese higher education.

At the time of the investigation there were 25 private colleges in the country. A number of cities had more than one private college. Therefore, despite the fact that there are thousands of institutions and hundreds of cities in the country, the list of candidate cities was not extensive. The institutions selected for this study are all located in a city in southeast China. The hosting province is home to more than 30 *Benke* institutions, 19 of which are located in the provincial capital – the fieldwork base city. The city features all four types of institution and these institutions are fairly large in terms of student population, therefore providing a large sample size for examining hypotheses and drawing conclusions.

This study fills a gap in the literature by exploring a new dataset of student backgrounds and experiences at a diverse set of institutions in China. One institution was chosen from each of the four ownership and official title categories, and throughout the study, these institutions are referred to as the Public University, the Independent College, the Public College, and the Private College.

The four specific institutions were selected for a number of reasons. First, they all have a sufficient enrolment of *Benke* students.

Because the study examines the same two fields of study at the four institutions, it was also important that the institutions offer these subjects and have a sufficient number of students studying them. The close geographic proximity of the four institutions means that the institutional managers have some knowledge about the position of their institution within the local system. Indeed, the institutional managers were interested in assessing their students' experiences compared to those of other institutions and therefore, were willing to provide access to students. Furthermore, the institutions are in the same province, and it is expected that the institutions all have large groups of local students, providing a base for the comparison of student entrance examination scores (as different provinces may use different papers in *Gaokao* and therefore the scores of students from different provinces are usually not directly comparable).

This study focuses on the four *Benke* institutions in one city only, and the research findings are not generalisable to all *Benke* institutions in the country. However, the study is deliberately explorative in nature and contributes to an understanding of what the diversification of institutions means for students in higher education in China.

In order to establish contact with the institutions, the deans or directors of higher education research at these institutions were contacted and given initial information about the study, and what participating in the research would entail. In particular, information was provided about the research design, including the number of questionnaires and interviews, the time and effort required from the institution, ethical considerations, the purposes of the study, and its potential benefits to the institution. All of the four institutions indicated strong interest in the study and its aims and agreed to participate in the study after receiving the first request to do so.

The timing of the data collection was designed to give students ample time to make judgments about their experiences at the institutions. Students' experiences are best assessed after a few weeks of re-exposure to the learning environment following a vacation or before the end of a term, when exam preparations dominate students' time. Therefore, the decision was made to undertake the interviews and administer the survey in the middle of the second term of the academic year. The institutions helped to identify the specific times and class periods during which the students could be surveyed.

Publishing the results of this study with the name of the institutions could be of interest to certain external stakeholders, especially prospective students and the media. NSSE's experience shows that roughly 25% of participating institutions voluntarily make their results publicly available, but other institutional participants primarily utilise the results on an internal basis. Some institutions assess their data and compare their results with other institutions before deciding on appropriate communication strategies (Center for Postsecondary Research at Indiana University Bloomington, 2007). For this study, it was made clear to the participating institutions that this study would guarantee the anonymity of the institutions.

Participating Institutions

At the time of writing, nine public colleges, two private colleges, and 13 independent colleges offered *Tongzhao Benke* programmes in the province, of which six universities, three public colleges, two private colleges, and eight independent colleges are located in the fieldwork base city, the provincial capital.

It should be noted that translations of the institutional names are not necessarily based on the translations adopted by the institutions. There are national requirements and procedures regulating institutions' use of titles, and institutions should not mislead applicants by "inflating" their authorised names. However, in practice, it seems that many institutional leaders interpret these regulations as applying only to the use of Chinese names, with institutions being free to decide their English name. To avoid confusion, this study adheres to the "real" title that reflects the institution's course level in translation, rather than directly using the English translation adopted by the institution.

A brief introduction of the four institutions is provided below. Most of the information was extracted from the respective institutional websites or brochures, while some was provided directly by the institutional contacts, and all of the information here has been verified by the institutions.

The Public University

The origin of the Public University can be traced back to the 1940s, when one of its predecessors was established. After several mergers, this institution has become a comprehensive university offering undergraduate and graduate courses encompassing virtually all academic disciplines.

The Public University's *Benke* enrolment size for 2008 was around 9,000. In 2008, the tuition fees for English and Computer Science programmes were 4,950 Yuan and 5,550 Yuan per annum, respectively. The tuition fee levels, as with all public universities and colleges in the country, are set by the administering authority, in this case the provincial government.

The university's main campus is located in a newly-built Higher Education Institution (HEI) Park in the city, which is a 35-minute drive from the city centre. This campus is very large in size and enjoys the benefits of being completely new; the buildings are modern and attractive. The HEI Park is one of two new HEI Parks in the city. The Public University is located in one park, while the Public College and the Private College in this study are located in the other. Previously, the (old) main campus of this public university was located in a central district in the city. The new campus opened in 2004 and the Public University has since designated the new campus as the main campus and moved all of its *Benke* students to the new campus. A half of the old main campus in the city centre was transferred to its independent college – the Independent College investigated in this study.

The Public University has a teaching force of over 2,600 full-time staff, of whom 49 are foreign nationals, over 1,200 are full professors or associate professors (accounting for 45.6% of full-time teachers), around 700 either hold PhD degrees or are pursuing PhD degrees, and over 1,500 hold Master's degree or above (accounting for 57.7% of full-time staff).

The institution's introduction on the website says it "... emphasises the importance of research". The institution has one national key laboratory and two Ministry of Education-level key laboratories. From 2005 to 2008, the institution led or participated in over one hundred research projects funded by the 863 programmes, the National Science Fund or the National Social Science Fund, and published over 6,000 papers. The university's institutional journals on arts and science are in the national key journal indices.

Regarding the education of undergraduate students, the institution claims that it "... strives to cultivate advanced professionals with high overall qualities, well balanced knowledge, solid [academic] grounding, wide scope of knowledge, and innovative spirits and practical abilities". Its self-proclaimed mission is "... to strive to build a high quality and modern comprehensive university, to make more and larger contributions to help the province rise in central China".

The Independent College

The Independent College is affiliated with the Public University in this study. It was established in 2001 and gained officially approved independent college status in 2003. As an approved independent college, it has an independent campus, independent financial accounts, and independent legal status from the Public University. However, compared to some other independent colleges in the country, this college's ties with its *Muxiao*, or mother institution, are strong; in fact, the Public University's business arm corporation owns it, and it moved to one of the Public University's campuses after the Public University moved to a new campus. The campus has a relatively central location in the city, and therefore enjoys easy access to transportation, entertainment, and other facilities. However, the campus is also constricted in size, and the buildings are mostly rather dated and do not have the attractive design that can be seen at many other newly-built higher education campuses.

The institution has around 40 *Benke* subjects, mostly concentrating in the fields of science and technology. The institution is mainly and traditionally focused on science and technology subjects but, as with other institutions, it has expanded its programme offerings to many other fields, as well, including English.

The *Benke* enrolment size for 2008 was around 3,000. In 2008, the tuition fees for English and Computer Science programmes were 8,000 and 10,000 Yuan per annum, respectively. The tuition fees are set by the institution within the upper limit determined by the government.

The college has more than 500 teachers, around 350 of whom are full-time staff. Of the full-time staff, 61 are full professors or associate professors (17.1%), and 106 have Master's degrees or higher (29.7%).

The college claims that its mission is to "... become a high quality, international, innovative, open, and nationally first-class independent college in the long term". It also emphasises that it "... relies on the high quality education resources of [the Public University]", and specifically cultivates four abilities in its students, namely "learning ability, practical ability, innovative ability and employability".

The Public College

The Public College included in this study was founded in the 1950s as a vocational college specialising in water conservation and hydroelectricity. It changed its name in 2003, when the college was promoted to the *Tongzhao Benke* level. The new name is a more general one, and shows that the institution aims to serve the whole region, instead of serving a specific industry. The college traditionally focused on engineering subjects, but has expanded to include English, economics, management, literature, science, agriculture, and other fields in recent years.

The college moved to a new campus in 2004. This HEI Park is about 40 minutes drive from the city centre. The campus is quite large and the buildings are new and attractive.

The college employs 1,100 staff members, 800 of whom are full-time teachers. Full and associate professors account for 30% of the teaching force. Over 50% of the staff hold Master's degrees or higher, and there are around 50 members of with PhDs.

The *Benke* enrolment size for 2008 at the Public College was around 2,000. In 2008, the tuition fees for English and Computer Science programmes were 4,950 and 5,500 Yuan per annum, respectively.

The college claims in its introduction that its mission is to "… become a high standard applied Engineering college that has advantages provincially and has influence nationally".

The Private College

The Private College was established in the 1990s and promoted to *Tongzhao Benke* level in 2005.

This college has two campuses. The new campus is next to the Public College in an HEI Park which is a 15-minute drive to the old campus. The old campus is relatively small and is located in a fairly central district of the city. The new campus now houses all of the college's *Tongzhao* students (including *Zhuanke* and *Benke*), while the old campus is for *Zikao* (self-test training) students. The new campus is very large in size; the buildings are new and attractive.

The vast majority of the Private College's students are enrolled in *Zhuanke* and *Zikao Benke* programmes. Unlike the *Zikao Benke* programmes, to which the institution can admit students freely, the admission quota for *Tongzhao Benke* programmes is determined by the government. Although the government quota has been growing steadily since 2005, it started from a very small base and is still small compared to other institutions.

The *Tongzhao Benke* enrolment size for 2008 at the Private College was 800. In 2008, the tuition fees for English and Computer

Science programmes were 8,000 and 10,000 Yuan per annum, respectively. The tuition fee level is determined by the institution and approved by the government.

The college claims that it has "... at all times adhered to the orientation of employment, adjusted the programmes according to market needs and cultivated high quality and application-oriented advanced professionals with innovation and creativity abilities". Its mission is to "... become a provincially leading and nationally first-class private *Benke* college".

Design of the Questionnaire

The new questionnaire was designed specifically to assess students' higher education experiences at their institutions. The learning scales of the questionnaire were constructed to be in accordance with learning theories and to fit the devised student experience conceptual framework devised for this study. The questionnaire was also designed to be general enough to apply to a variety of disciplines and institutions. The decision was made to devise a questionnaire that could be completed in 20 minutes and administered during class time, in order to maximise the response rate. However, this also meant that only a limited range of student experience could be explored.

In addition to the closed-response items, there were three open-ended questions to which respondents could, if they wished, add comments on aspects of their experience that may not have been adequately covered in the closed-response items.

Developing the items and scales of the questionnaire involved several stages. The first stage consisted of a review of current surveys in this field. As Harvey et al. note, in student surveys, students are more likely to respond and co-operate if the design process of the survey instrument involves the key "stakeholders" (i.e., the students and teachers):

> Any surveyed group is more likely to respond to a relevant survey than one that appears to miss the point. Students are much more likely to provide detailed information about issues that are important to students than those that teachers think ought to be important to students (Harvey et al, 1997, p. 11).

Therefore, in addition to creating, modifying, and using questionnaire items from the existing literature, students and teachers were consulted. In the second stage, a series of student focus groups and teacher interviews were conducted. The student focus groups were selected to reflect the variety of institutions and provision within the institutions. Student participants were drawn from different courses, and the groups reflected the gender balance at the institutions. Students and teachers in the focus groups were given a draft questionnaire and asked to provide their opinions. Students were also asked to discuss their student experience to inform the study.

The third stage involved an expert group reviewing the questionnaire. The field experts were invited to make suggestions about how to improve the questionnaire items. Furthermore, this process established the face validity of the items, eliminated uncertainties regarding interpretation, and analysed the adequacy of the item pool.

Fourth, the refined questionnaire was piloted at a small sample of institutions. The pilot helped to explore and refine the survey administration process. It also helped to reveal problems that could arise in actually administering the survey. Most importantly, it tested the statistical proprieties of the questionnaire.

During the development process, advice was sought from people outside the expert panel and student focus groups when the need arose. *Ad hoc* comments were sought from stakeholders, including prospective students, faculty, institutional administrators, and institutional career guidance staff, to ensure that the questionnaire reflected essential and valued student experiences.

A Chinese version of the questionnaire was used in the pilot, as well as in the final field survey. The nuances of translation were taken very seriously. To ensure that the statements on both the English and Chinese survey forms express identical meanings, the researcher gave the Chinese version to two university English teachers to translate back into English, then compared the English versions to see if there was any mistranslation and misunderstanding, and discussed the most appropriate translations with the English teachers.

Dimensions and Items of the Questionnaire

The conceptual learning framework of this investigation is presented in the chapter on *Student Experience in Higher Education*. This section further explains some of its key elements.

Personal Characteristics

This section of the questionnaire contains items related to student demographics, including gender and parents' level of education.

The questionnaire avoided asking students about their families' income. This is because, firstly, asking about income can be perceived as insensitive or rude by students; secondly, students are not necessarily aware of their families' actual level of income; and thirdly, the other socio-economic information collected this study, such as place of origin, parents' educational level, and, especially, the concern level for finance, are sufficient to indicate the student's socio-economic status in general.

Place of Origin

The questionnaire asks students for their place of origin, defined as the place they took their *Gaokao* exams. Since students can only take the *Gaokao* in the place where they are officially registered, this is equivalent to the registered residential place. There are a small number of cases in which students spend most of their childhood in one place, but register at another place and take the *Gaokao* there, usually for the purpose of getting better chances at admission (the so-called examination migration). Since the places students move to are usually of better status than the original place, and only relatively better-off students have the opportunity to move, the new places represent the students' socio-economic status better and are considered as the "place of origin" for the students here in this study.

In China, there are different classifications of "place". This study adopts the categorisation used by the *Expansion of Higher Education and the Labour Market* project at Peking University (Yue, Wen, & Ding, 2004), because the classifications are easily comprehensible by the students and they correlate well to the economic status of the place. In this classification, a "place" can be classified into five categories:

- *Shenghui Chengshi/Zhi Xiashi*: Provincial Capital or Municipality.
- *Dijishi*: Prefecture-level city.
- *Xianjishi*: County-level city.
- *Xiangzhen*: Township.
- *Nongcun*: Rural area.

In China, broadly speaking, the income of a resident is strongly associated with the type of place of residence. Residents of large and affluent cities are usually much wealthier than residents of smaller, less developed cities and towns, while residents of rural areas are the poorest. The respondent's place of origin, then, is considered a proxy for his or her socio-economic status, and is used in analysing the respondent's scores on other items.

Parental Occupation

The options under this question were designed to fit the Chinese context and are not directly comparable to the data and categorisation of other countries.

Parental occupation is used as another proxy for the respondent's socio-economic status. The occupation classification this study adopts is based primarily on two reports conducted by the Chinese Social Sciences Academy, namely the *Research Report of Social Classes in*

Contemporary China and *Social Mobility in Contemporary China* (Lu, 2002, 2004). The reports classify and rank social classes by occupation. Ten social classes (or occupations) are used in the reports, namely national and societal manager, managerial, professional, home/small business owner, staff in business/service industry, private business owner, industrial worker, farmer or off-farm worker and unemployed. The off-farm worker, or *Nongmingong* in Chinese, refers to a migrant worker who is from, and is still officially registered in a rural area but engages in remunerated non-farm work in a city. This group of people is of very low socio-economic status in China because the pay for their work is usually very low, and they do not enjoy pension, insurance and other benefits.

In the focus groups, students generally recognised the value of this classification, but felt that the first class, national and societal manager, was too vaguely defined, and noted that retirement was not included in the system of classification. Therefore, this study extended the classification to 13 classes by splitting the national and societal manager class into the official administrative personnel and public authority clerk classes, adding a retired category, and including an "other" option for which students could fill in detailed information.

However, occupation is not necessarily an accurate indicator of socio-economic status because a person's occupation does not necessarily reflect his or her income from other sources, or their social status. This is borne in mind in terms of data analysis; parental occupation was not used on its own as an indicator of students' socio-economic status, and other information was taken into consideration, such as place of origin, level of concern for finance and parental educational level.

Motivations for Studying in Higher Education

Ten items were included in this section. They ask students about their motivation for embracing on, and expectations of, the higher education experience.

Time Spent on Studying

Students' attitudes toward learning and their participation in the educational programme can be determinants of their academic engagement, and in turn of their academic achievement (Pascarella & Terenzini, 1991; Tinto, 1993). Class attendance is a behaviour that can be easily and precisely measured. Students are in command of their own attendance, and it makes sense to suggest that, provided that students who attend classes also engage in learning, the more a student attends classes, the more knowledge they acquire, the more they learn, and the better they do in their educational assessments (Newman-Ford et al., 2008). It is therefore useful for this study to assess and compare students' class attendance at the relevant institutions.

In this section, students were asked about their scheduled hours of classroom study (lectures and workshops), attended hours of study, and private hours of study for an average week. A class attendance rate is then calculated from the scheduled hours of study and the actual attended hours of study.

Perceptions of Learning Environment

The learning environment, arguably, has the greatest influence on students' learning and is the component over which the institution has overall control. This part of the questionnaire therefore encompassed measures that reflect a wide range of the facets of the learning environment.

Course Organisation and Structure

This scale measures the quality of course organisation and structure. The first two questions ("I understand the teaching goals in my subject" and "The actual teaching matches the goals of teaching") are widely used in the existing surveys in the literature, as they prove to be significant in determining the quality of the course and the quality of learning. The third and fourth items ("The overall teaching structure of the degree course is well-designed" and "The teaching activities are closely related and support each other") were suggested by students in the focus groups, and developed for the Chinese context of this study.

Class Teaching

The Class Teaching scale measures students' perceptions of their teachers' ability to contribute to student learning. It is characterised by practices that have been established in the literature to have a positive influence on student learning, such as making the course interesting to students, explaining things, motivating students, and understanding students' problems. There is a strong and direct link between teaching quality and learning quality. The presence of these teaching practices indicates a higher quality of teaching. The analysis of the UK National Student Survey reveals that this area has the greatest impact on students' overall satisfaction with the course (Surridge, 2006).

Learning Resources

This scale measures the quality and availability of learning resources for students. The learning resources include text books and teaching materials, teaching equipment (such as computers, laboratories), library resources, online resources, and public learning resources, such as public computers and information resources. The questions are framed in a manner that asks students to make judgements about the quality and availability of resources from *their* point of view, i.e., whether the learning resources are useful and available to *them*.

Xuanxiu Ke

The Chinese phrase *Xuanxiu Ke* refers to "optional modules". These modules are usually not directly relevant to the academic knowledge of the specific subject – for example, music can be a *Xuanxiu Ke* for

English and Computer Science students, but they carry some credits that can be counted towards the total credits required for the subject programme. Students are usually offered a list of *Xuanxiu Ke* from which they can choose the modules they would like to attend.

These classes are relevant for this research because they are usually provided by the institution to broaden the horizon of knowledge for students, to instil an interest in the Arts taste, or to make the students 'good citizens'. At first glance they appear irrelevant to vocational education and seem to be more connected to general education. Unlike the subject-specific classes, these classes are considered less important by many students (since they are irrelevant to the "real studies"). It is therefore interesting to see if students at different institutions and in different disciplines have different attitudes towards these "less important" classes.

Learning Approaches

The questions in this section are adopted from established questionnaires (Biggs, 1999; Ramsden, 2003; Trigwell & Prosser, 1991), with some minor adaptations and modifications to suit the Chinese context.

Educational Emphasis and Orientation

The Emphasis of Teaching scale contains four items that ask students to make judgements about the emphasis of teaching: the degree to which their teaching emphasises memorising, analysing, making judgements and applying knowledge. The Orientation of Teaching contains three sets of detailed questions: Academic Orientation, Practical Orientation, and General Orientation.

The items were developed based on a review of the literature on the characteristics of "applied colleges", and in consultation with administrators, teachers, and students in the interviews and focus groups.

Self-Evaluation

This scale indicates students' feelings of confidence in their own abilities to achieve the desired or required outcomes in the context of their studies. It is a scale adapted from self-efficacy items in the Motivated Strategies for Learning Questionnaire (MSLQ) developed at the National Center for Research on Improving Postsecondary Teaching and Learning (NCRIPTAL) (Pintrich, McKeachie, & Smith, 1989). Greater levels of self-efficacy are hypothesised as being related to better learning outcomes.

This scale contains one item that assesses students' prospects for employment after graduation. Because of the fierce competition in the employment market for graduates in China, this scale is particularly relevant in the Chinese context.

Overall Experience

These are two items covering students' overall experience of the course and institution. The two items provide useful summary measures, and can be compared across institutions and with the previously detailed measures of the specific learning experience. The experience of the UK National Student Survey suggests that satisfaction with the course and the institution need to be separated, and that the wording of the questions needs to be very clear on this separation; otherwise, many students may interpret this unit of reporting differently (Surridge, 2006).

Open-Ended Questions

Almost all of the questionnaires this study has reviewed contain an answer to at least one open-ended question. Open-ended questions in a survey provide richer data than quantitative items, and offer students an opportunity to give written comments on experiences that are not adequately covered by the closed-response questions. The Centre for Higher Education Research and Information at the Open University (Brennan et al., 2003) suggests that surveys should include quantifiable elements to allow statistical analysis, but should not be limited to quantifiable elements. Surveys should also give participants "… opportunities to comment, expand, and explain in their own words" (Brennan et al., 2003, p. 56). This questionnaire also asks students to suggest how the institution could improve their experience; the responses to this question are therefore of great interest to the institutions.

Presentation of the Item Scales

For most of the items in the questionnaire, respondents were asked to choose one of the following answers:

- Completely agree
- Mostly agree
- Neutral
- Mostly disagree
- Completely disagree

The questions are designed to reflect maximum applicability to every respondent. Options such as "I don't know" or "Not applicable" are not included because the questions are designed so that every student is in the position to provide an answer, and including these "I don't know" or "Not applicable" options increases the likelihood of attracting responses, even when a positive response would be more accurate (Brennan et al., 2003). The questionnaire contains questions expressed as both positive and negative statements, in order to encourage respondents to consider each item carefully.

Data Reporting

For the majority of the questions, the questionnaire generates responses on a five-point Likert scale. Numerical values are assigned to the responses, and these values range from 1 for "Completely Disagree" to 5 for "Completely Agree".

To represent the multidimensional nature of the student experience, a number of questions are grouped together to form scales, with each measure comprising one of the dimensions of student experience captured by the survey. The statistical properties of the scales allow an average of the scores to be computed as the score for that scale.

The data are reported at both the scale level and the individual question level. In the literature, the scale mean values and the individual item values are used to serve different purposes: the short and simple scale mean scores are usually used for summary evaluation, while the individual item scores have more details and are used for formative purposes (Braskamp & Ory, 1994; Cashin & Downey, 1992; Whitman & Weiss, 1982). In this study, both the scale mean values and the individual item values are used for analysis. The scale mean values give a general and broad image of the situation for a particular group of students, while the individual item values offer the opportunity to further investigate the situation.

The scale means are calculated by adding the students' responses to the items under each scale and then dividing the value by the number of items in the scale. In line with the individual questions, this yields measures ranging from 1 to 5. A score of 5 on a scale represents complete agreement with all constituent questions in that scale, while a score of 1 represents complete disagreement with all items in that scale. In addition to the scale means, a "broad agreement percentage" is computed for each scale, which equals the percentage of students whose scale mean score is greater than 3. Standard deviations are also calculated and used for analysis. In calculating the scales, any items with missing answers are excluded from analysis for that scale only, so that other valid scales in that questionnaire are still usable.

The answers to the open-ended questions were quantitatively analysed for patterns. Any information in the responses that may be used to identify the respondent was removed before reporting the results – either in this study or in the report to the institutions.

Ethical Considerations

Ethics approval for this study was obtained from the Social Sciences and Humanities Inter-divisional Research Ethics Committee (IDREC) of University of Oxford and the conduct of this study followed the Ethical Guidelines for Educational Research of the British Educational Research Association (2004).

Human subjects were involved in the study, but the study was expected to have little direct impact on them. Informed consent was obtained from the participants, including students and staff, before conducting the survey or interview. Participation in the survey was anonymous and participants were informed of their rights in relation to their participation. Survey participants were assured that no personal identifying information was required to answer the questionnaire. Participation was voluntary; they were able to withdraw without penalty, and any information provided was not related to their institutional records in any way. The study results will be shown in summary form only and the institutions and course tutors do not have access to any individual responses provided by students taking part in the study. The researcher did not obtain identifying information from focus group participants, and the information they provided in interviews was kept confidential.

The classroom setting for the survey raised ethical issues. Firstly, students may have felt pressured to contribute and that they would be penalised if they did not. Therefore, it was made clear that participation is completely voluntary and participants were free to withdraw without penalty. Secondly, students were assured of their anonymity, as personal contact with the researcher or institutional staff may make them feel vulnerable and have a negative impact on the quality of the data, as research has shown that students in this situation tend to give higher ratings (Feldman, 1978, 1986).

Students were informed that this project involved a number of institutions, and that data analysis would be conducted outside their institution. This was expected to increase the participants' confidence about confidentiality.

Response Rate

Response rate raises an important issue in student feedback studies, as a low response rate may lead to sample biases. If the selected sample differs systematically from the population, conclusions cannot be drawn about the population based on the sample. Research has shown that, in student surveys, non-respondents are usually different from respondents in terms of demographic characteristics, study behaviour, and academic attainment (Astin, 1970; Nielsen, Moos, & Lee, 1978; Watkins & Hattie, 1985). Therefore, it is reasonable to expect that the respondents and non-respondents may well have different experiences, and that the responses from survey participants do not necessarily represent the situation for non-participants (Brennan et al., 2003). The impact of this kind of sample bias can be reduced by minimising the number of non-respondents. Administering surveys during an in-class situation can significantly increase response rates and hence reduce the potential impact of sample bias.

Brennan et al. (2003) claim that for sample-surveyed courses, the usual cell size limit is between 50 to 100, below which no analysis should be reported, but for a census-surveyed course, a cell size as small as 10 is enough to convey meaningful information.

As will be discussed later in the *Results and Findings* chapter, the survey achieved a very high response rate – about 94%. This is very rare for any survey conducted in a Western context, and the potential ethical concerns are addressed here. The facilitation of the survey, including the administration process, strictly followed ethical guidelines. The researcher did not attempt to place any pressure on students filling in the questionnaire, and steps were taken to ensure that the institutional contacts, and the teachers present, did not create such pressures; this included reassuring students that the survey was anonymous, and requesting the teacher not to make demands on students. There are several reasons that the survey achieved such a high response rate. Firstly, the survey was administered in classrooms during self-study sessions. Students were available to fill in questionnaires at these sessions and, unlike during breaks between classes, students in self-study sessions do not expect to leave the classroom; therefore, students had adequate time to complete the questionnaire. Secondly, as found in the focus groups with students and in the returned questionnaires, students were extremely co-operative in this research because they appreciated the opportunities to share their experiences and have their voices heard. Therefore, students wanted to fill the questionnaire. In fact, one reason for low response rates in student surveys given in Western contexts is that students are usually over-surveyed. This is in contrast with the fact that very little attention has been paid to students in China, at least at the institutions surveyed.

Data Collection

For Phase 1 of the research, focus groups with students, focus groups with teachers, and interviews with field experts were conducted in November 2007. The students and teachers in the focus groups were from the sample institutions, but some of the field experts were external. Three focus group sessions were conducted with students at the Private College, the Independent College, and the Public College. These comprised 8, 9, and 7 students, respectively. Three discussion group sessions with teachers were conducted at the same colleges, and these comprised two, two, and three teachers, respectively. The students and teachers represented English and Computer Science subjects. Five interviews were conducted with field experts, including a professor of higher education at a university in Beijing, a professorial research fellow at a provincial Private Education Research Centre, a professor and director of the Higher Education Evaluation Research Center at the provincial Department of Education, a professor and director of the Higher Education Research Institute at the Public College, and a professor and vice-president (academic) at the Private College.

For Phase 2 of the research, the survey was conducted on-site at the institutions in classroom settings. Direct contact with students helped to yield higher response rates.

With advanced technology and increased access to computers, an online survey was a possibility. An online-based survey can minimise the efforts required of the researcher and instructors in terms of data collection and data entry, but there are also serious concerns about the ease of implementation, anonymity, response quality, and return rate for online-based surveys (Layne, DeCristoforo, & McGinty, 1999). Although it is reasonable to expect that most of today's higher education students are fairly familiar with computers, students who are more familiar with computers are more likely to participate, and this can potentially introduce sample bias.

The survey was administered in the spring semester of 2008. Traditionally, student surveys, especially surveys designed to assess teaching modules, are administered at the end of the term. However, there is concern that students receiving a satisfying grade, or a grade that is higher than expected, may give higher ratings to the course and vice versa (Richardson, 2005a, 2005c). Another issue is that because the course has concluded, the participants are unlikely to have the same instructor again in the future, and, in this case, they may feel that they will not benefit from completing the survey and hence will choose to withdraw from giving feedback or will not take the survey seriously, or will give unduly harsh criticism (Narasimhan, 2001). Therefore, this survey was conducted in the middle of the semester.

The survey was conducted at the four institutions within a time span of three weeks. Certainly, it would have been preferable for the survey to be administered at exactly the same point of the semester at the different institutions. But the institutional timetables needed to be co-ordinated, and the required presence of a researcher during the classroom visits meant that a time span is necessary to complete all of the institution and classroom visits. The time span of three weeks was considered acceptable in this case, as the small survey-administration time difference was not likely to have any significant effects on students' reports.

The surveys were conducted at the four institutions in *wanzixi*, or "evening self-study sessions". In these sessions, classrooms were provided for students' self-study activities. These sessions are a feature of higher education in China, as can be observed in almost all higher education institutions in the country. Attendance at these sessions is compulsory at some institutions, and recommended at others. It was decided to survey students during these sessions because students gather in classroom settings and are grouped according to study programmes at these sessions, which provides ideal access to students. Since the programmes at some of the institutions are modularised, students following the same programme may be studying different modules in different classrooms at any given time, thereby creating difficulty in terms of the survey's administration, but since students following the same programme have evening self-study in the same classroom, this potential problem was solved. The non-class evening timing also has the advantage of not interfering with the normal class schedule.

The researcher visited the institutions to administer the survey at times agreed with the institutions. In all four cases, the institutions appointed a staff member as the survey co-ordinator, who acted as the liaison with the researcher, and served as the contact point for the administration, collection and return of the survey. The survey co-ordinators were of sufficient seniority to ensure the smooth administration of the survey, and effective communication of the survey results to institutional managers.

To ensure consistency in the data collection procedures, the same survey protocol was applied to all of the classroom visits. A script was read out to students at all classroom visits. The script contained information that participating students should be aware of before answering the questionnaire. It introduced the purpose of the study, assured students of their anonymity and confidentiality, and instructed them on how to fill in the survey.

The survey data were analysed after collection and, to help interpret the survey findings, additional qualitative data were collected from interviews and document analysis. Course documentation, relevant student records, such as enrolment numbers, information on staff and resources, such as the number and qualifications of faculty, library resources, and so on, were collected from the relevant institutions through the institutional contact and website. National data on higher education, such as the number of students in each academic programme, the gender and socio-economic composition of students, and so on, were also collected to help analyse the institutions studied in the context of China's higher education system.

For Phase 3 of the research, focus groups with students were conducted at the four institutions in the autumn semester of 2008. At each institution, the focus group was attended by 12 to 15 students who were in the survey sample. The students were selected so that the group represented a good balance of male and female students, as well as students studying different programmes. The students were identified with the help of the institutional contacts. It should be noted that the students were not selected according to the returned questionnaires; as stated, the questionnaires were completed anonymously, and it was not possible to identify the respondent of any returned questionnaire. The institutional survey contact usually contacted the *Banzhuren,* or class director of the relevant subject programmes, and asked them to identify some students who could attend the focus group. *Banzhuren* act as pastoral advisors of students and are – as will be detailed in the findings chapter – a particular feature of higher education in China. Therefore, the focus group attendees were usually chosen by the *Banzhuren*. In the absence of intervention, this process poses a potential threat to the research because, in all probabilities, the students are not chosen randomly – the students chosen by the *Banzhuren* are likely to be the "better" students in the class. Therefore, it was requested of the institutional contacts that the students be chosen as randomly as possible, meaning that the *Banzhuren* should not simply choose his or her best students for the focus group. However, the student selection process was not controlled or verified by the researcher and, in order to protect the privacy of the attendees, personal information was not requested at the focus group.

The possible sample bias in the focus group attendees was borne in mind when the focus groups were conducted. The questions were framed to capture the widest possible range of information, and follow-up questions were used to check if the answer was widely agreed upon, or applicable only to the particular respondent. For example, after receiving an answer from a respondent, the researcher prompted him or her with questions such as: "Do you know anyone who would think otherwise?", or "Would some students, say, students with financial difficulties, have a different opinion?", and so on.

Semi-structured interviews were conducted with a small range of administrators at the four institutions. The interviewees were all senior staff who were considered well-informed on the subject matter at their institution. At the Public University, the vice-president (academic) and the deputy dean were interviewed; at the Public College, the director of students and the director of higher education research were interviewed; at the Private College, the interviewees included the board chairman, the vice-president (academic), and the dean; and at the Independent College, the president and the dean were interviewed.

For the interviews and the focus groups, the participants were informed of the study's purpose. Field notes were taken during the meeting, and the participants were given the right to check and make any deletion or alteration to the notes after the meeting. The participants could also ask the researcher any questions he or she had about the study. Interview schedules were developed for the interviews of teachers and administrators. The schedules contained questions that were relevant to the topic of this research and that were developed from reviewing the literature and field consultations. The interviews were organised as semi-structured and the interviewees were encouraged to comment on other issues that were relevant to the topic, and the researcher in many cases asked follow-up questions.

Data Analysis

Data compilation was conducted immediately after the completed questionnaires were collected from all four institutions. Student survey data were then entered into a computer database. The data analysis was aggregated with the Statistical Package for the Social Sciences (SPSS), Version 16.0. The data was cleaned and edited to prepare for analysis. Data were grouped into ranges to assist in analysis if necessary; for instance, the National Exams results were grouped into several score ranges to allow for comparison among the ranges of other variables. Missing values in the data were not used in computing mean scores. To answer the research questions, descriptive frequencies, means, standard deviations, cross-tabulations, analyses of variance (ANOVAs), and t-tests were utilised.

Following a common data preparation procedure, responses that did not meet certain criteria were rejected and not used in data analysis. These included blank questionnaires, "yea-sayers" (those who tick "completely agree" or "agree" for all items), and "middle category raters" (those who tick the middle option for all questions) (Richardson, 2005b). The result of this procedure is shown in the next chapter.

Interview and focus group transcripts and the open-ended questions in the questionnaire were analysed using a content analysis approach that categorises responses according to key terms (Weber,

1990). Participants' responses were coded by reviewing the field notes, which enabled the researcher to assess similarities between the interviewees' responses. Responses to the interviews, focus groups, and open-ended questions also provided explanations and a "thicker" description of the problem being investigated.

Testing of Reliability and Validity

Although the content validity of the questionnaire can be established through questionnaire design procedures, such as using learning theories to guide this design, careful borrowing from systematically reviewed existing literature, consultation with students, teachers, and experts, and the subsequent refinement of the questionnaire thereafter, and a pilot study was nevertheless required to test the instrument. The questionnaire design was thus pilot tested with a sample of *Benke* students at two of the four institutions. The revised questionnaire was then formally administered to the student samples at all four institutions.

The reliability and validity of the questionnaire was tested against the data from the pilot and formal administrations of survey. The reliability of the questionnaire scales must exceed the accepted values (Nunnaly, 1978; Schmitt, 1996). The internal consistency of each scale was examined using reliability coefficients (Cronbach's coefficient alpha). Cronbach's Alpha (1951) is the measure of reliability that indicates consistency between items in a scale. The higher the score, the more consistent the items are and the more reliable the scale is. The pilot and psychometric properties testing results are shown in the chapter on *Results and Findings*.

The questionnaire design procedure, which included using learning theories to guide the design, selecting items and scales from established surveys in the field, and consulting with expert panels and students and other stakeholders, provided a measure of construct validity. The content validity of the items was established by the expert panel's examination, and was further verified by student focus group discussions in Phase 1 research. The results of the Phase 1 research are shown in the next chapter.

Multilevel Methods

The study's survey data is multilevel in structure, with students placed within courses and institutions. The weakness of conventional regression models is that they contain the basic assumption that the responses are independent of one another. In a study of such student experience research, where students are grouped together by a higher level unit, this assumption often does not hold true. In statistical terms, this means that the error terms from a standard regression model are likely to correlate within institutions. Failing to recognise this may result in biased and invalid analysis (Goldstein, 1995, 2003; Hills, 2005). Multilevel modelling takes the hierarchical structure into account by incorporating variables at upper levels to adjust the regression of base-level variables. The conceptualisation of higher education student experiences as a multilevel phenomenon warrants the use of multilevel statistical methods.

However, researchers in the field have cautioned against the use of multilevel modelling when the sample size is small. They recommend group-level samples of at least 100. There is a rapid fall-off in statistical power as the number of groups and/or observations falls below the required threshold, as there is an unacceptable risk of not detecting cross-level interactions (Maas & Hox, 2005). The results presented in the *Results* chapter were produced by standard functions of SPSS. In fact, in the data analysis, the study applied multilevel methods to the data, but this did not add any significant findings to the results from the statistical analysis conducted by using SPSS. The relatively small sample size may have limited the power of the multilevel models, and, therefore, the SPSS results were used instead.

Chapter Six

Diversification to a Degree: The Research Findings

Introduction

The purpose of this study is to examine the diversity of students' experience at different institutions in China, and the differences between student groups, disciplines and institutions are of particular interest. The study therefore examines differences in the responses according to student characteristics, course characteristics and institutional characteristics. A wide range of these characteristics was considered, including gender, prior achievement, and socio-economic status, the course elements, and the institution's mission, history, and size. Data on student characteristics were collected from the survey questionnaires and interviews with students; data for courses and institutions were collected from individual institutions and public sources.

More specifically, as explained earlier, the research encompasses three phases, namely qualitative Phase 1, quantitative Phase 2, and qualitative Phase 3. The first phase explored the topic and informed the design of later phases of research. Phases 2 and 3 were designed to answer the research questions because the research methodology literature suggests that a questionnaire is not sufficient to reflect contextual factory while interviews are restricted in terms of sample size and generalisibility. Phases 2 and 3 were designed to complement each other. Therefore, this chapter presents the three research phases in two parts. Phase 1 comprises the first part, suggesting the main areas of interest and informing the design of the next stage of the investigation. The results of this Phase are described in the section *Field Consultations* below. Phase 2 and Phase 3 together form the other part, and investigate and answer the research questions for this study. The results of Phase 2 and Phase 3 are described later in this chapter and are used to answer the four research questions of this study. Therefore, multiple sources of data, including survey results, interview reporting, and document analysis, are used to answer the research questions in this chapter.

Field Consultations

Reflections and Implications for the Research

In Phase 1, the researcher conducted a series of focus groups with students and teachers, and interviews with institutional mangers and higher education researchers in China. Almost all of the participants showed great interest in this study and recognised the importance of looking at students' experiences, especially in the context of China's higher education system. Students and teachers commented on the draft questionnaire and offered insights and suggestions for improving the questionnaire and conducting the survey. A number of important findings emerged on the basis of these fieldwork consultations.

Most importantly, the student focus groups suggested that different institutions might be different in certain aspects of the teaching environment, which would affect students' learning. It was also found that students were able and willing to report their feelings and perceptions. Interview participants commented on the education provision at different institutions based on either theories or their experiences, but the evidence was not substantial.

Focus groups with Students

Three focus groups with students were conducted at three institutions with seven to nine third-year students studying in selected arts and engineering programmes at each institution. After introducing the study and discussing the research idea, a draft questionnaire was distributed to the participants. Students were asked to read through every statement in the questionnaire and raise questions if they felt any question was unclear or not applicable, or if they found the language to be awkward. Students were asked to offer ideas for any learning experience that they felt was important but not reflected in the questionnaire. Through this intense process, many questions were refined, and some were removed or added. For example, students reported that, in addition to the existing items, whether the teaching staff was perceived to be sufficiently prepared for classes was very important, so this component was added to the survey instrument. Furthermore, students reported confusion with terms such as "public", "foundation", and "elective" modules, as the terms were referred to differently at different institutions. As a result, more thorough explanations were added to the questionnaire to clarify these concepts. Students also suggested that, in addition to the extent of practical study, whether the practical element was assessed or not was very important, as this demonstrates the teachers' and institutions' attitudes towards the significance of practical elements. Some students also suggested that the discussion engaged them in thinking and reflecting on their own learning environment, process, and outcomes, which they had not done before and which they believed would be very helpful to their future studies.

The researcher found that none of the three institutions assigned institutional email addresses to their students, nor did they keep a register of all students' email addresses or require students to check their email regularly. The principal form of communication between institution and students was regular class meetings between the students and the *Banzhuren*, or class director. Many students meet their *Banzhuren* every weekday evening at the self-study sessions. This suggested that the survey should be conducted on paper at the evening self-study sessions.

Focus groups with Teachers

Three focus groups with teachers were conducted at three institutions. Participants were asked to review the questionnaire in the light of their own teaching experience. They believed that students' opinions on the specific factors would help them reflect on and improve their teaching in the future. One English teacher in the first meeting gave concrete examples of how communication with students had helped her and her colleagues to improve. The teachers' feedback resulted in changes to questionnaire items.

Interviews with Field Experts

In all five interviews, the interviewees argued that looking at higher education and higher education institutions from the students' perspective was of great significance and interest. The two interviewees from the sample institutions welcomed further research at their institution.

One interviewee suggested that organisational theories maintain that private institutions would be more efficient than public institutions. He hypothesised that private colleges in China were more student-oriented and more vocationally-oriented than public institutions. He also suggested that, in China, students were still sceptical of private higher education and private institutions did not have an established reputation; as a consequence, private institutions might advertise themselves as similar to public institutions to raise their status. He suggested that it was possible that, when compared to public colleges with similar entry requirements, private institutions achieve better teaching quality.

However, another interviewee, who worked at a public college in the city, believed otherwise. He thought that public colleges were more established and experienced in teaching, and also had more full-time teachers with high credentials; therefore, the public colleges were of superior quality. He thought that the private sector of higher education required more time to become competitive.

A vice-president at a private college, who had also formerly worked at a local public university, meaning that he had good knowledge of both sectors, told the researcher that, in his experience, although many private institutions claimed to be strong in practical teaching, this was not, in fact, necessarily the case. He said that, in some cases, he found that, although the curriculum clearly stated the hours of practical teaching required, it was not, in fact, achieved or implemented. For the study, this indicates that in order to compare different institutions, it is certainly not enough to examine the stated programmatic missions or curriculum and that, as the direct participants in education, students may offer better insight into the diversity of education provisions at different institutions.

Pilot Study of the Survey Instrument

A pilot study of the survey instrument was conducted after the focus groups and interviews. The pilot was conducted at the Private College and the Public College, and involved around 30 students from the computer science schools at each institution. English students were not involved to allow for a larger number of students in the same subject (computer science). The students were asked to comment on the content and clarity of the questionnaire after completing it. Some minor changes to the wording were applied after the pilot. The statistical properties of the questions were tested against the pilot data and were shown to be satisfactory, and it was decided to use the instrument for the main study, without major adaptation of the content.

Survey Sample

For research Phase 2, a survey of third-year *Benke* students at the four institutions was conducted in April 2008. The survey was conducted on-site at the institutions in a classroom setting. As expected, this direct contact with students helped to yield a high response rate. 1,345 questionnaires were distributed; of these, 1,264 non-empty questionnaires were returned, representing a response rate of about 94%.

The initial aim was to survey around 300 students at each institution, and that each discipline should include no fewer than fifty students. This aim was met at three institutions but not at the Private College, due to the small student base of the 2005 cohort at the institution, as 2005 was the institution's first year of enrolling *Benke* students. Although the college's enrolment had grown substantially in intervening years, the new enrolments were only in their first or second year at the time of survey and were therefore not in the sample. It was decided, to use a census approach, surveying all of the Languages and Engineering students in the 2005 *Benke* enrolment at the Private College. A total of 249 questionnaires were returned from this college; among these, 47 students were studying Languages and 202 students were studying Engineering. The number of Languages students was slightly below the threshold of 50 but this was considered acceptable since it represents the whole population of Languages students at this institution.

Figure 15. Distribution of survey respondents, by discipline and institution

Discipline	Private College	Public University	Independent College	Public College	Total
Languages	47	106	92	70	315
Engineering	202	208	276	263	949
Total	249	314	368	333	1,264

The 1,264 questionnaires constituted the focus of this investigation. These students were from two broad disciplines, Languages and Engineering, and represented ten degree programmes.

The figure above illustrates the distribution of responses across disciplines at the four institutions. It can be seen from the figure that, at all four institutions, Engineering accounted for the largest proportion of students in the sample. This does not mean that there is a sample bias toward Engineering students, but reflects two factors: first, all of the four institutions are relatively technology- and engineering-oriented, and have large numbers of students studying in related subjects; second, as technology- and engineering-related programmes offer strong occupational value and the advancement of technology and science is a priority for the country (Mohrman, 2003; Zhou, 2006), these subjects are extremely popular in China.

According to the Ministry of Education's statistical data (Ministry of Education, 1978–2009), in 2005 Chinese higher education institutions enrolled a total of 2.36 million *Benke* students. The largest proportion was studying Engineering (31.3%), the second largest group was Literature (including foreign languages) students, amounting to 18.4%; and Management, Science, and Economics students amounted to 15.7%, 11.3%, and 6.1% of the student population respectively. The smallest enrolments were in History and Philosophy, accounting for only 0.5% and 0.07% of the total enrolment.

The table below further breaks down the distribution of the responses into subjects, grouped according to disciplines and institutions.

Table 3. Distribution of survey respondents, by institution and programme

Discipline (Programme)	Private College	Public University	Independent College	Public College	Total
Languages	47	106	92	70	315
English	47	106	92	70	315
Engineering	202	208	276	263	949
Automobile Service Engineering	41	0	0	0	41
Electronic Information Engineering	46	0	12	0	58
Computer Science and Technology	26	108	46	64	244
Mechanical Engineering and Automation	89	100	0	0	189
Mechanical Design, Manufacturing and Automation	0	0	56	62	118
Electrical Engineering and Automation	0	0	82	70	152
Engineering Management	0	0	68	0	68
Hydroelectric Engineering	0	0	0	67	67
Architecture	0	0	12	0	12
Sample for this Study	249	314	368	333	1,264

Of the total 1,264 respondents:

- Around one-fifth (19.8%) did not give a response to the request for their *Gaokao* scores, perhaps due to the difficulty in recalling the exact score of the *Gaokao* three years previously. Some students might also have been unwilling to share this information.
- A significant percentage (8.9%) did not give a response to the item asking for their *Gaokao* place, possibly due to the concern that giving this information would make them identifiable.

- A small number of questionnaires were incomplete for some of the other items. The most common case was that a small number of questions were left blank, presumably because the question was not applicable to the respondent or the question was unintentionally skipped by the respondent.
- A very small number of questionnaires were half completed; for example, some students only answered the items on the first page of the questionnaire.
- A very small number of respondents gave more than one answer (usually two) to items for which only one answer was expected.

The decision was taken to include all usable responses. Students were only excluded from the analysis on a scale by scale basis; put another way, when comparing institutions on the different scales, questionnaires that provided full and valid responses to the specific scale were included in the analytical subsample. Therefore, the questionnaires that did not give valid responses to one scale are still used for the analysis of other scales for which the questionnaires did provide valid responses.

Throughout this chapter, the statistical findings produced from the quantitative data are of an associational nature; there are no formal causal models.

Survey Data Quality

The questionnaire contained Likert items on students' experience of course teaching, environment, resources and other aspects relating to the broader student experience of higher education. Many of these questions are grouped into scales. The rigorous development process of the questionnaire, including a review of existing instruments, numerous consultations and a pilot study, ensured that the questions within scales all had sufficient conceptual overlap. The reliability of the scales is measured using Cronbach's alpha (Cronbach, 1951).

Higher alpha scores indicate a greater correlation in item responses within a scale, suggesting that the items are measuring the same aspect of experience.

Table 4. The reliability coefficients of the scales

Questionnaire Scale	Cronbach's Alpha	Number of Items
Course Organisation	.739	4
Teaching	.861	7
Environment	.723	4
Resources	.805	5
Xuanxiu Ke	.733	3
Academic Orientation	.638	2
Practical Orientation	.761	3
General Orientation	.789	3

The table above presents the alpha values of the scales. All scales, except the scale of Academic Orientation, have alpha values exceeding 0.70. This indicates that the majority of the scales have satisfactory internal consistency, suggesting them to be reliable, with students responding similarly to each of the items on a given scale. The scale of Academic Orientation has an alpha value slightly below 0.70; this is due to the small number of items in that scale (only 2). A number of researchers (Nunnaly, 1978; Schmitt, 1996) have indicated that 0.70 and above is be highly reliable, but lower thresholds are also often used. It is concluded that, therefore, all the scales in the questionnaire are to be considered reliable.

A test for "Yea-Saying" was conducted to examine which respondents gave the same answer to all items. The result was that no student gave the same answer to all items from 5 to 66. However, it was not unusual for students to give the same answer to questions within the same scale. Considering the high correlation between items within the same scale, this type of response was expected, as it is reasonable for students to rate the specific part of their programme on the same point on the scale.

Research Question 1: Who studies at which type of higher education institution? What are students' social, economic, and academic backgrounds?

This section examines the demographic characteristics of the survey respondents. This demographic information is not only important in its own right, showing that different types of institutions have different composition of students, but these variations are also important in that students' characteristics may influence their experience of learning and of their institution, and should be taken into consideration when interpreting the responses to the experience items.

Gender

Of the 1,264 returned responses, 4.8% did not indicate their gender. The gender information is presented below, grouped in disciplines and institutions.

Table 5. Survey respondents' gender, by institution and discipline

	Institution (% within Institution)				
Discipline (Gender)	Private College	Public University	Independent College	Public College	Total
Languages					
Male	47.7%	8.6%	14.3%	17.6%	17.9%
Female	52.3%	91.4%	85.7%	82.4%	82.1%
Engineering					
Male	85.3%	97.9%	82.1%	81.4%	86.0%
Female	14.7%	2.1%	17.9%	18.6%	14.0%

The figures reaffirmed the hypothesis that female students are more concentrated in Humanity and Arts subjects, while male students are more inclined towards Engineering studies. It can be observed from the data that students' gender balance was quite varied across discipline areas. The vast majority of students studying Languages were female, accounting for 82.1% of the population. The trend for Engineering students was completely the opposite, with the vast majority being male students, accounting for 86% of the population. This imbalance was even more extreme in the Public University: of the 190 respondents studying Engineering, only 4, or 2.1%, were female; the percentage of female students studying Languages at the Public University was the highest among the four institutions, at 91.4%. These trends were evident in almost all institutions, with the only exception being the Languages discipline at the Private College, in which 52.3% of the students were female, remarkably lower than the other three institutions' data. Another phenomenon was that the gender patterns were stronger at the Public University than the rest of institutions. One possible explanation is that high-achieving students tend to be more inflexible with their subject choices, that they are determined to choose a programme that is consistent with their high school track, while low-achieving students are more flexible with their subject choices. However, it is unclear whether this was merely an individual case, or a more widespread phenomenon that prestigious institutions tend to have stronger disciplinary gender patterns.

Table 6. Survey respondents' gender, by *Gaokao* track and institution

	Institution (% within Institution)				
Track of *Gaokao* (Gender)	Private College	Public University	Independent College	Public College	Total
Science					
Male	83.2%	85.8%	70.2%	79.3%	78.2%
Female	16.8%	14.2%	29.8%	20.7%	21.8%
Total	100.0%	100.0%	100.0%	100.0%	100.0%
Arts					
Male	50.7%	34.1%	34.3%	33.7%	36.9%
Female	49.3%	65.9%	65.7%	66.3%	63.1%
Total	100.0%	100.0%	100.0%	100.0%	100.0%

A cross-tabulation of gender, institution and track of *Gaokao* shows that there was actually strong gender imbalance in the *Gaokao* track of students: male students in the sample were more likely to be on the Science track and female students were more likely to be on the Arts track in middle school and in *Gaokao*. Since students usually continue to study relevant subjects in their *Gaokao* track in higher education (as a result of institutional requirements and/or personal preference), e.g., students studying engineering subjects in university are usually from the Science *Gaokao* track, the gender imbalance in *Gaokao* tracks can in fact pass on into university disciplines, and therefore the gender imbalance in different disciplines in higher education institutions is rooted earlier in the education system.

There were also two outliers in the above table: in the Private College, slightly over half of the students from Arts track are male, which is significantly higher than other institutions; in the Independent College, only 70% of the students from the Science track are male, at least 9% lower than other institutions. There are two possible explanations for this. The first is that the less prestigious institutions tend to open their subjects to students from a different *Gaokao* track, e.g. allowing Arts track students to study Engineering at university. The Dean of the Private College noted:

> All of our subjects are open to students from both tracks today… in order to increase the enrolment figures and to help the institution meet its enrolment plan.
> (Dean, Private College)

Secondly, the researcher's previous research shows that male students are more likely than female students to accept the value of private higher education in China (Yu, 2005). This may suggest that, holding entering discipline and students' *Gaokao* track constant, male students are more likely than female students to apply to a private college.

The national statistics for the year 2005 suggest that gender mix in *Benke* education in China was very balanced, with a male to female ratio of around 1.07 to 1. This almost perfectly matched the overall gender mix of the country, with a ratio of 1.06 to 1 (National Bureau of Statistics of China, 2005). Although nationally the gender mix in *Benke* education was very balanced, figures from the survey have shown that the gender mix was very imbalanced across disciplines areas *within* institutions, and imbalanced, to a lesser extent, across disciplines *between* institutions. The different gender composition of the student body at different institutions is largely a result of the different composition of discipline areas at the institutions, e.g., institutions with larger engineering departments have a larger male student population, and in contrast, institutions focused on arts will have a larger female recruitment. However, new institutions with low prestige may have a more balanced gender composition *within* subject areas, as they tend to impose fewer restrictions on entering students' *Gaokao* tracks in an effort to recruit more students. Thus, the diversification of higher education institutions, especially the creation of new institutions, may have a small impact on the gender composition *within* subject areas, but this effect is considered to be small compared to the discipline and *Gaokao* track effects.

Gaokao Score

As discussed in the earlier chapter on *Higher Education in China*, many provinces compile their own examination papers, and thus the examination subjects and marking standards may vary between provinces. This makes comparing students' *Gaokao* scores between provinces problematic. However, it is assumed that, in terms of their students' relative position in their examination province, the institutions' enrolment profiles are similar across provinces. Considering that most of the students at the four institutions are from one single province (see the next section), this section focuses on students from that province only, comparing the *Gaokao* scores of in-province students at the four institutions.

Of the analytical sample, a total of 719 students indicated that they were from within the province, of whom 619 provided their *Gaokao* score and *Gaokao* track. Because the two tracks contain different examination subjects, marks are not directly comparable. The table below presents the *Gaokao* score of the respondents, grouped by *Gaokao* track and institution. The scores are classified into four groups: below 450, 450 to 499, 500 to 549, and above 549.

Table 7. Survey respondents' *Gaokao* score, by *Gaokao* track and institution

	Institution (% within Institution)				
Track of *Gaokao* (*Gaokao* Score Range)	Private College	Public University	Independent College	Public College	Total
Science					
Below 450	2.5%	–	5.5%	3.3%	3.3%
450–499	94.3%	1.0%	89.6%	20.7%	58.1%
500–549	2.5%	55.1%	4.9%	72.7%	29.4%
Above 549	8.0%	43.9%	–	3.3%	9.2%
Arts					
Below 450	–	–	–	3.8%	1.0%
450–499	82.1%	–	100.0%	30.8%	44.8%
500–549	17.9%	66.7%	–	61.5%	42.7%
Above 549	–	33.3%	–	3.8%	11.5%

The table shows that the four institutions had different patterns of students' *Gaokao* score. The Public University and Public College had the most high-performing students in terms of *Gaokao* score, while the Private College and Independent College's students were concentrated at the lower score end. This trend was evident in both Arts and Science tracks.

For both *Gaokao* tracks, almost all (99% and 100%) of the Public University's students had a *Gaokao* score of 500 or higher. The Public College's student score was lower, but was still concentrated in the higher margin: around 75% students in Science track and 65% students in Arts track had a score of 500 or higher.

The situation was different for the Private College and the Independent College. The vast majority (more than 80%) of both colleges' students, in both tracks, had a score of lower than 500. In the

Science track, the Independent College had slightly more students in the lower margin (below 450) and the higher margin (above 500) than the Private College; in the Arts track, all of the Independent College's students were in the 450–499 category, while the Private College had some students in the slightly higher 500–549 category.

The figures imply that the public institutions mainly cater for the high-achievers, while the newly-created private and independent institutions mainly enrol those who could not get into public institutions because of low achievement. The creation of new institutional types has increased the supply of higher education places through providing opportunities to the lower-achievers.

Province of Origin

The table below shows the students' home province. Since there are over thirty provinces in China (including provincial-level municipals such as Beijing and Shanghai), and most of the students came from within the province, the table groups the population into students from within the province and outside the province. In all disciplines and at all institutions, in-province students formed the largest group, accounting for over half of the student population.

Table 8. Survey respondents' province of origin, by institution and discipline

	Institution (% within Institution)				
Discipline (Province of Origin)	Private College	Public University	Independent College	Public College	Total
Languages					
In-province	63.8%	58.5%	53.3%	52.9%	56.5%
Out-province	32.2%	41.5%	46.7%	47.1%	43.5%
Engineering					
In-province	73.8%	54.8%	71.4%	59.3%	64.9%
Out-province	26.2%	45.2%	28.6%	40.7%	35.1%

Although the above trend can be observed in all institutions, the Private College's students were slightly more concentrated within the province than the other institutions' students. The enrolment of students from outside the province by the other three institutions was also much more diversified. For example, for the Engineering students, the Public College had students from 25 provinces, while the Private College's students were from 14 provinces only.

As the province's flagship institution and the only national key university in the province, it is interesting that the Public University's student enrolment was not significantly more diverse than other institutions' in terms of students' geographical origin. The university's percentage of in-province students in Languages programmes was above the average of the four institutions, and although its percentage of in-province students in Engineering programmes was the lowest among the four institution, it was nevertheless above the 50% threshold. Interviews with institutional mangers reveal that an institution's student origin composition was largely determined by the institution's administering authority, the Provincial Educational Bureau in this case, while the institution only has limited freedom in the allocation of enrolment places. The Public University is, in fact, designated by the provincial authority as a local institution, with the primary mission to serve the local economy and people, and this is reflected in its distribution of enrolment places:

> The figure [percentage of local province students in the student population] is as expected. We are required by the provincial authority to enrol around ten thousand students every year, of whom at least 50% must come from within the province.
> (Deputy Dean, Public University)

The provincial authority's control over institutions' student intake also applies to the Private College, but it is unclear whether all other provinces impose the same requirements on private institutions:

> 2005 was the first year for us to enrol *Tongzhao Benke* students, and we were given a small out-of-province quota. Other institutions have a longer history and more experience in recruitment, and are given larger out-of-province quotas. With

> our experience growing, we are also getting bigger and bigger out-of-province quotas and now recruit more students from other provinces than in 2005. However, the provincial educational bureau still requires that at least 50% of the quota remain in the province.
>
> (Dean, Private College)

It is understandable that provincial educational authorities are inclined to require the institutions under their administration to recruit substantial numbers of students from the local province, to better serve the local economy, and in return for the province's financial support (although private institutions do not receive direct funding from the province). As discussed in the background chapter, a number of universities in China are administered directly by the central government ministries, rather than by provincial authorities. A regulation of the Ministry of Education in 2008 mandates that directly-administered institutions shall recruit no more than 30% of their total intake from their respective local province. This regulation is aimed at making the directly-administered universities more "national" in terms of the regional pattern of students, and reflecting the fact that the central government provides significant funding to these institutions. Therefore, the diversification of the administration of institutions, i.e. some administered by the central government and others administered by their local authority, can result in a marked difference in student enrolment policy.

Where Students Come From

This section presents the type of the place where the respondents come from. As stated in the *Methodology* chapter, students were asked to select one of the five categories, namely *Shenghui Chengshi/Zhi Xiashi* (Provincial Capital or Municipality), *Dijishi* (Prefecture-level City), *Xianjishi*, *Xiangzhen* (Township), and *Nongcun* (Rural area).

The figure below illustrates the four institutions' student origin profile.

Figure 16. Where students come from, by institution

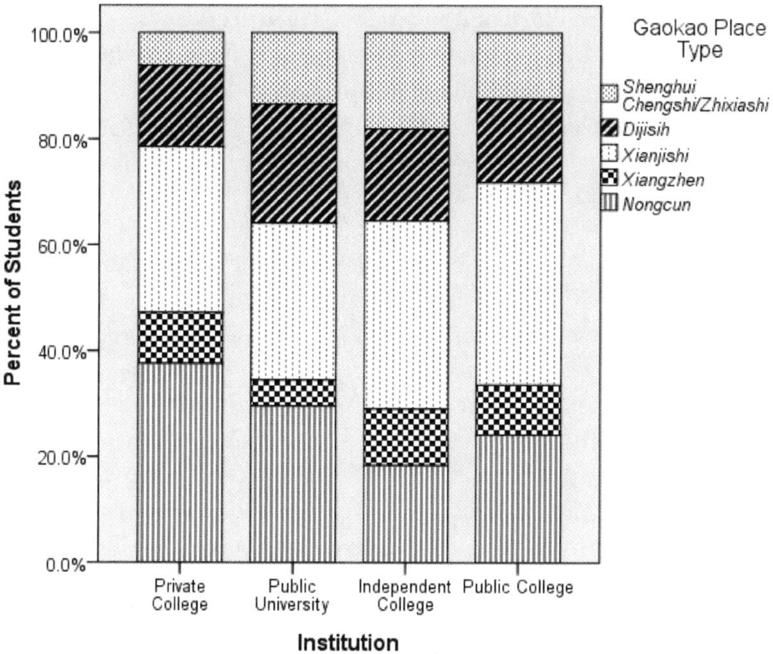

The above figure shows that the Private College and the Independent College represent the two extremes of the four institutions. The Private College had the smallest percentage of students from provincial capitals or municipalities, and the largest percentage of students from rural areas. The Independent College's situation was the opposite: it had the largest percentage of students from provincial capitals and municipalities of the four institutions, and the lowest percentage of students from rural areas. The association between place of residence and family income suggests that the Private College's students were among the poorest in the four institutions, a point which is reaffirmed by the analysis of the education and occupation of students' parents.

According to the national statistics, in 2005, 57% of the Chinese population were rural residents. In the fieldwork base province, over 60% of the population resided in rural areas (National Bureau of Statistics of China, 2005). However, at the Independent College students from rural areas accounted for just 18.3%, while at the Public University and Public College students from rural areas accounted for 29.6% and 24.2% respectively, and the Private College had the largest percentage of students from rural areas at 37.6%.

As stated earlier, institutions tend to recruit a large number of students from their respective province, and since most top public universities are located in affluent cities and provinces, top public universities will have a larger percentage of students coming from the affluent regions. This situation should not be interpreted as a result of institutional discrimination against rural students, because acceptance of eligible students is usually based purely on the *Gaokao* grades within provinces (although a larger quota being given to the local province may actually lower the percentage of rural students enrolled for higher education institutions in affluent and urban provinces). Instead, this is mostly because urban students receive more and better education and are more likely to achieve better *Gaokao* results; they also have more information about university choice, and therefore are more likely to get into prestigious institutions. Student from rural areas who do not meet the public institutions' admission requirements have no choice but to attend the less prestigious private institutions. However, the Independent College was different: its admission requirements were low, but it had the lowest percentage of students from rural areas. This may be because urban applicants have better information and prefer to enrol in an institution that has a "good name". The researcher's previous research shows that, compared to private colleges, independent colleges have a higher share of students who applied to the their college as their first choice (Yu, 2005). In that research, over 50% of the Independent College students reported that their current institution was their first choice in their selection of institutions, but for private college students the figure was less than 15%. This suggests that the Independent College students are more likely to be lower achieving but wealthy students who decided to enrol in expensive independent colleges in the first place, while the Private College students are more likely to be lower achieving and poorer students who initially applied to a cheaper public institution but were forced to go to the more expensive private college because of their failure to meet the admission requirements of that public institution.

Parental Education

Of the analytical sample, 1,191 respondents (94.2%) indicated their father's educational level and 1,187 (93.9%) provided their mother's educational level.

Table 9. Father's education level, by institution

	Institution (% within Institution)				
	Private College	Public University	Independent College	Public College	Total
Father's Education Level					
No Formal Education	11.1%	7.8%	7.2%	7.9%	8.3%
Primary School	17.9%	10.2%	7.2%	7.6%	10.2%
Junior Secondary School	39.3%	35.0%	24.7%	22.9%	29.6%
Senior Secondary School	27.8%	30.6%	42.2%	42.2%	36.5%
Zhuanke	2.1%	8.5%	12.1%	14.3%	9.8%
Benke	1.3%	6.1%	5.5%	4.8%	4.6%
Postgraduate	0.4%	1.7%	1.1%	0.3%	0.9%
Total	100.0%	100.0%	100.0%	100.0%	100.0%

The table shows that most of the students in the sample were first generation higher education students. This is consistent with the fact that universities and colleges in China only resumed enrolment in 1978, and the number of students enrolled was quite small in the earlier years. This was about the time when many of the parents of current university students were themselves at university-entering age.

Considering *Zhuanke* as a part of higher education, the proportion of students whose father had been to university or college was

3.8%, 16.3%, 18.7%, and 19.4% for the Private College, Public University, Independent College and Public College respectively. The Private College's profile again appeared markedly different from other institutions. Compared to the other three institutions, the Private College not only had fewer parents with high credentials, it also had more parents with low credentials: the proportion of students whose father had only received primary education or no formal education at all amounted to 29% at the Private College, compared with 18%, 14.4%, and 15.5% at the other three institutions.

The university participation rate in the late 1970s and earlier 1980s is estimated to be 5% or lower nationally, and so the father's educational level of students at the Public University, Independent College and Public College was many times higher than the national average. The trend in mothers' educational levels was broadly similar to the trend of fathers' educational level at the four institutions, in that the Private College mothers' educational background was much lower than the other three institutions. The difference was that, in general, mothers' educational level appeared to be lower than fathers' educational level.

Broadly speaking, the parents of Independent College students had the strongest educational backgrounds in the four institutions, and the parents of Private College students had on average the weakest; the Public University and Public College's profiles were somewhere between the two, but much closer to the Independent College's, that is, they had much better parents' educational backgrounds than the Private College.

Furthermore, the high percentage of first generation students in Chinese higher education has important implications for student advice and counselling. First generation students do not have parents who have experience of higher education to advise them on academic matters or university social issues. Students may feel that they are not getting support from parents who are unfamiliar with university life. Student advice and counselling services and student support programmes therefore become crucial in helping these students (Byrd & Macdonald, 2005; Pascarella et al., 2004).

Parental Occupation

Of the analytical sample, 1,185 respondents (93.7%) indicated their father's occupation and 1,172 (92.7%) provided a valid answer to the mother's occupation item.

Table 10. Father's occupation of the survey respondents, by institution

	Institution (% within Institution)				
	Private College	Public University	Independent College	Public College	Total
Father's Occupation					
Public Authority Administrative	1.3%	3.8%	5.2%	7.6%	4.7%
Managerial	.4%	1.0%	3.8%	1.9%	1.9%
Public Authority Clerk	6.9%	11.3%	14.0%	14.2%	12.0%
Professional	3.0%	4.4%	3.5%	4.4%	3.9%
Home/Small Business Owner	8.6%	8.9%	12.8%	5.7%	9.1%
Staff in Business/Service Industry	2.1%	1.4%	2.0%	.6%	1.5%
Private Business Owner	6.0%	6.1%	6.4%	4.7%	5.8%
Industrial Worker	13.7%	12.3%	11.1%	12.7%	12.3%
Farmer-worker	9.9%	4.4%	2.3%	6.6%	5.5%
Farmer	36.9%	32.8%	20.7%	28.5%	28.9%
Retired	2.1%	3.1%	2.0%	3.5%	2.7%
Unemployed	6.4%	6.8%	9.9%	4.1%	6.9%
Other	2.6%	3.8%	6.1%	5.4%	4.6%
Total	100.0%	100.0%	100.0%	100.0%	100.0%

The father's occupation figures were again consistent with the previous results on family residence and parents' educational background: on average, the Private College father's socio-economic status was much lower than at the other three institutions, particularly the Independent College. Compared with fathers of students at the Private College, fathers of students at the Independent College was 9.5 times more likely to be a manager at a business, four times more likely to be administrative personnel at a public authority, twice as likely to be a clerk at a public authority, and 48% more likely to run a home/small business, while fathers of students at the Private College were more likely to be an industrial worker, off-farm worker or farmer.

Fathers of students at the Independent College were more likely to be unemployed than fathers at other institutions. In fact, being unemployed does not necessarily indicate low socio-economic status, in contrast, it could imply that the person has income from other business, family, or personal channels to support them without the need to work, and in this case unemployment actually means high economic status.

The trend of mothers' occupation was broadly similar to the trend of fathers' occupation. The difference was that, in general, mothers' socio-economic status in terms of occupation seemed to be somewhat lower than fathers' occupation.

Concerns about Finances

The fee-paying ability item in the questionnaire asked whether students were concerned about their or their family's ability to finance their current education. Of the analytical sample, 1,143 respondents (90.4%) gave a valid answer to this question.

Before analysing the institutional result, it should be noted that nationally, private colleges and independent colleges' tuition fees are much higher than at public institutions, as they rely almost completely on student income, while public institutions receive public subsidies. In these four cases, the tuition fees of the Private College and the Independent College were almost double those of the public institutions.

Figure 17. Survey respondents' concerns about finances, by institution

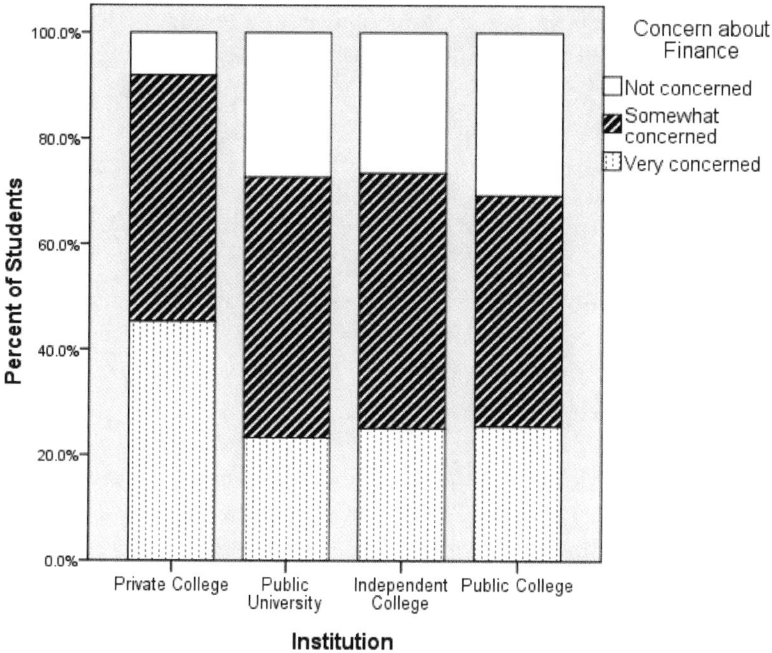

As the figure shows, the public institutions and the Independent College have very similar levels of student concern about finance. This demonstrates that, although the Independent College charges much higher tuition fees, the socio-economic status of the Independent College's parents also tends to be higher, and this higher level of tuition fees has been offset by the higher status and higher level of income of the students' parents. The result is that, although paying a much higher fee, the Independent College's students were not any more concerned about finance than their counterparts studying at cheaper public institutions.

Situation at the Private College was different. On the one hand, its tuition fees are higher than those of the public institutions; on the other hand, its students' socio-economic status was not only lower than the Independent College's, but even substantially lower than at the public institutions. The result is that there was a much greater tendency for the Private College students to be very concerned about finance. Only a minority of the Private College students, around 8%, indicated that they were not concerned about finance, compared to an average of 28% at the other three institutions; and almost half of its students, or 45%, were very concerned about finance, compared to around one quarter at the other three institutions.

Summary

Analysis of the demographics of students at the four different institutions suggests that in many aspects the diversification of higher education institutions has had a profound impact on the type of students that are admitted to the institutions.

The most notable differences between students at the four institutions were their *Gaokao* scores and socio-economic status. Not surprisingly, the most prestigious institution in the sample, the Public University, had the best students in terms of their prior academic achievement. The Public College was the second while the Private College and the Independent College were far behind. This suggests that the newly-established private and independent institutions are mainly providing higher education opportunities to students who cannot get into public institutions and who would previously have been rejected from higher education. In terms of socio-economic status, using type of residential place and parental education and occupation as proxies, the Independent College had the highest percentage of high-status students and the lowest percentage of low-status students. The socio-economic backgrounds of students at the Public College and the Public University were less favourable, but interestingly it was the Private College that enrolled the largest group of students from disadvantaged backgrounds. Combining the socio-economic backgrounds of students and the fee levels at the institutions, the Private College's students were the most concerned about finance.

Because admission standards are very similar at the Independent College and the Private College, an interesting question is why, given similar academic achievements, richer students decide on the Independent College and poorer students decide on the Private College. It is expected that this situation is not limited to the two colleges in the sample, but is a national phenomenon and that students at independent colleges are financially better-off, while students at private colleges are among the poorest. An investigation into the students' residential profiles shows that a substantial percentage of students at the Independent College come from the local city, while most students at the Private College come from poorer, further remote areas of the province. It is speculated that the local city's students are aware of and recognise the Public University's image more. Local wealthy students with better knowledge of the university and who recognise the brand more readily are the most likely to attend the Independent College of the Public University at the expense of paying higher tuition fees. Another possible reason for the different student profiles at the Independent College and the Private College is the clearing process of national admission: more students at the Independent College are more affluent and made up their mind to pay the extra expense and attend the Independent College before admission, while many students at the Private College are from poorer families and wanted to attend public institutions, but failed to receive any offers and ended up at the Private College through the clearing process (Yu, 2005).

These demographic differences have many policy implications. The differences between the two types of the newly introduced institutions under "private" control – private and independent – suggest that the two sectors are attracting different students. The fact that the public institutions received state subsides but clearly failed to enrol a significant number of students from disadvantaged backgrounds also has implications for policy.

Research Question 2: What are students' motivations for higher education study at different institutions?

This section presents the results of Section Two in the questionnaire, which asked about students' motivations for studying in higher education and their aspirations for postgraduate study.

Motivations for Studying in Higher Education

Item number five in the questionnaire, "I want to develop knowledge and skills I can use in a career", was given by 85.7% of the respondents as a motivation for entering higher education (ratings of 4 or 5 on the scale of 1 to 5). There was some variation between institutions, but the variations were generally small. Students with a higher level of concern about finance, and students at the colleges that seemed to be more career-oriented, were, perhaps surprisingly, not more motivated with regard to job prospects.

Overall, 89.4% of the respondents agreed with item six, "I hope the things I learn will help me to develop as a person and broaden my horizons". The Public University's students were least motivated by this – with 87.2% of the students indicating this, compared with 91% at the Private College, 88.9% at the Independent College and 90.6% at the Public College. However, these differences are small.

Item number twelve, "I mainly need the qualification to enable me to get a good job when I finish", was a less popular choice compared with the two motivations named above, with 61.6% respondents agreeing with the statement. The Private College's students seemed to be less qualification- or career-oriented. In the Private College, only 54.6% of the respondents chose this motivation, compared with 62.1%, 69.1%, and 58.9% at the Public University, the Independent College, and the Public College respectively. The marked difference between the Private College and the Independent College may suggest that the Independent College's students had high expectations that their institution's good name would lead them to a good career.

The motivation of "I'm mainly here because I did well academically in the past" was highly related to students' past achievement, as indicated by the *Gaokao* scores in the survey. Students with higher *Gaokao* scores were much more likely to agree with this item. Therefore, the Public University naturally achieved the highest figure on this. As many as 45.7% of the Public University's students indicated that they were motivated by this (notional agreement), compared with 20.5%, 26.3% and 25.6% at the Private, Independent and Public Colleges respectively.

When comparing reasons for attending higher education between different disciplines, it is interesting to note that, Languages students had a strong instrumentalist view toward higher education; many were even more career-oriented than the Engineering students. This indicates that students from both disciplines had very strong career goals. However, Languages students had slightly higher expectations of personal development and horizon broadening (94.2%) than Engineering students (87.7%).

The high importance students attach to employment considerations in deciding to enter higher education is also found in other countries. For example, in the US, a Higher Education Research Institute's (2004) report found that the most important reasons for deciding to go to higher education included "to get training for a career" (78.4%), "to make more money" (73.8%), and "to get a better job" (73.8%).

In the interviews for this study, a student put forward the following rationale:

> We have spent a large sum of our parents' hard-earned money; we certainly expect to learn useful knowledge and gain qualification that can help us get a better salary after graduation.
>
> (Female, English, Public College)

Some students also mentioned that they considered humanistic development very important or even as important as the vocational element. One student added that vocational success comes first and the guarantee of a proper job placement provides the foundation for humanistic development:

> To develop as a capable, knowledgeable and moral person is ideal for personal development and the society. But I think, gaining the necessary credentials for a future career has priority, and only when this is secured, can we start to talk about humanistic development.
>
> (Male, *Computer Science and Technology*, Public University)

This view is very much in line with Maslow's hierarchy of needs (Maslow, 1943), which presents people's needs in a hierarchy in order of importance. In the hierarchy, the lowest level is associated with physiological needs, while the uppermost level is associated with self-actualisation needs. Maslow argued that the higher needs in this hierarchy only come into focus when the lower needs in the hierarchy have been met. Another student had a similar point of view, showing the urgency that students at the Private College felt:

> There are some institutions, the ones that are the best in the country, their courses are not vocationally-oriented at all, and their students get paid very well after graduation. But for us, if our institution doesn't teach us something useful for work, many of us won't even be able to find a job.
>
> (Male, *Computer Science and Technology*, Private College)

In fact, although the different weight given to vocational and humanistic goals by institutions may reflect the course arrangements, these two developments are not mutually exclusive, as shown in the different responses to the fifth and the twelfth questions, i.e., "I want to develop knowledge and skills I can use in a career" and "I mainly need the qualification to enable me to get a good job when I finish". The agreement rate to the former question was much higher than to the latter question, suggesting that students considered vocational goals as very important, but not the only goals for higher education.

Aspirations for Postgraduate Study

1,238 students, or 98% of the analytical sample, answered the question about their planned studies after graduation. Overall, about one third (33.8%) of the respondents plan to continue to postgraduate studies after graduation. However, this figure varies greatly across institutions.

Table 11. Survey respondents' response to the statement "I am preparing to continue to postgraduate study after graduation", by institution and discipline

	Institution (% within Institution)				
Discipline (Response)	Private College	Public University	Independent College	Public College	Total
Languages					
Completely Disagree	4.5%	6.7%	2.2%	1.4%	3.9%
Disagree	59.1%	27.6%	44.4%	41.4%	40.1%
Neutral	29.5%	28.6%	31.1%	22.9%	28.2%
Agree	6.8%	22.9%	11.1%	21.4%	16.8%
Completely Agree	0%	14.3%	11.1%	12.9%	11.0%
Engineering					
Completely Disagree	7.9%	8.0%	8.1%	6.6%	7.6%
Disagree	23.6%	21.6%	17.6%	11.7%	18.0%
Neutral	39.8%	34.2%	38.1%	41.6%	38.6%
Agree	23.0%	25.1%	22.0%	26.5%	24.1%
Completely Agree	5.8%	11.1%	14.3%	13.6%	11.6%
Combined Total					
Completely Disagree	7.2%	7.6%	6.6%	5.5%	6.7%
Disagree	30.2%	23.7%	24.2%	18.0%	23.6%
Neutral	37.9%	32.2%	36.4%	37.6%	36.0%
Agree	20.0%	24.3%	19.3%	25.4%	22.3%
Completely Agree	4.7%	12.2%	13.5%	13.5%	11.5%

The Private College's students were the least likely to expect to continue to postgraduate study, with only 25% respondents planning to do so. The Public University and Public College's students were much more likely to want to continue, with 36.5% and 38.8% students indicating this. At the Independent College, 32.8% of the students were preparing for further studies. The Private College not only had the smallest proportion of students desiring further study; most of its students who did desire postgraduate study were not completely certain about the choice, with only 4.7% of the respondents strongly inclined towards further study, while this figure at the other three institutions was between 12% and 14%.

At the four institutions, on average around 36% of students were "neutral" to the statement concerning postgraduate aspirations. The students surveyed were in the third year of their *Benke* studies, and they still had more than one year before graduation. What remains unclear at this stage is their employment prospects. Through the interviews with students, it was found that some students had a "wait and see" attitude toward postgraduate study, and they wanted to wait until the last year of their *Benke* study, when they might have a better picture of their job prospects.

The table shows that Engineering students were on average more likely to indicate that they desired postgraduate education than were Languages students. On average, 35.7% of Engineering students were preparing to apply for postgraduate study, compared to 27.8% of Languages students. The percentage of "neutral" Engineering students was also higher than that of the Languages students. It is also noteworthy that the Languages students at the Private College showed an exceptionally low desire for postgraduate studies; only 6.8% of the students indicated that they would prepare to undertake postgraduate study, and none of them indicated so strongly.

The difference between the Languages and Engineering students' desire for postgraduate study is attributable to the difference between the two disciplines in general, and the difference between the two disciplines at these four institutions. As previously stated, China has placed priority on Engineering studies and there are more postgraduate places available in Engineering subjects than in Languages subjects.

Students' prior achievement, using their *Gaokao* score as a proxy, did not have any influence on students' desire for postgraduate study. However, students' current academic standing, using students' self-reported "always complete assignments with high quality" (see next section) as an indicator, had a strong influence on students' aspiration to postgraduate studies: those who completed assignments with high quality were more likely to indicate an aspiration for postgraduate studies than those who did not.

A further examination of the data revealed that a *Benke* student's desire to continue to postgraduate study was strongly related to his or her financial standing. Respondents who had more financial security and did not worry about financing their *Benke* study were much more likely to desire postgraduate study. The figure below shows the percentage of Engineering students preparing to take postgraduate study (those who chose Agree and Completely Agree to the item), classified by their level of concern about finance. Focusing on Engineering students, 43.2% of the students who were not concerned about finances indicated a desire for postgraduate study, in comparison to 35.4% of students who were somewhat concerned and 31.4% for students who were very concerned. This trend can be observed at all four institutions.

Table 12. Survey respondents' aspirations for postgraduate study, by concern about finance and institution

	Institution (% within Institution)				
Concern about Finance (Prepare to Take Postgraduate Study)	Private College	Public University	Independent College	Public College	Total
Not concerned	38.5%	42.8%	41.3%	46.6%	43.2%
Somewhat concerned	31.3%	33.7%	34.7%	40.6%	35.4%
Very concerned	25.9%	34.9%	35.3%	31.7%	31.4%

The financial standing's influence on students' desire for postgraduate study is understandable, as taking a postgraduate course not only means paying more years of tuition fees, but students also need to give up two or three years' income, compared with entering employment immediately after graduation. Furthermore, parents with higher earnings may also have higher expectations for their children and thus be more encouraging for them to continue their studies.

Since the Private College had a substantial proportion of low socio-economic status students, and the Independent College had a substantial proportion of high socio-economic status students, accounting for the financial influences would be expected to reduce the differences in students' desire for postgraduate studies across institutions. However, differences between institutions, especially between the Private College and other institutions, are still significant even after accounting for financial factors. This may indicate that there is a cultural difference between the institutions; the better reputation of the public and independent institutions may have encouraged students to aspire to postgraduate studies.

Meanwhile, students also indicated that their *Banzhuren*, or class director, can have a significant impact on students' decision to proceed toward further study.

> Sometimes it is all about the *Banzhuren*. Most students are not certain about whether they should continue to postgraduate study or not. But if the *Banzhuren* strongly favours postgraduate study, he will tell his students that they definitely should, and the students will be persuaded to do so. In our Department, in some classes a very high percentage of students are preparing to apply for postgraduate study because their *Banzhuren* strongly encourages them to do so; in some other classes only very few people [are preparing for applying for postgraduate study].
>
> (Male Student, Mechanical Engineering, Private College)

Another student from the same subject continued the conversation to explain why *Banzhuren* have such a strong influence:

> *Banzhuren* have a very big influence on students' decisions regarding postgraduate study. For example, the *Banzhuren* of our class has experience of postgraduate study himself, he is very experienced, he tutors us for the postgraduate admission

> examinations and teaches us the specific methods that we shall use to study and prepare for the admission test. In the main library we have a self-study room dedicated to students who are preparing for the postgraduate admission test; this is all organised by our *Banzhuren* and is not possible without his efforts.
>
> (Male Student, Mechanical Engineering, Private College)

As will be outlined in a later section, *Banzhuren* at different institutions tend to have different levels of influence on their students, and there seems to be an institutional culture around the influence of *Banzhuren* on their students.

An earlier study in the Chinese context investigated and compared undergraduate students' aspirations for postgraduate education at two north-western universities (Li, Li, & Zong, 2007). One was in the 985 project and was considered a top-ten university nationally, while the other was a 211 project university of a similar status to the Public University in this study, but directly administered by the Ministry of Education. The investigation showed similar results to the ones presented here, in that the more prestigious university had a higher percentage of students planning to pursue postgraduate study (59.5%) than did the less prestigious university (44%). Overall, around one third of the respondents planned to continue to postgraduate study. This is a high level compared to data from other countries. For example, only slightly more than one fifth of students in the US intend to continue their study to a higher level (Higher Education Research Institute, 2004; OECD, 2003a).

Several market factors may also explain why many students in China desire to pursue postgraduate studies. The competition among *Benke* graduates for better-paid jobs has become more intense. As discussed in the chapter on *Higher Education in China*, the expansion of higher education has resulted in a sharp rise in higher education enrolments and, correspondingly, a sharp increase in the supply of university graduates. However, at the same time, demand for new graduates in the labour market has increased only marginally and is insufficient to absorb all the new *Benke* graduates. In view of the continuous abundant supply of graduates each year, employers have gained bargaining power to increase the credential requirements for job candidates (Chen, 2004). Therefore, pressure from the labour market compels many *Benke* students to aspire to postgraduate education (Li et al., 2007).

Interviews with students and institutional management revealed that there is a widespread culture in the Private College, that students are encouraged to lower their expectations for their first job and to seek better opportunities only after gaining initial employment, or the so-called "get employed first and seek career later" principle *(xian jiuye, zai zeye)*. This may explain, to some extent, why students at the Private College are less likely to aspire to postgraduate study.

Furthermore, the question about aspiration to postgraduate study in the questionnaire specifically asked students whether they are preparing to apply for postgraduate studies; this figure may be rather very different from the final figure of how many students pass the examination and actually enter postgraduate education.

Summary

This section shows that the main motivating factors for entering higher education include: gaining knowledge and skills that can be used in a career, developing as a person and becoming more independent and self-confident. The comparisons in this section show that students at the Colleges, which might be expected to be more career-oriented, were in fact not more career-oriented than students at the Public University. The Public University students' motivation towards personal development was also relatively low compared to students at the Colleges. The impression from these findings is that the College students were more strongly intrinsically motivated for studying than the University students. Interestingly, this finding is consistent with an examination of the former binary higher education system in Britain, which showed that students at polytechnics were more concerned with the intrinsic interest of what they were learning than were university students (Ramsden, 1983).

One notable difference between the students' aspirations was their desire for postgraduate study. The Private College's students were the least likely to expect to continue to postgraduate study, while the Public University and Public College's students were much more likely to want to continue, with the Independent College's students between the two extremes. Examination of the data shows that aspirations to postgraduate study were different among subjects of study: Engineering students were, on average, more likely to indicate that they desired postgraduate education than were Languages students. Furthermore, students' desire to continue to postgraduate study was strongly related to their financial standing, as the more socio-economically privileged students were more likely to desire to continue to further studies. The cultures of the different institutions may also partly explain the different aspirations among students.

Research Question 3: What are students' experiences of the learning environment at different institutions? What can the institutions do to improve students' learning experiences?

This section examines the diversity of the experience of the students surveyed. The areas of experience covered include: hours of study, perceptions of teaching (including course organisation and structure, teaching, resources and *Xuanxiu Ke*), areas of educational emphasis, self-evaluation, learning approaches and overall experience. The open-ended questions in the survey are also analysed here.

Class Attendance Rate

Two items in the questionnaire requested respondents to indicate the number of their scheduled class hours, and the number of hours that they actually attended on campus per week. 959 responses were valid for this analysis. The purpose of asking about both scheduled and actual class hours was so that a class attendance rate could be calculated.

Table 13. Survey respondents' class attendance rate, by institution

Institution	Average Class Attendance Rate
Private College	97.40%
Public University	95.49%
Independent College	96.17%
Public College	96.35%
Total	96.28%

As illustrated in the table, the overall average class attendance rate was quite high, at 96%. Overall, the mean differences between institutions were very small.

The Private College had the highest proportion of students (almost 80%) who indicated their full attendance, compared with the Independent College at 69%, and Public College and Public University at 67%. The Public University not only had the smallest proportion of students reporting full attendance; its proportion of students reporting an attendance rate below 70% was also the highest among the four institutions, at 3.2%, compared with 1.9% at the Independent College, 1.6% at the Public College and zero at the Private College.

Figure 18. Survey respondents' class attendance rate, by institution

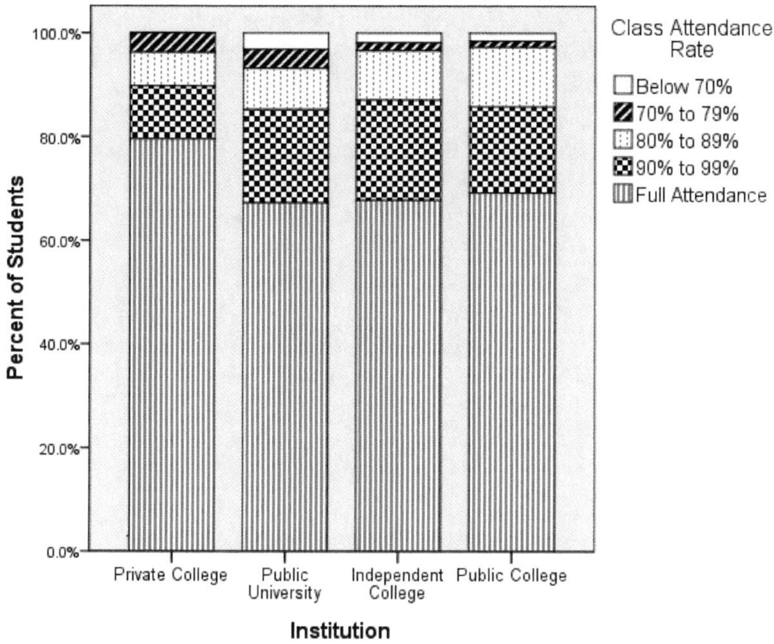

A cross-tabulation of Class Attendance Rate, Institution and Concern about Finance shows that there is a significant association between financial concern and class attendance rate in the Independent College: students concerned with finance were more likely to report a higher class attendance rate. However, this association was not the case in the Public University and Public College, where fees were lower. This may suggest that the level of tuition fees and the perceived financial burden in paying the fees have an impact on students' attitudes towards studying, but this impact only becomes significant when the financial concern exceeds a certain threshold.

For example, students from higher socio-economic groups at the Independent College had the lowest class attendance rates among all groups at all institutions. Their class attendance rate was on average 3.9% lower than the average student in the total sample.

Furthermore, another specific group – students studying Languages at the Independent College – had significantly different attendance patterns than other students: their attendance rate was on average 8.2% lower than the average student in the total sample. As shown below, this difference was highly significant.

Table 14. Effects of institution and discipline on survey respondents' class attendance rate

Dependent Variable: Class attendance rate

					95% Confidence Interval	
Parameter	B	Std. Error	t	Sig.	Lower Bound	Upper Bound
Intercept	.956	.005	186.462	.000	.946	.966
Private College	.016	.008	2.037	.042	.001	.031
Public University	-.009	.008	-1.167	.244	-.024	.006
Independent College	.019	.007	2.547	.011	.004	.033
Public College	0P[a]	.	.	.	.	.
Languages	.034	.011	3.089	.002	.012	.055
Engineering	0P[a]	.	.	.	.	.
Independent College * Languages	-.082	.015	-5.554	.000	-.111	-.053

a. This parameter is set to zero because it is redundant.

After taking into account the effects of institutions and disciplines, male students' class attendance rate was lower than that of female students. This is consistent with Satry and Bekhradnia's (2007) study of the academic experience of students in English universities. This survey found that female students are, in general, more industrious than their male counterparts, in terms of both private study hours and class attendance rate.

Table 15. Effects of gender on survey respondents' class attendance rate

Parameter Estimates

Dependent Variable: Class attendancerate

Parameter	B	Std. Error	t	Sig.	95% Confidence Interval Lower Bound	95% Confidence Interval Upper Bound
Intercept	.978	.012	82.235	.000	.955	1.002
Male	-.029	.013	-2.191	.029	-.055	-.003
Female	0P[a]	.	.	.	.	.

a. This parameter is set to zero because it is redundant.

Furthermore, after controlling for gender, institution and discipline, students' prior achievement, using the *Gaokao* score as a proxy, had little impact on their class attendance rate.

Private Study Hours

The figure below shows that students had different patterns of private study habits. The mean private study hours of students at the Independent College and the Public College appeared to be lower than those of the students at Private College and Public University. The Private College's students reported the highest figure of private study hours, at 15.27 hours per week on average, students at the Public University reported an average 14.97 hours, students at the Public College reported 13.83 hours, and students at the Independent College reported 12.96 hours. This shows that, although the Public University students' class attendance rates were lower than at the other institutions, they reported more private study time.

Analysing the sample by discipline reveals that Languages students reported spending more time on private study. Dividing the sample by gender shows that female students did more hours of private study than male students. As previously indicated, the subject of study and gender are associated: the Languages discipline has more female students than male students. The above two trends (the gender trend and the subject trend) can be observed at all of the four institutions, i.e., at all of the four institutions, Languages students spend more time in private study than Engineering students, and female students spend more time in private study than male students.

It is worth noting that the standard variations among students' reported private study hours were quite high. As shown below, on average the percentage of students whose reported private study hours were below 10, between 11 and 20, and above 20 accounted for 28.8%, 41.1%, and 30.2% of the population respectively.

Figure 19. Survey respondents' private study hours per week, by institution

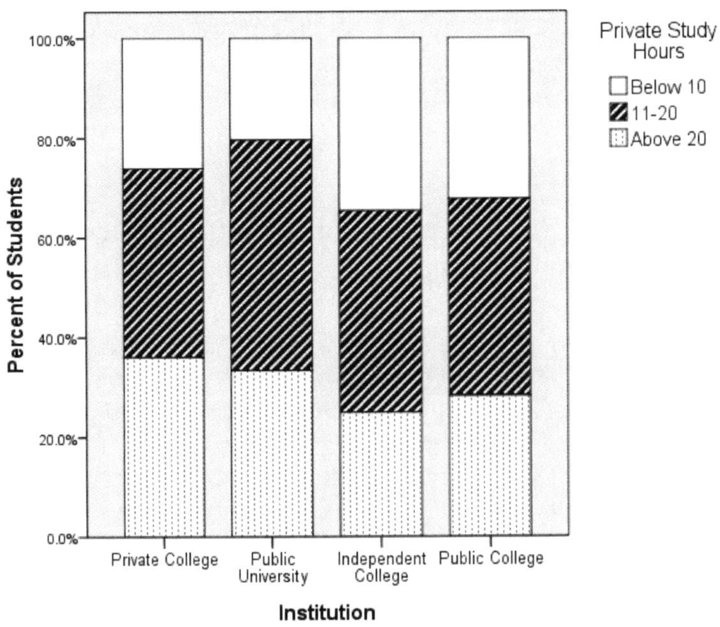

The association between students' financial concerns and private study hours was unclear across and within the four institutions, indicating that financial concerns have little influence on students' private study patterns. It may also be the case that, students with financial pressures had more additional responsibilities, such as part-time employment, and therefore they had less time to increase their private study hours.

Compared with the UK data (Sastry & Bekhradnia, 2007), Chinese students appeared to have higher class attendance rates. According to the English survey, the average class attendance rate was 92%, slightly lower than the 96% in this study. It is not clear from this study whether the Chinese students were genuinely more industrious than their English counterparts, but the study shows that a number of factors may have contributed to the difference. The first is the student management system: the *Banzhuren* system not only engages students in studying, it also allows close monitoring of students, also, given the strict regulations on class attendance in general, students feel obliged to attend the classes. The relatively high cost of attending higher education may have also contributed to Chinese students' higher class attendance. However, the survey respondents in this study did not appear to spend more time engaged in private study than UK students. Considering that their institutions have formally organised private study sessions, Chinese students seem to spend even fewer hours on "voluntary" private study than UK students.

Further Investigation

In China, private institutions have been considered to be of inferior quality compared with public institutions (Pan, 2005; Zhongguo Zhiliang Wanlixing, 2007). Private institutions have shorter histories, lower reputation, less-qualified teaching staff, students whose prior academic achievement is lower and are considered to offer an inferior study environment. However, in this study, the Private College's students reported the highest class attendance rate and the largest number of hours spent on private study. Admittedly, the differences between the institutions were small, but this finding warranted further investigation. The topic was one of the foci in the later interviews with students and institutional administrators.

The research literature provides evidence about the causes of absenteeism in higher education. The factors that may cause non-attendance include assessment pressures, poor lecturing, inconvenient timing of lectures, poor quality of lecture content, low motivation, work overload, and work and family commitments (Fleming, 1992, 1995; Longhurst, 1999; Winn, 2002)

Within the context of Chinese higher education and the four specific institutions, a number of hypotheses are put forward:

1) Students' prior achievement. This can influence students' attitude towards studying. The more successful students have more positive views about studying and demonstrate higher class attendance and more self-study time.
2) Quality of teaching. High quality of teaching, including the use of technology, a focus on relevant content, and employing humour, can attract students to attend class and develop interest in the course.
3) Students' socio-economic status and the level of tuition fees. On the one hand, the pressures for financing higher education can make students feel more obliged to attend classes and achieve results; on the other hand, commitments to part-time jobs can distract students from classes and private study.
4) Study atmosphere. Students are influenced by their environment, and especially by their peers.
5) Regulations. Institutions can impose regulations on students' study, which may include control of class attendance.

For the first hypothesis, the Private College's student intake was among the academically weakest (using the *Gaokao* score as a proxy of prior achievement) in *Benke* institutions, while the Public University students were the best. However, the Public University had the lowest class attendance rates. Statistical analysis has shown that students' prior achievement in terms of *Gaokao* score played little role in determining students' class attendance.

The analysis of the data did not support the second hypothesis as, although the quality of teaching at the Public University was considered to be better than that of the Private College, attendance rates at the Public University were lower.

For the third hypothesis, the above results have suggested that, in some circumstances, there is an association between financial pressures and class attendance.

The fourth hypothesis proposes that a student's study attitudes are influenced by the study environment, which includes IT resources and support, as well as the influence of the study patterns of peers. Interviews with students and institutional mangers revealed that the study environment is also managed by the institution – and the different institutions approached this in different ways. The most important difference found in the institutions was the placement of *Banzhuren* and their influence.

Banzhuren, or class directors, are an integral part of student life at many higher education institutions in China. They remain in close and constant contact with students through regular class meetings and private consultations. They are expected to manage, lead, organise and monitor the students, and are also responsible for their students' academic, moral and personal development. *Banzhuren* may be in full-time posts dedicated to this role, and this position can also be held by academic staff as a concurrent post.

Because of their close contacts with students, although they may not be the actual faculty members who teach the students, *Banzhuren* can still exert significant influence on students' study. Different responsibilities, and expectations of *Banzhuren* can result in different levels of contact between *Banzhuren* and students, and different levels of influence. At the Public University, although all *Banzhuren* are dedicated full-time staff, each *Banzhuren* is responsible for around two hundred students. This certainly reduces the contact quality between *Banzhuren* and students. The *Banzhuren* at the Private College, however, have closer contact because of smaller student numbers:

> In [the Public University], one *Banzhuren* may need to supervise as many as six classes, but here in [the Private College] it is two.
>
> (Dean, Private College)

The Deputy Dean at the Public University claimed that the institution's *Banzhuren* system was among the better ones in public universities, but the number of students each *Banzhuren* supervises is still large compared to the Private College:

> All of our *Banzhuren* are dedicated full-time staff. Our *Banzhuren* team is quite good among the institutions and have won many prizes. Currently the *Banzhuren* to student ratio is at 1 to 200; we used to have a ratio as low as 1 to 180 in the past.
>
> (Deputy Dean, Public University)

The number of students that a single *Banzhuren* supervises has a clear influence on the frequency of contact between the *Banzhuren* and his or her students. For example, one student at the Private College reported frequent and close contact with his *Banzhuren*:

> In a public institution, it may be counted as lucky for a student to see his *Banzhuren* a couple of times every year. But here [in the Private College], we see our *Banzhuren* every day. They live among us. They actually visit our dormitory three or four times a week.
>
> (Male, English, Private College)

In addition to the frequency of contact between *Banzhuren* and students, the level and type of contact is also important. Although it is not the responsibility of *Banzhuren* to teach students, they may actively organise academic and non-academic activities that are beneficial for students' studies and social lives. These activities can also increase students' engagement with their academic and social lives at campus.

> Most *Banzhuren* [at this institution] are not much older than us. Standing behind the teacher's desk they are our teacher, after the class we are brothers and sisters. Our class meetings [organised by *Banzhuren*] are rich and colourful; for example, we have had all-English class meetings.
>
> (Female Student, English, Private College)

> Every evening before the term begins, our *Banzhuren* will come to our dormitory to see if we have arrived safely. This is like returning home, there is a feeling of home.
>
> (Male Student, Art Design, Private College)

The interviews with the Private College's students show that their *Banzhuren* exerted a significant positive influence on them:

> When I entered this college I had no goals… my *Banzhuren* once told me in a one-to-one conversation that I should make goals for the future. She said that the

life of a person without goals is just to help people who have goals in achieving their goals. She is very nice to me; I respect her as much as I respect my mother.
(Male Student, Automobile Service Engineering, Private College)

When I entered the institution I was depressed, I didn't like studying. My *Banzhuren* found this out. She appointed me to a student management position in the class. This increased my communication with classmates, and I have become more alive and now am no longer depressed.
(Male Student, Computer Science and Technology, Private College)

Frequent and active contacts between *Banzhuren* and students are clearly important for creating and maintaining an atmosphere that fosters the academic and personal development of students. Through frequent contacts, *Banzhuren* are always aware of the situation and progress of his or her students, and understand the academic and non-academic difficulties the students are facing. Through close contact, *Banzhuren* can engage their students academically and socially, helping them tackle academic and non-academic challenges.

Furthermore, different institutions also had different provision concerning study regulations (hypothesis 5). At the Private College, for example, the regulations on skipping class are strict:

Here in [the Private College], students skipping more than 15 classes per term, or skipping two consecutive weeks of classes without a good reason, will be expelled.
(Dean, Private College)

Banzhuren and regulations have an impact on students' private study hours as well. Many higher education institutions in China, as a general rule, have the so-called *wanzixi* sessions, or evening self-study sessions, during which classrooms are provided for students' self-study activities. Although *wanzixi* sessions are offered at almost all higher education institutions in China, different higher education institutions, departments and *Banzhuren* can have different requirements about attendance at these sessions. This study found that it is both a requirement of the institution and of the *Banzhuren* at the Private College that students attend these sessions. At the institution, *Banzhuren* regularly visit the *wanzixi* to see if students are there.

However, at the other three institutions, *wanzixi* attendance is either not a requirement or is a requirement that is poorly enforced. This contributes to the lower number of hours students at these three institutions reported spending on private study.

The differences in the use of *Banzhuren* and the provision of regulations for students' study may in fact reflect different institutions' philosophy of education. Interviews with the relevant Deans showed that, at the Public University, students had high levels of past academic achievement as proof of their ability to study; the institution therefore tends to give students more freedom and expect that they will study hard. In contrast, students at the Private College had poor records of academic achievement, and this institution imposed strict regulations and supervision on its students.

The study environment may also be relevant to the different student groups within institutions. For example, at the Colleges, *Benke* is the highest level of their programmes and efforts are focused on the *Benke* programmes and students. However, at the Public University, priority is always given to postgraduate education and research, and the evaluation of staff is also more focused on research output rather than teaching quality. Different institutions' management attach different levels of importance to *Benke* programmes and students, and therefore create differences in terms of input to the programmes. From the students' perspective, Public University's *Benke* students may feel marginalised. In contrast, the Dean at the Private College argued:

> *Benke* students are treasured in our institution. They are our top priority. We dedicate our best resources to them. *Benke* students in major universities certainly do not enjoy this privilege. The research universities are more inclined to cherish their research faculty and students. Research receives priority over *Benke* education in research universities ... just like in our institution *Benke* education receives priority over *Zhuanke* education.
>
> (Dean, Private College)

Of course, students' attitudes toward studying can also be affected by the quality of institutional management and students' personal characteristics.

Course Organisation and Structure

The Course Organisation and Structure scale is the first scale in Section Three (Student Experience: Perception of Teaching) of the questionnaire. Of the overall analytical sample of this section, 1,217 students provided valid answers to all items in the Course Organisation and Structure scale. An aggregation score of the scale is calculated by adding up the value of the four items and dividing by four (the number of items). The table below shows the mean of the scale score, number of cases, and standard deviation of each institution and discipline.

Table 16. Report of the Course Organisation and Structure scale

Institution (Discipline)	Mean	N	Std. Deviation
Private College			
Languages	2.9889	45	.64833
Engineering	2.9347	199	.70092
Total	2.9447	244	.69055
Public University			
Languages	3.1690	105	.59596
Engineering	3.1878	193	.70804
Total	3.1812	298	.66973
Independent College			
Languages	2.8624	89	.63179
Engineering	3.2592	272	.67124
Total	3.1614	361	.68270
Public College			
Languages	3.1500	70	.68021
Engineering	3.0571	254	.71970
Total	3.0772	324	.71135
Total			
Languages	3.0502	309	.64459
Engineering	3.1179	918	.70878
Total	3.1009	1227	.69354

Comparing the mean values of the institutions, the Public University received the highest score in this scale as reported by students, and the Private College received the lowest rating. This is not surprising, as the Public University had the best teachers (in terms of qualification and experience) and the longest history in offering *Benke* programmes. However, the standard deviations were very large, while the mean differences were small (around 8% differences on average). This trend becomes even smaller when gender and *Gaokao* score are controlled for. The Independent College attained a relatively high score close to that of the Public University, and the Public College' score was slightly below average.

At the Independent College, there were differences between the Languages and Engineering disciplines. The College's Languages programmes received the lowest rating of all disciplines in all institutions and its Engineering discipline, in contrast, received the highest rating. The Independent College benefits from the Public University's experience and teacher expertise, but it may be that, the College has given insufficient attention to its Languages programme, and this is reflected in the low scores it received on the Course Organisation and Structure scale for this programme. As will be shown later, the College's Languages students also received the least practical education and gave the lowest rating on this aspect.

A further analysis was carried out to assess the significance of the differences between institutions and disciplines. As the table below shows, taking into account the influence of programmes (Languages and Engineering) and using the Public College as a reference, the Private College achieved a slightly lower score, but the difference was insignificant at the 95% confidence level. The Public University and Independent College achieved slightly higher scores and the differences were significant at the 95% confidence level. Looking at this from a different perception, when controlling for the influence of institutions, in general the differences between Languages and Engineering subjects were small and insignificant. However, the Languages programme at the Independent College showed very different score patterns than other programmes and other institutions; the programme at this institution received much lower scores than other programmes and institutions, and the difference was strongly significant.

Table 17. Effects of institution and discipline on survey respondents' rating to the Course Organisation and Structure scale

Dependent Variable: Aggregated Value of the Course Organisation and Structure Scale

Parameter	B	Std. Error	t	Sig.	95% Confidence Interval Lower Bound	95% Confidence Interval Upper Bound	Partial Eta Squared
Intercept	3.057	.043	71.210	.000	2.973	3.141	.807
Private College	-.120	.066	-1.830	.068	-.248	.009	.003
Public University	.131	.065	2.001	.046	.003	.259	.003
Independent College	.202	.060	3.385	.001	.085	.319	.009
Public College	0P[a]	.	.	.	.	.	.
Languages	.093	.092	1.006	.315	-.088	.274	.001
Engineering	0P[a]	.	.	.	.	.	.
Independent College Languages	-.490	.125	-3.932	.000	-.734	-.245	.013

a. This parameter is set to zero because it is redundant.

Common problems in course organisation and structure as reported by students in interviews included: timetable clashes of classes, insufficient time for revision, and courses not being designed in an incremental and progressive way that supports learning.

> We have encountered a lot of timetable issues. Sometimes you feel that the timetabling is not very systematic.
>
> (Female Student, English, Independent College)

> The lecturers are passionate and responsible, but the course arrangements are not ideal.
>
> (Female Student, English, Public University)

These two responses are typical of the responses received in interviews. Many students reported that there were flaws with the course delivery and design; some problems were at the programme level and some were at the module level. This problem is prevalent in all of the four sampled institutions, suggesting that there is room for improvement in this regard in the institutions. Furthermore, many students also reported that class arrangements change due to other events going on at the institution or department. This situation is better managed and solved in the institutions that control the course elements more tightly (by offering fewer module choices, for example) than in institutions where course elements are organised in a more complex way (such as highly modularised programmes).

Teaching

The Teaching Scale asked about students' perceptions of the teaching of their programme. Of the overall analytical sample of this section, 1,218 students provided valid answers to all items in the Teaching scale. The table below presents the mean value, number of cases, and standard deviation of the aggregated scale score.

Generally speaking, the Private College scored lower than the other three institutions, with a difference of around 6% below the highest rated Public College, but the standard deviations were large. The Languages students at the Independent College again gave significantly lower scores on this aspect than their Engineering peers.

Across institutions, the weakest area lies in the "the teaching staff always make the teaching interesting" item, where the average score was only 2.85, while the highest score was 3.61 for "the teaching staff are always prepared to answer students' questions after class".

Table 18. Report of the Teaching scale

Institution (Discipline)	Mean	N	Std. Deviation
Private College			
Languages	3.0877	44	.43376
Engineering	3.1355	195	.59519
Total	3.1267	239	.56842
Public University			
Languages	3.4272	106	.50747
Engineering	3.2208	198	.71863
Total	3.2928	304	.65933
Independent College			
Languages	3.0673	87	.58491
Engineering	3.3379	271	.64809
Total	3.2721	358	.64310
Public College			
Languages	3.2898	70	.56149
Engineering	3.3386	254	.68242
Total	3.3280	324	.65767
Total			
Languages	3.2452	307	.55367
Engineering	3.2698	918	.66714
Total	3.2637	1225	.64046

It should be noted again that the differences between disciplines *within* institutions are often much larger than the differences *between* institutions. Using "the teaching staff are always prepared to answer students' questions after class" as an example (see the table below), the differences between notional agreements at different institutions (the percentage of respondents who rated 4 or 5 for the statement) were no larger than 5.6% (between the Private College and the Public College), but differences between the two disciplines within institutions ranged from 9% (the Independent College) to 22.3% (the Private

College). The differences were more associated with the institutional effects on the discipline rather than discipline effects *per se*, as at the Public University the Languages discipline scored higher than Engineering but at the other institutions it was the reverse.

Table 19. Notional agreement with the statement "The teaching staff is always prepared to answer students' questions after class", by institution

Institution	Languages	Engineering	Total
Private College	80%	57.7%	61.8%
Public University	76.4%	66.5%	63.4%
Independent College	56.1%	65.1%	62.9%
Public College	80%	64%	67.4%

Further analysis was carried out to examine the differences between institutions and disciplines on this scale. The table below shows that, controlling for the effects of disciplines and using Public College as a reference for comparison, the Private College's score on this scale was significantly lower. The Public University's score was slightly lower as well but this was not significant. The Independent College's score was about the same as the Public College.

Table 20. Effects of institution and discipline on survey respondents' rating to the Teaching scale

Dependent Variable: Aggregated Value of the Teaching Scale

					95% Confidence Interval	
Parameter	B	Std. Error	t	Sig.	Lower Bound	Upper Bound
Intercept	3.339	.040	83.810	.000	3.260	3.417
Private College	-.203	.061	-3.333	.001	-.323	-.084
Public University	-.118	.060	-1.957	.051	-.236	.000
Independent College	.000	.055	-.012	.990	-.109	.108
Public College	0P[a]	.	.	.	.	.

Table 20. Effects of institution and discipline on survey respondents' rating to the Teaching scale (cont.)

Dependent Variable: Aggregated Value of the Teaching Scale

Languages	-.049	.086	-.569	.569	-.217	.119
Engineering	0P[a]	.	.	.	.	.
Public University Languages	.255	.115	2.223	.026	.030	.480
Independent College Languages	-.222	.116	-1.911	.056	-.449	.006

a. This parameter is set to zero because it is redundant.

Resources

The Resources scale asked students to rate the learning resources provided by the institution, including textbooks, teaching equipment, library resources and online resources. Of the overall analytical sample, 1,209 students provided valid answers to all items in this scale.

The average rating for this scale (3.44) is the highest of all the scales in terms of absolute value. Although the assessment area of each scale is different and direct comparison is not necessarily appropriate, this seems to suggest that students are more satisfied with the resources provided by the institutions, than with other factors. A high level of satisfaction with institutional libraries and computing facilities was also found in both the UK and Australian national student experience studies. Less than 10% of the students in the two studies indicated dissatisfaction with either of these aspects of provision (Krause et al., 2005).

Table 21. Report of the Resources scale

Institution (Discipline)	Mean	N	Std. Deviation
Private College			
Languages	3.4698	43	.55012
Engineering	3.5309	188	.64824
Total	3.5195	231	.63047
Public University			
Languages	3.5495	103	.59390
Engineering	3.4808	193	.69048
Total	3.5047	296	.65828
Independent College			
Languages	2.8067	89	.74434
Engineering	3.4541	270	.75044
Total	3.2936	359	.79856
Public College			
Languages	3.6571	70	.54708
Engineering	3.4775	253	.71359
Total	3.5164	323	.68421
Total			
Languages	3.3462	305	.71561
Engineering	3.4823	904	.70640
Total	3.4480	1209	.71090

The Private College achieved the highest rating among all institutions in this aspect, although only slightly higher than the Public University and Public College. The Independent College, however, showed a lower rating on this, with a nearly 9% difference to other three institutions. The large difference was, again, due to the difference between Languages and Engineering subjects at the Independent College. The Engineering students' rating, of 3.45, was only slightly lower than the average level of the other institutions, but the Languages students gave a rating of 2.8, showing an overall negative opinion towards the institutions' resources.

Table 22. Mean scores of the Resources scale items, by institution and discipline

Institution / Discipline	The textbooks or teaching materials of my courses are very helpful to my learning	The teaching equipments (e.g. computers, labs) are helpful to my learning	The library resources and services are helpful to my learning	The institution provides convenient and ample learning resources (public computers, information resources, etc.)
Private College				
Languages	3.36	3.27	3.91	3.32
Engineering	3.30	3.49	3.94	3.45
Total	3.31	3.45	3.93	3.43
Public University				
Languages	3.74	3.43	3.68	3.23
Engineering	3.44	3.41	3.67	3.41
Total	3.54	3.42	3.67	3.35
Independent College				
Languages	3.07	2.66	3.22	2.18
Engineering	3.48	3.44	3.68	3.25
Total	3.38	3.25	3.56	2.99
Public College				
Languages	3.53	3.46	4.09	3.47
Engineering	3.52	3.39	3.80	3.26
Total	3.52	3.40	3.87	3.31
Total				
Languages	3.44	3.19	3.67	2.99
Engineering	3.45	3.43	3.77	3.33
Total	3.44	3.37	3.74	3.25

An examination of the specific items shows that the Independent College's Languages students gave lower ratings than its Engineering students on all the items within this scale. Four items have been selected in the above table for further analysis. It can be seen from the table that the largest difference between the Independent College's Languages and Engineering disciplines, and also the largest difference between the Independent College and other institutions, occurred in the library resources, computers and equipments-related aspects.

Further analysis, as shown in the table below, reveals that, using the Public College as a reference for comparison, after controlling for the disciplinary effects, the Private College's score on the resources scale was slightly higher, but not significantly so. The Public University and the Independent College's scores were about the same or slightly lower, and insignificant as well. Controlling for the institutional effects, the Languages discipline in general receives a higher rating from students than Engineering, but the difference was also insignificant. The only exception to the above result is the Languages discipline at the Independent College, which scored significantly lower than other programmes and institutions.

Table 23. Effects of institution and discipline on survey respondents' rating to the Resources scale

Dependent Variable: Aggregated Value of the Resources Scale

Parameter	B	Std. Error	t	Sig.	95% Confidence Interval Lower Bound	95% Confidence Interval Upper Bound	Partial Eta Squared
Intercept	3.477	.043	80.429	.000	3.393	3.562	.843
Private College	.053	.066	.806	.420	-.077	.183	.001
Public University	.003	.066	.051	.959	-.126	.132	.000
Independent College	-.023	.060	-.389	.697	-.141	.095	.000
Public College	0P[a]	.	.	.	.	.	.
Languages	.180	.093	1.935	.053	-.003	.362	.003
Engineering	0P[a]	.	.	.	.	.	.
Independent College Languages	-.827	.125	-6.602	.000	-1.073	-.581	.035

a. This parameter is set to zero because it is redundant.

Detailed information about the library resources were collected from the four institutions and a comparison was made:

Table 24. Library provisions of the participating institutions

	Private College	Public University	Independent College	Public College
Space (m²)	34,000	60,000	10,370	36,422
Books (Paper-based)	1,410,000	2,560,000	500,000	720,000
Books (Electronic)	1,380,000	1,080,000	N.A.	460,000
Seats	3,000	4,321	1000	3,800
Computers in Library	200	N.A.	N.A.	500
Open Hours per week (term time)	98	88	88	98

N.A. indicates the data are not available.

Data source: Institutional websites and information leaflets.

It can be seen from the table that the Independent College's library had the smallest space, the smallest volume of books, and the fewest seats for students. Unsurprisingly, the Independent College's students were not satisfied with their library resources.

In addition, the experience of students is not necessarily consistent with the simple numbers in the table; there are other factors that can influence the actual experience of students with regard to resources. The first factor is the usefulness of the resources to the particular student. For example, students may not find the library useful if the library mostly contains books about other subjects, or books that are not up-to-date or relevant to the needs of the students, even if the library's book collection is large. This may explain, in the case of the Independent College, why the Languages students rated the resources significantly lower than their Engineering peers. A student majoring in Languages at the Independent College confirmed this:

> Literature studies require lots of reading, but the volume of books available for us in the library is clearly insufficient… there are plenty of books for the Electronics, Engineering, and Comic Design subjects, but much fewer books for us.
> (Female Student, English, Independent College)

Interviews with the President and the Dean of the Independent College also confirmed this influence, because they were particularly proud of the facilities for Engineering and Technology-related studies, mentioning that these facilities are "more and better" than that of their *Muxiao*, the Public University, and they acknowledged that the other programmes at the institution received less attention and resources. Through interviews with managers at other institutions, it became clear that this situation is prevalent in all four institutions. The institutions have "key" subject areas, which receive the most support from the institution in terms of attention, facilities, resources, faculty, and so forth. It is not surprising that students of these "key" subject areas are likely to report higher scores and levels of satisfaction with their programmes and institutions than students of other subjects.

The second factor is the number and type of students sharing the library resources. A "resources per capita" measure can be calculated by dividing the total resources by the number of students; this is, in fact, an indicator that is assessed in the national evaluation of higher education institutions in China. However, the students in this study did not seem to adjust the rating according to the student numbers. For example, although the Independent College's library was smaller, the College itself also accommodated fewer students and, according to the President of the Independent College, their educational resources per capita was higher than that of the Public University. However, the College nevertheless received lower ratings.

As well as the student numbers, the type of student also influences the students' needs. For example, although the Private College had a large number of students sharing the library resources, most of the students were *Zhuanke* students who may have fewer requirements for book resources, thereby increasing library access for the *Benke* students.

In contrast, although the Public University had a very large book collection, its large research student base also meant more frequent use of the library resources, reducing the books and space available for *Benke* students. The Public University received a low rating on its library resources, despite its large book collection and number of spaces available. As two students of the Public University noted:

> Library resources are sometimes insufficient as there is a large volume of students wishing to use the same books.
>
> (Male Student, English, Public University)

> Many of the books are clearly not provided for us [the *Benke* students]... they are too advanced, some are old too, only maybe research students and professors will use them.
>
> (Male Student, Mechanical Engineering and Automation, Public University)

Third, the learning environment of the library is also crucial. During the interviews, students at the Private College frequently praised its library, and the statements immediately received widespread agreement from other students: students mentioned the beautiful design of the building and the large volume of books in it.

In the case of the Independent College, it is expected that this year's third-year students and next year's third-year students will have different experiences with regard to the resources, because the institution only made a large investment in the library in the intervening period:

> It is true that the resources were lacking in 2006 and 2007, but we have put in fifty million [yuan] this year... Students enrolled in 2005 experienced difficult times of the institution. When they entered the institution, we did not have our own laboratories, we had to use buses to send them to the [*Muxiao* Public University's new campus, which is about one hour's drive away] for them to attend some classes. They have not enjoyed the new facilities we bought later. Students enrolled in 2006 and 2007 certainly have.
>
> (Dean, Independent College)

This situation is also prevalent in other institutions. As introduced in the background chapter, Chinese higher education experienced rapid development in the past decade. Many higher education institutions are developing and changing quickly. It is likely that the students of later years will have a better experience with regard to resources than students of the earlier years have.

The resource scale and figures on numbers of books and spaces are only a very crude proxy for what is available to students and how satisfied they are. Simple quantitative measures of space and volume of resources do not easily translate to an understanding of the student experience. But it also points to a limitation of the student questionnaires, which is that real complexities (like how students actually work and learn) cannot be captured easily.

Xuanxiu Ke

The Chinese phrase *Xuanxiu Ke* refers to the "optional modules". The scale has three items. Of the overall analytical sample of this section, 1,197 students provided valid answers to all items in the *Xuanxiu Ke* scale.

Table 25. Mean scores of the *Xuanxiu Ke* scale items, by institution

Institution		I think the learning in *Xuanxiu Ke* is very significant	The teaching staff of *Xuanxiu Ke* take the teaching very seriously	My classmates take the *Xuanxiu Ke* very seriously
Private College	Mean	3.44	3.04	2.71
	Std. Deviation	.976	.892	.882
Public University	Mean	3.20	2.97	2.58
	Std. Deviation	1.012	.988	1.033
Independent College	Mean	3.22	3.01	2.68
	Std. Deviation	1.096	.965	.992
Public College	Mean	3.20	2.95	2.34
	Std. Deviation	1.094	.935	.950
Total	Mean	3.25	2.99	2.57
	Std. Deviation	1.055	.949	.981

The table shows that, perhaps surprisingly, students of the more applied-learning-oriented Private College felt *Xuanxiu Ke* to be more important, and the students of the more academic Public University reported the lowest level of significance for *Xuanxiu Ke*. The differences, however, are not substantial and the standard deviations are large.

The overall picture of students' attitudes toward *Xuanxiu Ke* can be seen from the responses to the item "my classmates take the *Xuanxiu Ke* very seriously". The table below shows the percentages of students ticking the relevant score (1 to 5) at the four institutions.

Table 26. Responses to the statement "My classmates take the *Xuanxiu Ke* very seriously", by institution

	Responses to the statement "My classmates take the *Xuanxiu Ke* very seriously"					
	Completely Disagree	Disagree	Neutral	Agree	Completely Agree	Total
Private College	7.8%	33.2%	40.1%	18.1%	.9%	100.0%
Public University	18.3%	25.0%	40.0%	13.7%	3.0%	100.0%
Independent College	12.7%	28.9%	39.9%	15.0%	3.5%	100.0%
Public College	18.6%	41.8%	28.2%	9.6%	1.9%	100.0%
Total	14.7%	32.2%	36.8%	13.8%	2.4%	100.0%

The vast majority of students (over 80%) did not agree with the statement. Of course the use of "very" in the statement has heightened the standards, but institutions and the higher education sector in China still need to pay attention to this. The Public College should especially be concerned about its students' attitudes to *Xuanxiu Ke*, as it had the largest percentage of students disagreeing with the statement (60.4%) and the smallest percentage of students agreeing with the statement (11.5%).

Areas of Educational Emphasis

The students were asked two sets of questions on this area. The first set requested the respondents to indicate their agreement to the "teaching emphasis" statements; these questions were broad and general in nature. The second set was more specific, containing nine items, which could be classified into three groups: Academic Orientation, Practical Orientation and General Orientation.

Of the analytical sample, 1,221 provided valid answers to all these items. The table below shows a cross-tabulation of institutions, disciplines and the scores of the educational emphasis items.

Table 27. Emphasis of subject teaching, by institution and discipline

Discipline (Institution)	The subject teaching emphasises memorising knowledge	The subject teaching emphasises analysing knowledge	The subject teaching emphasises making judgements of information	The subject teaching emphasises applying knowledge
Languages				
Private College	3.28	3.63	3.49	3.95
Public University	3.75	3.90	3.72	4.00
Independent College	3.66	3.58	3.41	3.53
Public College	3.72	3.84	3.57	3.85
Engineering				
Private College	3.20	3.87	3.62	3.91
Public University	3.16	3.65	3.52	3.65
Independent College	3.44	3.89	3.79	3.91
Public College	3.22	3.80	3.58	3.92
Total				
Private College	3.21	3.83	3.60	3.92
Public University	3.37	3.74	3.59	3.77
Independent College	3.49	3.81	3.69	3.81
Public College	3.33	3.81	3.58	3.90

The subject variations are significant in the knowledge memorising item, but less significant on the application of knowledge item. The Languages students felt that they were required to memorise more information (3.65) in studying than were the Engineering students (3.27), but overall the ratings on this item were lower than that of other items, and students across both disciplines gave much higher ratings to the application of knowledge they learnt at their institution (3.82 and 3.86).

Most of the institutional variances were small after taking the above discipline variances into account. The Private College's ratings on memorising knowledge were consistently at the lower margin and its ratings on application of knowledge were consistently at the higher margin, indicating that the institution had a stronger emphasis on the vocational applicability of knowledge. Overall, however, the difference is small. For example, the Private College's "emphasis on applying knowledge" item received a score of 3.92, which is not much higher than the average value of 3.85. However, the Private College's Languages students rated memorising knowledge considerably lower than the average: its score of 3.28 was lower than the average value of 3.65.

The other three institutions' scores were closer to the average value and most variants from the average were less than 5%. Larger differences did exist, but they did not appear to indicate systematic institutional differences. For example, the rating given by the Independent College's Languages students for knowledge applicability was 7% lower than the average, but the rating given by its Engineering students was 1% higher than the average. The rating given by the Public University's Languages students for knowledge memorising was 3% higher than the average, but the rating given by Engineering students was 4% lower than the average. On the knowledge applicability item, Languages students at the Public University reported the highest value (4.0) among the four institutions, but Engineering students at the same institution reported the lowest value (3.65) of the four institutions.

Overall, students at the Private College and Public College reported a lower emphasis on the memorisation of knowledge in teaching, while students at the Independent College reported a higher emphasis on memorisation. However, it should be stressed that most differences were small. It can be said that, according to the students, all four institutions place great importance on the applicability of knowledge.

There were considerable variations between the two disciplines, but most variations occurred within institutions. The only variation that generalises across institutions was that Languages students were subject to more knowledge memorisation than Engineering students. However, students from both disciplines reported that their institutions placed high importance on the applicability of knowledge.

As stated, there were considerable variations between disciplines within institutions. For example, at the Public University, Languages students rated applicability of knowledge (4.0) much higher than Engineering students (3.65), but the trend was reversed at the Independent College, where Engineering students gave a much higher score (3.91) than Languages students (3.53).

In summary, students from all four institutions agreed that their institution placed more emphasis on the application of knowledge than on memorising knowledge. The patterns are less clear when comparing the four institutions' level of importance placed on application of knowledge. The Private College and the Public College seemed to have placed the most importance on this aspect, while the Public University gave the least importance to application of knowledge. It is critical to note that even for the Public University, students' scores given to the applicability of knowledge were still quite positive compared with scores given to other items, and the overall score differences between institutions on this aspect are not large.

Students' opinions of their institution and course's emphasis on applicability of knowledge were consistently high and varied only a little from institution to institution. This finding contradicts the expectation that colleges at the lower end of the hierarchy, which publicly label themselves as "applied colleges", are more vocational- and career-oriented than the major universities at the upper end of the hierarchy. However, as stated, the reality is that, according to the reports from students, the institutions all place similarly high emphasis on the applicability of knowledge.

Students' responses to the second set of questions yielded similar results, in that the four institutions received very similar scores on their educational orientations. Therefore, the results are not presented here, but the data on educational orientations are used in other sections of the analysis of the questionnaire data, for example, in calculating their influence on students' overall experience.

"General" and "specific" objectives in undergraduate education are contradictions that are difficult to coordinate. Many institutions in China, especially those with a certain prestige and history, such as the Public University under study, find themselves bewildered in identifying a priority educational objective, and most have included both the general and specific aims as objectives. However, students' time is limited; it is immensely difficult, if at all possible, for students to excel at both general knowledge and specific knowledge, or at both humanistic development and practical ability, in just four years. Some recent critiques have mirrored this embarrassing position. Some critics argue that current undergraduate education in China is too practical and vocational, and, as a result, students' minds are not developed and their potential is not utilised (Huang & Feng, 2003; Wang, 2006; Zhao & Yao, 2004). At the same time, others criticise the undergraduate curriculum as too generalised and not useful, as offering little value to society, and as being responsible for the difficult employment situation graduates face today (Fan & Wu, 2004; Shi & Wang, 2008). This contradiction is surely of great interest and necessitates a solution.

Self-Evaluation

The self-evaluation scale contains four items. They ask students to evaluate their own study progress at the institution and their job prospects against four statements. Of the overall analytical sample of this section, 1,218 students provided valid answers to all items in the self-evaluation scale. The mean values of the four statements at the four institutions are presented in the table below:

Table 28. Survey respondents' scores on the self-evaluation scale items, by institution

	Institution				
	Private College	Public University	Independent College	Public College	Total
I always complete the coursework assignments on time	3.62	3.55	3.59	3.61	3.59
I always complete the coursework assignments to a high level of quality	3.34	3.19	3.31	3.29	3.28
I master the knowledge and skills taught by teachers and books	3.18	3.21	3.20	3.17	3.19
I am fully confident that my studies will provide me with good career prospects	3.03	3.15	3.12	3.09	3.10
Self Evaluation Scale	3.2926	3.2737	3.3136	3.2892	3.2930

The differences on the self-evaluation aspects between institutions were all very small. In general, students were more confident about completing their assignments on time, rather less confident about being able to master knowledge and skills, and even less confident about obtaining a job after graduation. Interestingly, within institutions, a student's confidence about future employment was not significantly related to his or her *Gaokao* score. Between institutions, the institution and its status may play a part in students' confidence about future employment. One student from the Private College noted:

> I am a little worried about my job prospects after graduation. I mean, even if we study really hard and achieve good scores in the exams, and gain other technical qualifications or credentials as well, I will still worry that my resume and job application will not even pass the screening because the human resource manager has not heard of my institution.
>
> (Male Student, Computer Science and Technology, Private College)

The research literature shows that relationships and networks play an important role in students' job-seeking in China. It is very common in China for students to obtain job opportunities through the relationships and networks their parents have (Yue et al., 2004). Since, in general, students at the Public University and the Independent College are from better-off families, they and their parents are likely to have wider and more useful networks, and this resource can help them ease their concerns over employment.

Learning Approaches

The questionnaire asked students a set of questions relating to their learning approaches. The questions can be divided into two sets, the first is related to the Deep Learning Approach and the second is related to the Surface Learning Approach (see the *Methodology* chapter for the explanation and theories of these concepts). An aggregated mean value is calculated for each approach for every respondent.

The following table gives the results of the values:

Table 29. Survey respondents' learning approaches, by institution and discipline

Institution	Discipline		Deep Learning Scale	Surface Learning Scale
Private College	Languages	Mean	3.3167	2.5737
		Std. Deviation	.42332	.68524
	Engineering	Mean	3.3737	2.7581
		Std. Deviation	.60554	.75507
	Total	Mean	3.3636	2.7268
		Std. Deviation	.57709	.74545
Public University	Languages	Mean	3.5000	2.4321
		Std. Deviation	.55997	.72408
	Engineering	Mean	3.4054	2.7856
		Std. Deviation	.57799	.80552
	Total	Mean	3.4388	2.6611
		Std. Deviation	.57253	.79481

Table 29. Survey respondents' learning approaches, by institution and discipline (cont.).

Independent College	Languages	Mean	3.3506	2.4375
		Std. Deviation	.55918	.62528
	Engineering	Mean	3.4189	2.7521
		Std. Deviation	.59027	.77851
	Total	Mean	3.4018	2.6779
		Std. Deviation	.58261	.75624
Public College	Languages	Mean	3.4357	2.5072
		Std. Deviation	.64036	.64496
	Engineering	Mean	3.3191	2.6084
		Std. Deviation	.59507	.72955
	Total	Mean	3.3449	2.5857
		Std. Deviation	.60629	.71166
Total	Languages	Mean	3.4178	2.4696
		Std. Deviation	.56568	.67321
	Engineering	Mean	3.3787	2.7219
		Std. Deviation	.59259	.76869
	Total	Mean	3.3887	2.6588
		Std. Deviation	.58587	.75363

The results show that there were some disparities between the two disciplines. In general, Languages students were more likely to report a deep learning approach toward learning and less likely to report a surface learning approach than Engineering students. Across institutions, the Public University students' score on the deep learning approach was slightly higher than the College average. But the differences were very small and insignificant.

This finding indicates that students' learning approaches were not significantly associated with their institution of study. The Public University's students were not significantly more likely to report an "academic" approach to studying – interest in what is being studied for its own sake and an active, critical stance towards learning (Ramsden, 1983).

Overall Experience

The two measures on overall experience do not form a scale in the same way as those previously analysed. They provide useful summary measures, and can be compared across institutions and with the previous measures on the specific learning experience. The table below shows the mean value for the two items, grouped by institution and discipline.

Table 30. Survey respondents' overall experience, by institution and discipline

Institution (Discipline)	I think the educational and social experience at this institution is excellent.	If I could start all over again, I definitely would go to the same institution I am now attending.
Private College		
Languages	2.80	2.17
Engineering	2.93	2.60
Total	2.91	2.52
Public University		
Languages	3.31	2.62
Engineering	3.29	2.97
Total	3.30	2.85
Independent College		
Languages	2.55	2.22
Engineering	3.10	2.75
Total	2.96	2.62
Public College		
Languages	3.13	2.43
Engineering	2.96	2.58
Total	3.00	2.54
Total		
Languages	2.98	2.40
Engineering	3.07	2.72
Total	3.05	2.64

The table shows that the Public University students' reported levels of satisfaction with the overall experience were much higher than the colleges' students, and the Private College students' reported levels of satisfaction were the lowest. There was a significant difference between the scores of the Public University and of the Private College of 13%.

The question on whether the students would choose their institution again if given the chance yielded even lower scores with an average of only 2.64, overall, the students' opinions were quite negative. Students' overall experience varies greatly according to subject, and these subject effects are not generalisable across institutions – on the contrary, they are specific to the institutions. Institutions that designated some subjects as a priority for development are likely to receive lower satisfaction from students of other subjects. This is clearly the case in the Languages and Engineering subjects at the Independent College in this study.

Students at the Independent and Private Colleges pay much higher tuition fees, but reported lower levels of satisfaction with the educational and social experience at their institutions than students who have paid less at the public institutions. Students' expectations increase with the increase of tuition fees, so the more expensive institutions may be likely to receive lower scores because their students' expectations were higher.

This statement is also true elsewhere. For example, in student surveys in the UK, international students, who pay higher fees than home and EU students, are generally less satisfied with the course and university experience (Surridge, 2006, 2008; UKCOSA, 2004). If students take account of value-for-money and difficulty in financing their studies when considering their overall satisfaction with the course or university, it is understandable that students in China would report a higher level of dissatisfaction compared with that of the UK or Australia, since students and the general public have little confidence in the quality of the higher education system in China and therefore teaching quality in China may be considered by students as inferior compared to that of developed countries, and at the same time the fees are high in terms of their percentage in the household disposable income.

However, there are also examples of more expensive institutions receiving higher scores than less expensive institutions. Buckingham University in England is such an example: it charges higher fees, the tuition for a UK or European Union undergraduate student at Buckingham University is around £8,000 pounds per annum compared with £3,100 pounds in other universities in England (University of Buckingham, 2008), but it still received very favourable scores in the recent administrations of NSS (Newman, 2008a; University of Buckingham, 2006). However, the duration of a Bachelor's degree programme at Buckingham is shorter than at other UK institutions, the total expenses including tuition fees and living expenses at Buckingham may be lower than at other institutions.

Comparing the score with the previous specific experience measures, it seems that this overall experience score is not necessarily associated with the measures of learning. Using the Private College as an example, compared with other institutions, it received fairly good results in the learning environment measures (relative to other three institutions), but it received the lowest score in the overall experience questions. In terms of absolute values, the other two Colleges had overall scores that were much lower than the scores on the teaching and learning measures, and only the Public University had an overall score that was close to its scores on the teaching and learning measures. This shows that factors other than learning and teaching can influence students' overall towards the institution in which they study.

As shown in the table below, it was found that students' concerns about finance in general have an impact on their perception of experience at the institution. Students with the lowest level of financial concerns tended to be more satisfied with their institution. However, the Public University is an exception here; students with high levels of financial concern at the Public University were, on the contrary, more satisfied with the institution than those with lower or no financial concerns. Therefore, it is suggested that an institution's composition of students, in terms of socio-economic status, has a complex influence on the average satisfaction rating that the institution receives from its students.

Table 31. Survey respondents' overall experience, by institution and concern about finance

Institution (Concern about finance)	I think the educational and social experience at this institution is excellent.	If I could start all over again, I definitely would go to the same institution I am now attending.
Private College		
Not concerned	3.06	2.69
Somewhat concerned	2.93	2.56
Very concerned	2.87	2.39
Public University		
Not concerned	3.29	2.88
Somewhat concerned	3.22	2.83
Very concerned	3.43	2.79
Independent College		
Not concerned	3.06	2.65
Somewhat concerned	2.92	2.60
Very concerned	2.95	2.66
Public College		
Not concerned	3.02	2.56
Somewhat concerned	3.02	2.43
Very concerned	2.86	2.59
Total		
Not concerned	3.11	2.69
Somewhat concerned	3.03	2.61
Very concerned	3.00	2.59

There were other factors that the students may have taken into account when considering the overall experience with their institution. It is possible that students' confidence in the institution played a role and, that the College students had less confidence in their institution because of its relatively low status, and therefore tended to give a low score on this measure. The sense of being enrolled in an academically inferior institution was displayed repeatedly in the interviews with the College students, and it was clear that the students at the Colleges lacked the confidence that their University counterparts had. In the discussions with students, it was found that students' information about other institutions was often incorrect. In this context, the reputation of the Independent College is complex. As discussed in the background chapter on *Higher Education in China*, previously independent colleges could confer degree credentials that were exactly identical to those of their *Muxiaos*, and therefore these graduates would enjoy the reputation of the established *Muxiaos*. However, the new policy mandates that independent colleges confer degrees in their own names; this certainly reduces the value to some extent, but how employers and students perceive the reputation of independent colleges in comparison to the reputation of private and public colleges is still unclear. Future research in this field is warranted.

Effects of other scales on overall experience

The contribution made by each of the other areas covered by the questionnaire was examined in the analysis of students' overall experience with the course and institution. This gives an indication of the importance of the respective areas when students come to an overall assessment of their experience with their course and institution. For example, it may be the case that despite very positive evaluations of Learning Resources, this is not a key element for students and so does not have a large impact on the overall assessment of the experience.

Table 32. Effects of the questionnaires scales on survey respondents' overall experience (item 1)

Dependent Variable: I think the educational and social experience at this institution is excellent.

					95% Confidence Interval	
Parameter	B	Std. Error	t	Sig.	Lower Bound	Upper Bound
Organisation Scale	.210	.048	4.402	.000	.117	.304
Teaching Scale	.060	.053	1.118	.264	-.045	.165
Environment Scale	.049	.047	1.058	.290	-.042	.141
Resources Scale	.064	.046	1.406	.160	-.025	.154
Xuanxiuke Scale	.046	.037	1.228	.220	-.027	.119
Self-evaluation Scale	.414	.041	10.023	.000	.333	.495
Concern about finance	-.055	.033	-1.684	.093	-.119	.009
Orientation-Academic	.057	.043	1.321	.187	-.027	.141
Orientation-Practical	-.027	.042	-.644	.519	-.111	.056
Orientation-General	.219	.041	5.397	.000	.139	.299

The coefficients in the above table can be used to make comparisons between the analytical scales, as each analytical scale is measured on the same numeric scale. It can be seen that most of the analytical scale generated only a small influence on the overall experience assessment. The table suggests that course organisation had a significant, and by far the strongest, effect on overall experience. Regarding the students' characteristics, there is a strong association between students' self evaluation and their overall experience; students who reported better academic performance tended to report a better overall experience.

Furthermore, there is also a negative association between level of financial concern and overall experience, e.g., students who were more concerned about finance tended to report lower level of satisfaction. Academic orientation appeared to have a positive effect on overall experience, while Practical orientation appeared to have a negative effect on overall experience, but both effects were not significant. However, the general orientation had a significant and strong positive effect on overall experience, indicating that an institution's emphasis on inter-disciplinary learning, education on learning to learn, and the development of students' values and ethics are important for students' overall assessment of their experience.

The result suggests that students who perceive their course organisation favourably are more satisfied with their courses. But the effects of most other factors in the questionnaire on students' overall experience with the institution are not significant. This indicates that the levels of association are not high enough to suggest that the scales in the questionnaire are simply a proxy measure for general satisfaction.

The relationship between the questionnaire scales and the second overall experience statement, that is, whether the student would go to the same institution he or she was attending if he or she could start all over again, is also assessed. None of the questionnaire scales shows significant association with students' answers to the second overall experience question.

Table 33. Effects of the questionnaires scales on survey respondents' overall experience (item 2)

Dependent Variable: If I could start all over again, I definitely would go to the same institution I am now attending.

Parameter	B	Std. Error	t	Sig.	95% Confidence Interval	
					Lower Bound	Upper Bound
Intercept	.328	1.966	.167	.868	-3.551	4.207
Organisation Scale	.249	.408	.611	.542	-.555	1.054
Teaching Scale	-.851	.522	-1.628	.105	-1.881	.180
Environment Scale	-.149	.428	-.349	.728	-.993	.695
Resources Scale	.285	.474	.602	.548	-.649	1.219
Xuanxiu Ke Scale	.098	.421	.232	.817	-.733	.929
Orientation (Academic)	-.085	.428	-.200	.842	-.929	.758
Orientation (Practical)	.253	.405	.626	.532	-.545	1.051
Orientation (General)	.687	.356	1.931	.055	-.015	1.388
Self-evaluation Scale	.262	.403	.649	.517	-.533	1.056
Concern about finance	-.019	.379	-.051	.960	-.766	.728

The ranking order of the four institutions on students' overall experience, that is, the Public University at the top, Public College and Independent College in the middle, and Private College at the bottom, seems to reflect the reputational hierarchy of the institutions. Students' overall experience of their institution, are more affected by the reputation and the tuition fees level of the institution, and less affected by the academic aspects of the institution. In this context, students in the interviews commented that:

> I feel lucky to be able to study at [the Public University]...yes, because of its top position in the province. There aren't any better choices in the province. Studying here can't be wrong.
>
> (Female Student, English, Public University)

> Actually, this institution was my second choice. I wanted to attend another better university, but I didn't get a place... because I didn't get the required grades... but this one is good too, it is a good choice for the grades I got.
>
> (Male Student, Computer Science and Technology, Public College)

The attitude that "this is a good choice for the marks I attained" is widespread among the students at the Independent College. The students in the interviews clearly attached high importance to the reputation of the institution. The students did not have plenty of choices of institutions on the basis of their *Gaokao* scores and, in the past, they would have been denied the opportunity to attend higher education. But, by paying higher tuition fees than they would in public institutions, they could now study at an institution with a good name. Compared with private institutions, independent colleges have more prestige and become these students' top choices.

> I see that the teaching and environment here is not better than at many other institutions, but I am happy to study at a [independent] college of [the Public University]. This is a good choice for the marks I attained.
>
> (Male Student, Engineering Management, Independent College)

At the Private College, many students had the same attitude: that their choices were limited and, although they would prefer other institutions, they could not get in. In the interviews, some students talked about the attractive environment of the campus, and said that, although they were not certain about their choice of this institution, they enjoyed their studies and living there. But some students who were allocated to this college through the clearing process and had difficulties with finance still hoped that they could get into a public institution that is less expensive:

> I admit that the campus is beautiful and I feel good studying here. But I wish I had studied harder and attained better marks, that way I could study at some other public institution for less money.
>
> (Male Student, Computer Science and Technology, Private College)

Since the Private College has a larger proportion of "clearing" students, it is also to be expected that the college has a higher percentage of students wishing for change. However, in practice, the current regulations do not encourage, if not forbid, the transfer of students between institutions, and it is very unusual for students to change institution.

As with the results of other scales, the differences between the two disciplines are larger than the differences between institutions. In almost all institutions, the Languages students were less satisfied with their course and institution than the Engineering students, and had more desire for a change of institution. The primary reason for this could be the difference in relative strength of the two disciplines at the four institutions and the status of the Languages discipline in these institutions.

As well as the academic experience of the course, Astin (1993) also points out in his research in the US that "… the strongest positive effect on overall satisfaction is leaving home to attend college: the distance of the student's college from home is also positively related to overall satisfaction, over and above the effects of living away from home" (p. 279). However, this study did not find an effect of living away from home. Overall, the mean values for the overall experience of the in-province students and the students from outside the province are identical (3.04). Looking at individual institutions, the local province's students at the Private College are slightly more satisfied than the students from outside the province (2.98 compared with 2.73), but the differences are small and insignificant, and are not present at other institutions.

Table 34. Survey respondents' overall experience (item 1), by institution and *Gaokao* place

Institution	Students' *Gaokao* Place	Mean	N	Std. Deviation
Private College	Out-province	2.73	64	1.058
	In-province	2.98	164	.978
	Total	2.91	228	1.005
Public University	Out-province	3.28	134	.779
	In-province	3.30	174	.883
	Total	3.29	308	.838
Independent College	Out-province	2.96	119	.986
	In-province	2.95	240	1.011
	Total	2.96	359	1.002
Public College	Out-province	3.02	134	.880
	In-province	2.98	189	.934
	Total	3.00	323	.911
Total	Out-province	3.04	451	.923
	In-province	3.04	767	.966
	Total	3.04	1218	.950

Open-ended Questions

In addition to the quantitative questions, the questionnaire also asked two open-ended questions. The two questions were "What do you like most about your institution?" and "In your opinion, what could your institution do to improve your learning experience?"

The openness of the questions represented an attempt to collect the widest possible responses from students. It was also anticipated that few students would take the time to comment in any detailed fashion. The advantages of an open response are well documented in the literature: these include the potential richness of data, the avoidance of the constraint of pre-specified questions or items, and that data can be grouped inductively. However, it must be borne in mind that the responses are produced rapidly and only reflect what is uppermost in the respondent's mind at the time (Eley, 2001).

Of the 1,264 students in the analytical sample, 863 and 793 students gave answers to the first and second question respectively, representing response rates of 68.1% and 62.7%. These are fairly high for open-ended questions, and indicate that the students were eager to comment on their experience of higher education.

The responses are grouped according to the institution, and then classified into different categories based on the area they commented on, such as environment, teaching, learning, and so forth. Responses often mention several different areas, and the response is used in the analysis of all the areas mentioned. For the analysis of the classified responses, a response count is provided in some cases, giving an idea of how many students mentioned this aspect; the key words students used and some typical responses are also presented. In the analysis, the background of the respondent, including prior achievement, the programme studied, family status, and so on is also considered.

Private College: the open-ended items

At the Private College, most comments on what students liked about the institution were on the campus environment and facilities; some also mentioned the teaching staff, management, and practice learning opportunities. Most comments on what improvements could be made to the learning experience focused on practical learning and teachers.

In the 182 responses to the first question from the Private College, the term "environment" was mentioned as many as 77 times, "facilities" were mentioned 87 times, and "library" or "books" were mentioned 23 times.

With regard to the environment, "beautiful", "scenic view", "cleanliness" and "fresh air" were mentioned many times. One student commented that: "the environment is very beautiful, the Botanic Garden and the Pavilion are ideal for morning reading or strolling for everyone", and "the beautiful campus environment delights people". With regard to the facilities, many quoted "modern", "first-class" and "wide ranging".

The *Banzhuren* system is also a topic touched upon by a number of students, and clearly the *Banzhuren*s' work has been much appreciated by their students, as students commented that "*Banzhuren* are very conscientious in their work", and "*Banzhuren* treat students well". One student, however, described the *Banzhuren*'s management of students as "nanny-like", but still in a positive tone, as the student followed on by saying that "it is good for students' studies and parents are reassured."

Students' opinions on the teachers and teaching are somewhat contradictory. Some students praised the teachers, saying, for example, that "there are many experienced teachers, they are very good", and "the teaching staff is strong", but others gave completely different opinions, observing that "the teaching staff is not good", and "the teachers are not of a high level standard". These differences cannot be explained by the subjects – some students in the same discipline, or even in the same programme, provided completely contradictory comments, suggesting that, even within the same class, students' expectations and experiences of the teaching and their subjective perceptions, can be very different.

Most comments on the improvement of teaching and teachers were very superficial: "[the institution] should improve the teaching staff" and "we need good teachers" were cited by most students who responded to this aspect and, in most cases, no details were provided, such as in what sense improvements should be made. One student of English was more specific, mentioning that teachers should have more interaction with students in training students' speaking ability. One student expressed concern about the institution's large investment in the campus environment while little attention was being paid to "the development of the quality of the teaching staff", but no further details were provided here either. Some more specific comments about teaching and teachers included "do not use teachers who have no experience and do not know how to teach", "make teachers more professional… invite some high class experts to give lectures", "invite good professors to give lectures", and "the teaching staff is not good, mostly reliant on part-time teachers and newly graduated Master's students".

A total of 159 responses to the second question ("what could your institution do to improve your learning experience?") were collected from the Private College. The terms "practical learning" and "practical training" had occurred frequently. All students who mentioned this aspect indicated their wish that the practical learning opportunities be increased. Examples are "adjust the contents of the specialisation courses, to make them more connected to future work, provide more opportunities for field training and field practice, the focus should be on cultivating students' practical abilities in the field", "… more visits to factories and work experience to factories", "Theory should be integrated with practice, like in Engineering classes, there are many special terms, teachers focusing on the books, it is monotonous and difficult to comprehend. If theory and practice can be integrated it will be more lively and easy to understand and command"; "Don't offer unnecessary courses, offer courses that are relevant to practice; practice training should strengthen students' abilities to apply their knowledge", and "it is necessary to have more co-operation with industry, to strengthen students' practical abilities". Only one student gave a completely different opinion, that "*Benke* education should be primarily centred on the teaching of theories".

There were also some comments regarding the student body. Most of these comments cited "improving the quality of students". Comments made by students included "not shouting in the library and using mobile phones loudly", and "increase students' passion for studying". Some students wished the institution would improve the quality of the student intake and would pay more attention to them as a group in the institution; the quotes included "Raise the admission requirements", "Stop admitting *Zikao* [Self-Study] students", and "Focus on *Benke*, not *Zhuanke*". It appears that students connected the student intake with the overall impression of quality, or the reputation of the institution, and regarded improving the student intake as a way of improving the reputation of the institution as a whole.

Public University: the open-ended items

Most comments on what the students liked at the Public University (first question) were about its campus environment, facilities, teaching, the study environment, and the university's reputation. Some factors also mentioned by students referred to social aspects and general living conditions, such as student union activities, accommodation, transportation and the availability of shops. With regard to possible improvements of student learning, the most frequently mentioned area pertained to practice and practical learning. Increasing extracurricular activities and improving teaching quality were also mentioned by some students.

In the 297 open comments about what students like about this institution, the term "environment" was mentioned as many as 173 times; terms used to describe the environment included "beautiful", "good view", and "clean". Students also mentioned that the beautiful scenery of the campus puts students a "good frame of mind" for studying.

It was somewhat surprising that the library was only mentioned by 20 students as a good aspect of the institution. All comments on the library were about its "ample resources", but only one student mentioned that it was "convenient for study", and another student mentioned that the library was "too far away".

Students also commented positively on their teachers and the teaching at the university. "Teachers", "teach" and "teaching" were mentioned 119 times, but many students mentioned these terms multiple times in their response. Almost all comments on teaching and the teachers described the "high quality teaching" and "high quality teachers", but comparatively few students gave a detailed description of what specific aspects they liked about the teaching and teachers and what describe them as "high quality". Students who gave more specific accounts described the teachers as "first class in the province", "the relationship between teachers and students is good", "teachers are kind", and "teachers are earnest with regard to their work attitude", and one student mentioned that teachers prepared classes well. One student mentioned as a negative aspect that "teachers only appear when there are classes".

The terms "studying" or "learning" were frequently mentioned in what students liked about their university, and appeared 70 times in the 297 responses. A number of students mentioned the contribution of the quality of students, that students engage in learning and create a good study environment for others.

Students seemed to be aware of and satisfied with the reputation and prestige of the university. The term "211" was mentioned by ten students, indicating that students are aware of and value the prestige of being at a national key university.

As an area for improvement, the terms "practice", "practical learning" and "internship" were mentioned as many as 134 times out of the 289 responses to the second question ("what could your institution do to improve your learning experience?"). Students stressed that the university should improve the frequency of various practical elements in the curriculum and strengthen the connection between theory and practice. The following statements were typical: "offer more opportunities for internships, focus on improving students' practical ability"; "the university should place more focus on the cultivation of students' practical ability"; "practice-based courses should have stronger experiment-based teaching and field practice"; "more practice, less theory"; "open practice-based courses, especially for humanities students'; "combine theories with practice, and more emphasis on the learning of useful knowledge"; and "increase practical activities, for Engineering students like us, it is best to do practice in factories every year from year one to year four, even visiting is important, rather than only doing this in year three or year four". In terms of discipline, Engineering students accounted for a larger percentage of the students who raised these concerns. Compared to the Private College students at the Public University had a stronger desire for the strengthening of practical elements in their teaching, especially Engineering students.

In the 289 responses to the second question, the term "communication" also appeared 41 times. Most of these referred to the "communication between teachers and students', but some referred to "communication between disciplines". With regard to the former, most students did not specify for what reason they considered the communication with teachers to be insufficient, but one student mentioned that the university "... should relocate most teachers' home to the new campus". The background for this comment is that the students are studying in the new campus of the university, which was built in a suburban area, but many teachers still live in university-provided accommodation in the city area. This has certainly reduced the after-class communication between teachers and students; one student mentioned that "... teachers all disappear after class". Two students specifically mentioned that the institution should "... encourage more communication between different disciplines", and one of these students went on to say that it "... should not separate the Arts and Science and Engineering geographically", referring to the fact that many schools within the university have their own buildings and are grouped according to discipline or field.

A number of students considered the quality of teaching to be an area for improvement as well. However, besides the "communication" aspect, most students were vague about the specific areas in which improvement was needed, as most students just mentioned that "... the teaching staff needs to be improved". Those who were more specific mentioned the need for "well-known and respected" teachers as a way to improve the teaching staff.

Despite the university's relatively high-quality student intake (in terms of *Gaokao* scores), some students requested the university to "improve students' studying attitudes, and start with improving discipline in classroom", and "strengthen the management of the students".

Independent College: the open-ended items

The students at the Independent College were less enthusiastic about talking about their institution, then the students at the other three institutions. The percentages of students answering the two open-ended questions were far lower than the percentages at the other three institutions. In fact, even in the 173 valid responses to the first question, a very large number of students responded "nothing", "don't know", and "no strong opinion". This might indicate that students at this institution were relatively disengaged from their institution, as compared to students at the other institutions. With regard to the second question about areas for improvement, students' participation level was low as well. For those students who did answer this second open-ended question, practical learning was again at the top of the list of areas for improvement; other areas included teaching facilities, living facilities and teaching.

The term "environment" was mentioned by 29 students out of the 173 responses. On the positive side, students commented favourably upon the central location within the city, and therefore the convenience of shopping and transportation, and the availability of "food stalls outside the campus"; students also mentioned the trees and lawns in the campus. But one student said that although the city centre location was good for entertainment needs and job-seeking, it was also accompanied by the negative aspect of distracting students from studying. Some students considered the compact size of the campus to be an advantage – "small means less walking time to classroom".

The terms "teach", "teachers" and "studying" appeared 67 times. Many students praised the academic atmosphere as "suitable for studying"; one student specified that the college was strict about students' class attendance, and that this was "beneficial for creating a good studying environment". A few students mentioned that the college had the "teaching experience from the [the Public University]", and that the teaching in the College is deeply influenced by that of the Public University. However, most students who praised the teaching staff again did not give more specific reasons. In the interviews, students said that they have some teachers who are from the Public University, but work part-time at this Independent College. There are also designated formal or informal channels for communication between the staff of the two institutions; therefore, students felt that the teaching at their institution was inherited from or influenced by the teaching at the Public University.

Of the 150 responses to the second question, the terms "practice", "practical learning" and "internship" were mentioned 47 times by students as the most frequent area needing improvement. Most comments on this aspect called for "more practice-based courses"; "connecting the subject knowledge to practice", and "more internships outside the campus". One student specifically mentioned that the many courses at the institution "deviated from societal and vocational needs" as there were too many "non-useful" courses.

Resources were also high on the students' agenda. Students suggested that the institution needed "to improve facilities", as "the current conditions are too poor". This is understandable, in that this College is using a relatively out-dated and small campus, and investment in renovations may be limited. To be more specific, students mentioned that "… the institution's current teaching facilities are obsolete"; other students focused on the library, suggesting making the library larger and increasing the holdings. A few students suggested the opening of overnight reading rooms. Since most *Tongzhao Benke* students live in shared dormitory accommodation, they are in greater need of such studying space than students in the UK, who usually have single rooms. Compared with the teaching facilities, it seems that more students were concerned about the living facilities. Students frequently suggested the improvement of the accommodation and the sports venues. Another 13 students specifically mentioned that the dining hall and the food offered needed improvement.

The term "teacher" was mentioned 12 times out of the 150 responses, which was still less frequent than the numbers of responses at other institutions. But, like other institutions, most students identified the need to "improve the quality of teachers", without pointing out the specific areas to which they were referring. One student specifically mentioned that the institution should "hire more young teachers", but another said the institution should "hire more teachers who have practical skills, and fire those young teachers who have a postgraduate degree but have no real learning".

A student of English specifically opined that the institution "… should treat students of different disciplines equally", indicating that the student may have felt that those studying different subjects were treated differently at the institution. This mirrored the quantitative results, in that the Languages and the Engineering students gave very different ratings to their course and institutions.

Public College: the open-ended items

On the first open-ended question, students mentioned that they liked the institution's environment, facilities, teachers and the management of students. With regard to the areas for improvement, practical-based learning was again at the top of the list. Students also mentioned the improvement of teaching, time organisation, and the studying environment.

Of the 209 responses to the first open-ended question, the term "environment" was mentioned 85 times. Almost all students who mentioned the environment aspect described it as "beautiful"; some students were more specific and mentioned the trees and lawns, the cleanliness and the planning. One student wrote that the "greenery makes people feel very comfortable"; another student wrote that the distance from the city centre makes the campus quiet and therefore good for studying.

Students also made positive comments on the facilities, including the teaching facilities and the living facilities. The college uses a new campus, where most facilities are newly built or purchased, and are up-to-date. Students commented that the teaching facilities, computers and laboratory equipment were wide-ranging and adequate. One student also mentioned the large variety of the sports venues, while another student commented that the opening hours of the sporting facilities are insufficient. A substantial number of students referred to the "good" or "excellent" accommodation conditions, and two students also specifically praised the management of the accommodation.

In responses to the first question, "teachers" were mentioned 26 times in the responses, a lower number compared with the Private College. Like students at other institutions, most students stated that "the teaching staff is good" and, at this institution, the terms "earnest" and "responsible" were used much more often in describing the teachers.

"Students" and "management" also appeared frequently in students' answers to this question. Many respondents praised the management of students at the institution, claiming that the institution cared about its students, and were strict with students' studying attitudes. A small number of students described the institution as "applied," and as good at combining theory with practice.

A student of English student showed her dissatisfaction with the English programme and the institution's input to the programme. The student described this as "failing the English programme", and argued that "the college only supports the main and big subjects", again indicating that substantial differences exist between subjects within the same institution.

With regard to improvement areas, 195 students answered the second question. The terms "practice" and "internship" were mentioned 89 times in the answers. Like the answers at other institutions, students at the Public College called for more practice activities, and the combination of theory and practice in teaching. One student said that practical activities "... can give us real practical and working abilities, and can make us more competitive in society after graduation".

Most comments about teaching were very general, simply stating "Improve the quality of teachers". Some students suggested improvements in teaching methods, and some others suggested inviting well-known teachers to give lectures.

A small number of students mentioned that the institution should improve the study environment. One student suggested that the attendance of evening self-study hours (*wanzixi*) should be compulsory for every student; another student suggested strengthening the enforcement of discipline in self-study rooms to create a better study environment.

Summary

This study investigated the students' experience of various aspects of higher education. There were disparities between different institutions' students' experiences, but in most cases the differences between institutions were quite small and insignificant. Where there were significant differences, it is common that the differences were often caused by students' subject of study and socio-economic and academic background, and other factors over which the institutions had less control.

With regard to students' commitment to studying, students at the Private College, who were the weakest in terms of prior attainment (as measured by the proxy of their *Gaokao* scores), did not spend less time on studying; on the contrary, many of them attended more classes than students in other more prestigious institutions. Further investigation revealed the importance and potential of *Banzhuren* or class directors in students' university life. The four institutions also had differing philosophies towards the management of students because they had different student populations in terms of prior attainment.

With regard to students' perceptions of teaching at their institution, the Public University was usually rated highest by the students. The Private College's ratings were relatively low compared with the other four institutions, but it received very good scores for the resources aspect. The differences between institutions, however, were mostly very small and insignificant. In many cases, the differences between disciplines within the same institutions were larger than the differences within the same discipline between different institutions. Most notable were the differences between the Languages and Engineering disciplines at the Independent College, where the Languages students usually gave much lower scores than their Engineering counterparts.

There were significant differences between the students' overall experience of their institution. The Public University students' levels of satisfaction were much higher than the colleges' students, and the students at the Private College rated their experience lowest. This may be connected with the institutional reputation and level of tuition fees, rather than the actual experience perceived.

Regarding what students' liked most about their institution, and the potential areas for improvement, the three areas that attracted the most comment were: the campus environment and facilities; teaching and faculty, and employment-related practice-oriented curriculum and teaching.

Three of the four institutions – namely the Public University, the Private College and the Public College – had built new campuses within the previous five years, and all of the respondents were using and living in these new campuses. Students at these three institutions were very positive about their new and modern campus environment, and they commented on this aspect positively. Students also mentioned the connection between the campus environment and the study environment, claiming that a clean, green, peaceful, and well-designed environment is beneficial for studying. In contrast, the Independent College in this study uses an old campus in the city centre previously used by the Public University. Although it enjoyed a central location and therefore proximity to entertainment and living facilities, the outdated buildings failed to enthuse students. There were some positive comments about the environment, but very few students at the Independent College commented on this aspect.

Facilities were mentioned by many students. This aspect is connected in part to the previous aspect of campus environment, as new campuses tend to have new, modern, and more spacious classrooms, libraries, and laboratories. This aspect was an area for improvement mentioned by the students of the Independent College, but an area praised by students at the other three institutions. However, when commenting on this aspect, students' descriptions were usually vague, such as “new” and “complete”; this is probably due to the fact that students know relatively little about the provision of facilities at other institutions and had no reference point for comparison.

Another area that attracted comment was the teaching and faculty. This is an area for improvement reported by students at all four of the institutions. In this study, except for a few Public University students who specifically mentioned that there was a problem of communication between teachers and students, few students offered concrete opinions or suggestions regarding the specific areas for improvement in teaching. Most students simply reported that this was an area for improvement, or that the institution should improve its teaching or teaching staff. A number of students mentioned that the current teaching staff was too young and inexperienced, and desired more renowned teachers, but these students did not suggest the specific reason for their preference for well-known teachers over young faculty. It appeared that students assumed that reputation was an indication of instruction quality.

The third area was employment-related curriculum and teaching. Students reported that this area was indicated in need of improvement at all of the four institutions. Students’ desire for improvement in this area seemed stronger at the Public University than at the Colleges, as reflected in the high percentage of its students who suggested this area for improvement. However, as indicated, this area was flagged up at all four institutions as in need of improvement, suggesting that, although the Colleges may have made more effort strengthening the practicability and applicability of the knowledge taught, students still desired more practical opportunities and quality. At the Public University, although it is more prestigious and its students had better prior achievements, and therefore its students should be more attractive to employers compared to the students at Colleges, its students had the strongest desire for improvement in employment-related teaching, suggesting that employment is also a critical issue for these students and the Public University’s provision of employment-related teaching does not meet the students’ requirements.

Research Question 4: How can we explain the similarities and differences found in the students' experiences at different institutions?

As shown in the previous sections, although the four institutions vary greatly in ownership, status, and prestige, they received very similar scores in most aspects from the students in the survey. In other words, in most aspects, there are few differences between the institutions, as perceived and reported by their students. To further investigate this phenomenon, the study collected and analysed data from additional sources, including the institutions' teaching planning documents – *Benke Jiaoxue Jihua*, or the *Benke Programme Handbook*, the official statistics of facilities, and interviews with students and institutional managers. The *Benke Programme Handbook* is an institutional document that introduces and regulates the delivery of a *Benke* course programme. It outlines the purpose and objective of the course, specifies the course structure and content, sets the credits required for the course, and so forth. This document is usually compiled at the course or departmental level, and approved by a committee at the university or college level.

As previously discussed in the chapter on *Higher Education in China*, China began to rapidly expand higher education enrolments from 1998. A large part of this expansion was achieved through creating new institutions. Between 1998 and 2004, as many as 171 new public *Benke* colleges were established. Most of these newly-established *Benke* colleges had previously been vocational colleges, and were upgraded to the *Benke* level in the national expansion (Ministry of Education, 1978–2004).

Although these new *Benke* colleges used to be the better vocational colleges among their vocational peers, they now found they had to compete with the more established and traditional *Benke* universities and colleges. In order to avoid direct competition with the established colleges and university, a new concept of "applied *Benke* education" was created in the market, and has since been adopted by almost all new *Benke* colleges (Xu, 2008). This was described by an institutional leader in the interview as "... an application of Michael Porter's differentiation strategy to build competitive advantage in a realistic context" (Vice-President (Academic), Private College).

Michael Porter, the Harvard Business School professor mentioned by the Vice-President, researched how a corporation can develop a competitive strategy and build a competitive advantage over its rivals. According to Porter, a company can gain competitive advantage over its competitors by offering consumers greater value, either by means of lower prices (cost minimisation strategies) or by providing greater benefits and services that are valued by buyers, thus justifying higher prices (product differentiation strategies). The differentiation can be associated with product design, brand image, technology, product features, network or customer service. In order to compete successfully, new entrants to the market must develop their own distinctive competence to differentiate their products in order to break the buyers' loyalty to traditional products and firms (Porter, 1980, 1985).

In higher education in China, by creating "applied *Benke* education", new colleges have attempted to create a product image that is fresh and new within the sector. However, as shown above, the survey of students from the four institutions shows that the educational emphases of the four institutions, as perceived by students, were not substantially different.

This section has discussed four possible explanations for this phenomenon:

(1) New institutions are unable to differentiate their education significantly

Although new institutions have attempted to create a new product to compete with the established institutions (Xu, 2008), and they had the experience of offering high quality vocational programmes as vocational colleges, their ability to offer differentiated *Benke* programmes is nevertheless limited by a number of factors.

Firstly, "applied *Benke* education" is not an official type of provision; it is a concept created purely by the institutions in the market. Not being officially recognised by the state means that there is no separate regulatory provision for this type of education. The state has two provisions for higher education: one is the vocationally-oriented *Zhuanke* track, and the other is the more academically-oriented *Benke* track. All *Benke* institutions, whether claiming to provide applied *Benke* or traditional and academic *Benke*, are subject to exactly the same regulations; in other words, all *Benke* programmes, applied or not, must conform to the same set of state standards.

The state has clear and detailed criteria for *Benke* programmes, and conducts evaluations of the institutions and the programmes they offer. Failure to comply with the state standards or to pass the evaluation can mean termination of the programmes and even suspension of institutional enrolment. Since the standards were created for the established *Benke* programmes, new institutions may find it difficult to offer applied *Benke* while meeting the state standards at the same time. For example, the state mandates that all *Benke* teachers must hold postgraduate qualifications. This creates a barrier for new institutions in recruiting professionals to teach students applied elements of the course. These professionals have practical experience but may lack academic qualifications. Students are also required to complete paper-based assignments and examinations. This limits institutions' ability to make practicality and applicability central to teaching and assessment.

There are also state regulations on the establishment of *Benke* programmes. The Ministry of Education publishes a *Catalogue of Benke Programmes*, listing 249 programmes classified into disciplines. Institutions in China are required to set up programmes according to this Catalogue. It is not possible for institutions to offer a new programme outside the Catalogue, unless specially approved by the Ministry. The limited number of programme choices means that institutions are highly convergent in their programme provision.

New institutions also have difficulty obtaining enough resources to offer a different kind of *Benke* provision. First, a large proportion of teachers at new institutions are in fact part-time or retired staff who primarily work, or previously worked, at established institutions. It would be unrealistic to expect them to teach in an academic manner at one institution and then teach in a vocational manner at the other. Although new institutions may recruit newly graduated teachers, these new teachers do not necessarily form a "new workforce", not only because their teaching is subject to the same evaluation standards as required by the state, but also because they are usually trained by senior staff and undertake teaching internships at established institutions as part of the requirements of their qualification. In addition to issues of human resources, it is also difficult for new institutions to obtain sufficient resources to support diversification. Applied teaching would involve more sessions devoted to practice and experiments. This means more equipment is needed, which can be more expensive than human resources in China. However, since "applied *Benke*" is not an official provision, institutions offering this type of education do not receive extra funding for this from the state. Price regulation at public colleges and their relatively low reputation mean that they cannot charge a premium on fees for "applied *Benke*" education either.

Some other factors may also influence the culture of new institutions, including the national reorganisation of institutions. The presidents of public institutions, as bureaucrats, are appointed by the authorities. The Director for Higher Education Research at the Public College argued that:

> Different ownership could bring differences to institutions. For example, our college was previously financed by the Ministry of Water Resources, and as a result we had to offer relevant programmes to serve the interests of the Ministry. But now it has changed, the college has been assigned to the local educational authority [in the national higher education reorganisation], we have lost the characteristic features and our course provision is now very similar to others… Another reason is the appointment of presidents. The authority regularly shifts the leaders of public institutions [as they shift leaders of other public bureaus], and appoints someone from the major universities here. Of course we all become similar in the end.
>
> (Director for Higher Education Research, Public College)

Furthermore, the new institutions cater for the broader personal development of students. For example, the Private College has made significant investment in the personal development of students:

> We have a Department of Sports here at our college. Sports departments are not common among private institutions, because according to the regulations, many sporting facilities are required for an institution to establish a sports department; this is not considered economical. But we think a good institution should develop its students in all aspects; just reading books and acquiring skills is not enough. For us, the sporting facilities we built can benefit all of our students in exercising the body. The campus also gets a better cultural environment when there are students majoring in sports, music, dancing and arts. This is good for developing students comprehensively; this will be good for their future.
>
> (Director of the Board, Private College)

The Independent College has displayed a strong vocational orientation in its *Benke Programme Handbook*, but at the same time emphasises learning to learn skills, which will have long-term benefits for students and the development of person:

> To be clear and definite about the positioning of [our] education: cultivating the applied talents. Independent colleges as the bottom end of *Benke* education and the top end of vocational education shall give prominence to practical education and field working abilities ...
>
> [The fundamental principle of the education is] to provide life-learning education, all-round development education and to improve the talents' continuous adaptability to the economic society. To strengthen foundational teaching, subject teaching, and subject foundational teaching, broaden students' knowledge field. Shall increase humanity and social science knowledge for engineering and science students ... shall increase science and technology knowledge for humanity and arts students.
>
> (*Benke Programme Handbook*, Independent College)

The Public College's *Benke Programme Handbook* states in a familiar tone:

> The teaching plan shall handle well the relationship between "becoming a [cultured] person" and "becoming a [useful] talent", and use "becoming both a person and a talent" as the institution's educational standard… to be clear with the objec-

tive of education, that is, to cultivate applied *Benke* talents who have "a solid theoretical foundation, broad subject knowledge, strong practical abilities, and highly comprehensive [personal] characteristics".

(*Benke Programme Handbook*, Public College)

With both professional (vocational) development and personal development in mind, it is not surprising that the colleges may be confronted with contradictory interests. For example, the *Benke Programme Handbook* of the Public College has displayed such a contradiction between "increasing theoretical education" and "cutting down theoretical education":

[The third Fundamental Principle] Reinforcing foundation, integrating arts and science.
A strong foundation provides applied talents with the ability to develop sustainably and transfer knowledge, thereby meeting the needs of employment market changes. Therefore, we must reinforce the foundational knowledge, foundational theories and foundational skills education in Science, Engineering and Arts and Social Science subjects, organically integrating these three basic disciplines in teaching practices, to improve students' culture as well as improving students' ability to conduct actual work…

[The fourth Fundamental Principle] Strengthening practice, stressing innovation. The cultivation of ability of applied talents is mainly achieved through practical education. Therefore, we must further reduce theoretical education, and strengthen practical education…

(*Benke Programme Handbook*, Public College)

An examination of the titles and descriptions of course provision at the four institutions in this study found that course provision at the four institutions are highly similar. Using English as an example, the Independent College offered courses on Critical Appreciation of English and American Literature, while the Private College offered a similar course in English Literature, and the Public College offered a course in Society and Culture of Major English-Speaking Countries. The Public University offered more "academic" courses, such as Lexicology, and more general courses, such as History of American Literature in the course list, but these were also found at the other three colleges.

On the more vocational courses, the provision at the four institutions were very similar as well. All four of the institutions divided their English subject into sub-categories based on focus or track. For example, there were two tracks for the English *Benke* programme at the Public University, namely, the Literature, Culture and Translation track, and the Linguistics, Communication and Specialisation track. Students in different tracks had different choices of modules. At the Public College there were three tracks, namely, Engineering English Translation, International Business, and Linguistics and Literature. There were similar tracks at the Private College. Although it offered no specific track choices, the Independent College offered a wide range of English modules, and students of English were free to choose without the limitation of tracks. Technical and vocational courses could be found at all four institutions. For example, the Public College offered courses such as English for Technology; the Private College offered Cambridge Business English, and similar vocational courses, such as English for Foreign Trade Negotiation, or English for Tourism, and Advanced Interpretation could also be found at the Public University. Similar patterns can also be found in Engineering courses.

The similarities found in the structure of courses across the four institutions in this study seem surprising, in the light of the literature on diversification of curricula at different types of higher education institutions. For instance, Bernstein's concepts of "vertical" and "horizontal" discourses in higher education are used by Abbas and McLean in investigating the pedagogical differences between two British universities of different prestige (Abbas & McLean, 2007). Vertical discourse, in this context, is the specialised language of academic disciplines that carries a sense of the "sacred or esoteric", whereas horizontal discourse refers to everyday, non-academic discourse (p. 732). Abbas and McLean found that the elite university maintained the primacy of vertical discourse within its disciplines, while the former polytechnic engaged with more non-academic contexts. The above examination of the titles and descriptions of the course provision at the four institutions in this study, although necessarily only a snapshot of the orientation of the course provision, contributes to the degree of understanding of the similarities and differences found in student experience at the institutions. It indicates the broad convergence of the titles of the course provision at the four institutions.

(2) Established institutions are becoming more vocational

The high levels of unemployment in China mean that it has become very difficult for graduates to find jobs. Students and the government can add pressure to institutions to be more employment-oriented. Students certainly look for returns on their investment in four years' education, and since the most immediate return for students is a job that meets expectations, making the courses relevant to the employment market is crucial for institutions to meet students' employment expectations.

The government has also put pressure on institutions. The Ministry of Education collects graduate employment data from institutions on a regular basis. The Ministry considers an institution's graduate employment situation when deciding the enrolment quota for the institution. It can reduce the enrolment quota or even suspend the enrolment for a course, if that course failed to send an appropriate percentage of students into employment. The Ministry also uses employment as a quality indicator in the evaluation of institutions (Higher Education Evaluation Center, 2008). The Ministry requires specifically that "When formulating and implementing the developmental plan of higher education institutions, [institutions] must establish "employment orientation" and fully consider employment factors. The administration authority must consider graduate employment rates as an important factor in approving the institutions' mid- and long-term developmental plan" (Ministry of Education, 2003). The Public University certainly feels this pressure:

> Students' first priority is to find a job. If the employment rate is low, it will still look very bad for us despite the fact that we are a 211 [national key] university.
> (Deputy Dean, Public University)

The Public University's education objectives for students clearly show its focus on knowledge applicability and graduate employment. Below is an extract from the *English Subject Benke Programme Handbook* of the Public University:

> Education Objectives: This subject focuses on offering a solid foundation and basic skills in listening, speaking, reading, writing and translating the English language, and on cultivating multiple-competences and applied English language talents who ... can use English proficiently in translation, teaching, management and research positions in academic, foreign affairs, education, economics and trade, culture, science, tourism and military organisations.
>
> (*Benke Programme Handbook for English Subject*, Public University)

The Public University also regards practical elements in education as important. The institution's official document *Views on Further Strengthening and Improving Teaching* puts great emphasis on practical lessons:

> According to the requirements on cultivation of talented people demanded by the new era's economic development and the societal development... the following views are brought forward:
>
> Strengthen the idea of "practical training"... practical education is a crucial element in carrying out the Party's education policy and in developing talented people in higher education... the quality of practical education has an impact on the overall quality of higher education teaching and talent cultivation of the institution... strengthening practical education is particularly significant in cultivating the high quality professionals needed for building a harmonious society...
> All schools and departments of the university shall strengthen the idea of "practical training", pay great attention to practical teaching...
> All schools shall... develop a practical teaching system that is beneficial to developing students' practical ability and innovative ability...
> Strengthen the evaluation and inspection of practical teaching. The university's teaching affairs department shall strengthen the evaluation and inspection of practical teaching, make improving practical teaching quality a priority... shall formulate further practical teaching indicators to evaluate the practical teaching effectiveness in a comprehensive, real and robust manner.
>
> (*Views on Further Strengthening and Improving Teaching*, Public University)

The Deputy Dean at the Public University commented on this as a "practical choice". She mentioned the institution's aspiration to be oriented toward intensive research and liberal education, and therefore not address vocational demands too much. However, this was not possible because of the reality of poor student intake and lack of reputation and resources:

> We are not like other top universities [in China], we face really large pressures on graduates' employment. The authority requires us to enrol ten thousand students every year, of whom at least 50% must come from within the province. This certainly reduces the quality of incoming students. Even for universities like Peking University, if it had to enrol ten thousand students from our province, it will get poor students. We want to learn from the model of Fudan University [to offer general education], but our ability is very limited.
>
> (Deputy Dean, Public University)

Peking, Tsinghua, Fudan and other top universities in China have attempted to follow the US elite institutions' model of offering general education. Although they still offer professional guidance and career development courses to students, their philosophy of developing the whole person first is in sharp contrast with other institutions' struggles to send graduates into the workplace. This suggests that there has been a divide between institutions in China, even within the national key universities – only the top universities have the luxury of being able to offer a more general curriculum, while national key universities lower down in the rankings are becoming homogenously vocational. The Public University in this case, although a national key university, had nevertheless been confronted by enormous employment pressures and had to add vocational elements to respond to the students' needs and governmental requirements.

(3) The definitions of academic teaching and practical teaching are unclear

Shijian Ke, or practical classes, is a term used in all of the four institutions' *Programme Handbooks*. It refers to modules or classes with significant practical elements. Based on the information in *Benke Pro-*

gramme Handbooks from the institutions, the researcher calculated the importance attached to practical teaching at the institutions, using the time and credits devoted to practical elements as the indicator:

Table 35. Time/credits of practical elements as a percentage of the total time/credits

	Public College	Private College	Independent College	Public University
Computer Science and Technology	35%	44.5%	40.7%	Not less than 25% (2008)
English	28.85%	43.8%	15.8%	18% (2006)

The table shows that, within institutions, the Computer Science subject always attaches more importance to practical teaching than does English. However, the variation between the two subjects was very different across institutions, ranging from less than 1% (the Private College) to 25% (the Independent College). Furthermore, the question of the definition of "practical teaching" is very complex.

Across institutions, it is also clear that the Private College attached the most importance to practical elements, accounting for nearly half of the total teaching. The Independent College displayed sharp contrasts between its Computer Science and English subjects, with the former placing much more emphasis on practical learning than the latter. The Public University attached the lowest importance to knowledge practicability, in terms of time and credits attached to practical teaching.

These differences are due to several reasons. Firstly, there are differences in the course requirements. For example, English students at the Private College were required to take Computer Operation Practice, Computer Language Practice, Office Automation Practice and other practical modules, which were not required at some other institutions.

Secondly, there are differences within the modules. For example, the 30 classes for the module Oral Interpretation were all labelled by the institution as "practice-based" at the Private College, but the

32 classes for the same module were all labelled as "teaching-based" at the Public University.

The third is the difference in understanding and labelling of a module. For example, the 120 classes for Physical Education at the Public University were all counted as "teaching-based", while 96 of the 126 classes for Physical Education at the Private College were counted as "practice-based". At the Private College, Education Orientation, Employment, Entrepreneurship, Professional Practices and Vocational Ethics Education count towards "practice-based" elements, although these same programmes at the Public University are given few credits and do not count towards "practice-based" learning.

Therefore, the lack of universal standards of which classes should count toward "practical classes" has resulted in different interpretations and uses of the term in different institutions. In fact, the division between the broader terms of academic study and practical study is ambiguous and not necessarily mutually exclusive.

(4) Students are not well-positioned to compares different institutions

It would seem that students are not able to identify the differences between institutions. This might have two possible explanations: the first is that the differences did exist, but students just did not experience them; the second possible explanation is that differences did exist across institutions, but since students only had experience of one institution, they could not tell the differences in a comparative way.

Triangulating the documentary evidence of a number of practical sessions above with the survey data collected from students, it is easy to see why the Independent College students had different responses to the college's Computer Science and English subjects in terms of practical training: within the same institution, the Computer Science students received much more practical training than the English students.

However, the trend becomes obscure when comparing different institutions. English at the Public University, clearly being the least practice-oriented course at any institution by the number of hours and credits given to practical sessions, was rated high by its students for emphasis on practicability. Computer Science at the Public University, which had given more hours and credits to practical sessions, was in contrast given a very low rating on the emphasis on applicability of knowledge.

This shows that a students' feeling about his or her course's emphasis on the applicability of knowledge was not influenced only by the number of hours and credits of the practical sessions; there are certainly other factors that can influence students' feeling.

One factor is the quality of the practical sessions. As just explained above, some identical modules were labelled differently at different institutions. Although modules like Education Orientation, Physical Education, etc. are counted towards "practice-based" in the labelling system at the Private College, they do not automatically make students feel that the institution places great emphasis on the practicability or applicability of knowledge. In addition, the instruction quality and the real connection to practice and application of the same module can be different at different institutions. For example, for the modules that are expected to be highly practical, poor teaching and poor connections to the field can result students in considering these modules as impractical.

The second factor is the student expectations of applicability of their courses. Students from different backgrounds bring with them differing expectations regarding knowledge applicability. In the student interviews and the open-ended section of the questionnaire, it is often the financially poorer students who are more concerned about the applicability of knowledge and the expectation that the institution reinforce the connection between study and the workplace. Students in this situation place more importance on immediate employment prospects and therefore have higher expectations for knowledge applicability than students from higher socio-economic background. With this expectation, they tended to give a lower rating than their counterparts from higher socio-economic background. The institutions' ratings are therefore influenced by the composition of students.

Students' ratings are also influenced by their perceptions of the institutions:

> In China, private institutions lack the history and reputation… at [the Private College], many students think that public institutions are superior… although without knowing what the public institutions are really like and whether they would be better for them. But because of their name, students believe they are better and may give lower ratings to [the Private College]…
> (Male Student, English, Private College)

Relating to the second factor, everything being equal, a student's job prospect may influenced by the name and reputation of his or her institution. The more prestigious the institutions are, the better job prospects their students will likely to have. A better job prospect eases the Public University students' employment concerns and lowers their requirements for knowledge applicability (but in a fiercely competitive market these students are still under enormous pressure). With lower expectations, they may tend to give a higher rating on their institutions' emphasis on practical education than students do at less prestigious institutions, even if the programmes are the same:

> I know that finding employment is difficult at this time, and practical ability adds an advantage to us in finding a job. But after all we are good students in a good university, this is our advantage. I don't think our course should be overly vocational. We may continue to postgraduate studies or find a job that is not relevant to our course.
> (Male Student, Mechanical Engineering and Automation, Private College)

The method for calculating customer satisfaction in business may be borrowed here. Spreng et al. (1996) suggest deconstructing the traditional expectations measure into two measures: (1) predictive expectations: beliefs about the likelihood that attributes, benefits, or outcomes are associated with a product or service, and (2) desires: evaluations of desirability of an attribute, benefit, or outcome, that is, the extent to which the attribute, benefit, or outcome leads to the attainment of the customer's values. Both the predictive expectations and desires can be affected by students' prior experience. Unlike many consumption products for which the customers have plenty of opportunities to try the different varieties available, and some items that are expensive but offer customers trial periods (like automobiles), higher education is a much more complicated process, and most students have little prior experience with higher education and their awareness of higher education life is poor. In addition, it is believed that if the experience with the course or institution after enrolment becomes more and more satisfying, expectations for future performance are adjusted ever higher. This is frequently referred to as "raising the hurdle" (Vavra, 1997).

Evidence from the survey and interviews reveals that students are proficient at distinguishing the differences between courses within institutions. This is perhaps due to the greater frequency of contact with students from other majors. When asked about their awareness of teaching at other institutions, some students responded positively. The institutions are all situated in higher education parks; this means the institutions are geographically close to each other. This makes students' contact across institutions easier. Some students said that they had even attended classes at the neighbouring institutions. Additionally, students also often get information about other institutions through contacts with middle school classmates who are studying at other institutions. However, even though there are some channels for students to receive information about teaching at other institutions, it is often the case that students' information about other institutions is inaccurate or not up-to-date.

Because students only had experience with one institution, they lacked the experience to accurately assess the situation at other institutions and therefore their ability to tell the differences in a comparative way is limited. Furthermore, even if they had complete information, different students would give different ratings because they had different backgrounds and different expectations. The lack of "comparable experience" may be a limitation of student questionnaires in general.

Summary

Although the four institutions vary greatly in ownership, status, and prestige, they received very similar scores in most aspects from students in the survey. This section discussed in detail four possible explanations, including (1) Because their ability to offer differentiated *Benke* programmes is limited by a number of factors, including state regulations, lack of human and hardware resources, and the objective to develop all-round person, new institutions are unable to differentiate their education significantly; (2) Mostly because of pressures from the employers, established institutions are becoming more applied and vocational in their educational orientation; (3) The boundary of and difference between academic teaching and practice teaching is unclear; and (4) Students are not well-positioned to compare different institutions, and their perceptions are influenced by many other factors.

Chapter Seven

Discussion and Conclusions

Summary and Discussion of the Findings

This study offers a detailed picture of the ways that students and their experiences vary at the selected higher education institutions. The study offers a rich resource for understanding the impact of the diversification of higher education institutions in China on students and their experiences, which is the overarching research question of this study. Through analysing student experiences, the study provides a further perspective for researchers and policymakers to examine and understand the effects of institutional diversification.

In programmatic, systematic, reputational, and financial terms, higher education in China has become diversified. At the programmatic level, there are the different academically-oriented *Benke* and vocationally-oriented *Zhuanke* tracks of undergraduate education, and there are also different routes to admission into these programmes, such as the standard national exams or *Putong Gaokao*, the self-study exams or *Zixue Kaoshi*, and the adult exams or *Chengren Gaokao*. This study is restricted to the *Tongzhao Benke* programmes – the *Benke* programmes that admit students from the national unified admission channel, as this is the standard or "golden" route to undergraduate education in China.

At the systemic level, there are institutions of different ownership, namely public, private, and independent, and there are institutions of different administrative affiliations – some institutions are "national", as they are administered directly by the Ministry of Education of the central government, while others are "regional", as they are administered by the provincial authority. The institutions also have varying student population sizes and varying campus sizes.

Largely for historical reasons, some institutions have particular focus areas at the *Tongzhao Benke* programme level. The names of many institutions in China illustrate this focus quite clearly, such as Normal University, University of Agriculture, University of Finance and Economics, University of Medicine, University of Sports, and so on. However, numerous institutional mergers and the attractiveness of being "comprehensive" have reduced the level of focus in this respect. Many institutions have opted for more "general" names, and even those institutions that have kept names reflecting specialisation have, in fact, become more "comprehensive" in their course provision. Although all institutions have expanded their enrolments since 1998, the elite universities have focused more on the postgraduate sector, while the expansion of *Benke* enrolments has largely been absorbed by the regional and newly-established institutions. Meanwhile, many *Benke* level institutions have a strong wish to upgrade to the postgraduate level.

Diversification is also highly visible at the reputational level. The "national key university" and "provincial key university" are important terms. The 985 and 211 projects, which aimed at compiling a small list of institutions that are "world class universities", have now become a label for the prestigous universities. Administrative affiliation with the Ministry of Education is also frequently interpreted as a symbol of high prestige. This reputational hierarchy is further reinforced in the admissions system through the admission tiers. In most provinces, the top universities admit the best students from the first tier, while less prestigious institutions admit students from the second and third tiers. Vocational institutes admit the lowest-scoring students on the *Gaokao* into their *Zhuanke* programmes.

At the financial level, higher education institutions have also become more diverse since the 1990s. Substantial funding provided to elite universities through the 211 and 985 projects, and the elite universities' participation in business ventures and executive education, has resulted in wider income ranges for institutions. The structure of income has also diversified. Previously, institutions in China relied exclusively on state funding, but with the tuition fees reform of the late 1990s, institutions have been able to generate revenue from tuition fees. The establishment of private and independent institutions financially diversified the sector by creating institutions that rely almost exclusively on tuition fees, compared to the public institutions, which receive mixed income from state funding and tuition fees.

This study is interested in a particular kind of diversity – diversity in student experience – and the association between student experience diversity and diversity at other levels. This study demonstrates the "constituential diversity" level (Birnbaum, 1983; van Vught, 2009), or the differences in students served at the institutions. At this level, there are diversities in terms of students' prior attainment, socio-economic background, regions of residence, and so on. Not surprisingly, the prestigious Public University has the best students in terms of *Gaokao* scores, students at the Public College come in second, and the Independent College and the Private College have the students with the lowest scores. In terms of students' socio-economic backgrounds, different institutions – as classified by ownership and reputation – also have very different profiles. The Independent College has students from the highest socio-economic groups, followed by students at the Public University and the Public College, and students from the Private College. Regarding the regional profile of the student population, the study has found that almost all institutions had an inclination to recruit more local students, usually as a reflection of, and in return for, local government support. The state regulation requiring Ministry of Education-administered institutions to limit their percentage of local students will create sharp differences between national and regional institutions in their students' regional composition.

The relationship between an institution's ownership type and its subject focus is not straightforward. Some critics have pointed out that private and independent institutions tend to be more focused on arts and humanities subjects, since these subjects require less laboratory equipment and are cheaper to teach, and therefore generate higher financial returns (Guo, Qiao, & Fu, 2005; Mao, 2006). However, other researchers argue that this tendency towards inexpensive subjects is not found only in private and independent colleges, but also in the newly promoted public colleges (Zong et al., 2007). The Private College and the Independent College in this study actually both concentrate mainly on engineering studies.

There are also some differences in the gender mix of students at the different institutions, but these differences are primarily a result of the subject mix. Another factor that causes a difference in the gender mix may come from the individual institution's restrictions on or requirements for students' secondary school study track; those institutions and programmes with no restrictions on the study track tend to be more balanced in terms of the gender of applicants, as students' study track in secondary school is often associated with their gender. The newer and less well-known institutions may be less restrictive on this requirement as a strategy to solicit more applications.

In summary, the empirical and conceptual analysis of this study has shown that institutions of different types, as classified by ownership and prestige, can have very different student compositions. This finding has important implications. With regard to issues of equity, it suggests that students of different socio-economic status are channelled into different institutions, and many students do not bear a reasonable share of the cost of their study, based on their ability to pay. State subsidies to public institutions are frequently given to students who are less in need of them, while poorer students have to pay more to attend less prestigious institutions. With regard to issues of quality, this suggests that it may be inappropriate to use a single universal standard to assess different institutions, given that students at different institutions are very different. It is unreasonable to expect institutions that admit lower-achievers to train their students to a standard comparable to institutions that admit high-achievers. Therefore, a "value-added" approach towards measuring students' success seems more appropriate.

However, despite all of these clear diversities across the *Benke* education sector, this study has found few differences in students' reported experiences at the four different institutions. This is reflected in the students' experience in terms of the quality of teaching, and in their perceptions of the educational orientation and emphasis of the course programmes and institutions. This study has found larger differences between disciplines *within* institutions than within disciplines *between* institutions.

The recent establishment of private and independent colleges has resulted in a significant new sector, and shifted the higher education system in China from being almost homogeneously public to a system where a significant proportion of students are enrolled in non-public institutions. However, this study shows that, in terms of programme provision and student experience, the two private and independent institutions operate in a way that does not differ substantially from the Public College or even the Public University.

As Levy (1999, p. 15) notes, "To make a difference, for better or worse, private higher education must bring something important not otherwise found in the higher education system". In the US and some other countries, the more successful private and, in particular, for-profit institutions seem to have found ways to benefit from flexibility of course provision and delivery. These institutions emphasise convenient scheduling, have a broader range of evening courses, larger recruitment of mature working students, or rapid growth of popular areas in response to demand (Teixeira & Amaral, 2001). In addition to flexibility, accelerated programme completion is an attractive feature offered by many well-known for-profit institutions (Bailey et al., 2001). However, none of these characteristics was found in the Private and Independent Colleges in this study. The programme provision, course delivery modes and student ages at the Private and Independent Colleges do not significantly differ from those at the other institutions.

A more visible difference between the three different types of colleges in the study appears to be the number of practice-based classes offered. The Private College offers a significantly larger proportion of practice-based classes than the Independent and Public Colleges in this study. However, this study has pointed out that there are differences in the labelling of classes in institutional handbooks; some classes with similar structures are labelled as practice-based at the

Private College, but as teaching-based at others. Furthermore, this difference appears to have little impact on students' experience – students reported similar levels of practical orientation of classes at the institutions.

The Public University in the study has a high level of prestige. As the only national key university in the province, it might be assumed that its course provision is somewhat different from other institutions in the province. However, this study found very limited differences, even in comparison with the newly-created colleges in terms of teaching philosophy, course structure and student experience. However, there are differences in philosophies concerning student management, in that students at the Public University appeared to have more autonomy in studying.

There is arguably diversity of reputation within the national key university category, for example, the 985 project universities are more prestigious than the 211 project universities, and among the 985 universities, there are top institutions, like Peking, Tsinghua, Fudan, and Shanghai Jiao Tong universities. The Public University in this study, although an older, established national key university from the 211 project group, is nevertheless different from the universities at the very top of the list. Therefore, a limitation of this study is that the behaviours of the sampled public university do not necessarily resemble those of the elite universities.

The lack of diversity found in this study is the product of many normative forces, including uniform state standards and evaluations, and the reliance of newly founded colleges on retired professors from public universities for their teaching strategy. The separation of *Benke* programmes (and, in many cases, institutions) through the admissions criteria has created different segments for school-leavers and for adults who aspire to undergraduate education. The strict regulation of the course provision and delivery means that institutions are generally unable to open innovative programmes in a timely fashion or to offer part-time options. Governmental control of the admissions process (unlike in the UK, for example) means that institutions are unable to expand to the mature student market, as they cannot recruit mature students into their *Tongzhao Benke* programmes. In the rather conformist Chinese society, it appears that private higher education institutions may be "duplicates" of the public ones. Their efforts to develop their reputation in the conformist existing structures have also contributed to the convergence of *Benke* education, as "[e]veryone, it seems, wants to be more like Peking University or Fudan University" (Mohrman, 2003, p. 5). Indeed, it appears that all higher education institutions, of whatever tradition, are seeking to become more comprehensive in their subject range, and more research-intensive. As Birnbaum (1983) speculates, programmatic expansion at the institutional level can result in a negative correlation with institutional diversity at the systematic level. In other words, when institutions become more internally diversified, they tend to become more alike externally. There is clearly a convergence of programme provision at Chinese universities, particularly in areas such as computer science, languages, and management studies, and this has led to overlap in programme enrolment across the system and to a reduction in institutional diversity.

The institutions that have labelled themselves as "applied" have also faced many difficulties in achieving this objective. The danger is that the brand or image of these institutions reflects market needs, but not the institution's capacity, and that the institutions cannot fulfil the expectations raised by their marketing messages. Market pressures, especially pressures from the labour market and competition within higher education, have contributed to the convergence of different institutions' behaviours. Because of the pressures from the labour market, the older universities have become more concerned with the industry demands (vocational drift). Because of the pressures of competition, it is common for newly-created colleges to aspire to university status and to recruit more academic professors and faculty with doctoral degrees, in the same way as they aspired to upgrade from the vocational education level to the *Benke* level (academic drift). These drifts have resulted in a blurring of the mission and function of the institutions and private and public institutions becoming increasingly similar. Therefore, in practice, the diversity in *Benke* teaching at the institutions is eroded by factors that tend to promote convergence.

The force of national regulations contributes to this situation. The *Benke* system is governed by the same rules and administered in a common way; the evaluation assessments judge all institutions by a single set of rules. The quality assurance system emphasises compliance and box-ticking, rather than originality and innovation, and this has served to discourage innovation and constrain the dynamic development of subject areas. There are no financial incentives to encourage further diversity. The governance rules discourage, if not forbid, institutions from pursuing a more diverse provision.

International comparisons suggest that clear and publicly acknowledged mission differences between institutions, and the government's determination to defend such differences, are central to the encouragement of diversity in higher education (Taylor, 2003). Although the Chinese government could impose diversity, it is not inclined to take the necessary steps. For the purpose of assuring quality, it appears that the government values convergence more than diversity in *Benke* education.

From a governmental point of view, strict control over the *Benke* programmes has helped to maintain quality standards at hundreds of newly-created institutions. For the government and the public to acknowledge diversity, and to conduct restructuring and strategic planning in the higher education system to promote diversity, an important step would be redefining and identifying broader ideas about quality. Part of this process would involve moving away from traditional definitions of quality and promoting innovation in *Benke* education.

The findings of this study do not support the common assumption that the curriculum, pedagogy, and learning experience at prestigious universities are perceived by students as of a higher quality than that of less prestigious institutions. The study also shows that there are important factors within institutions that can differ significantly between departments within the same institution; this implies that when comparing institutions, it is of crucial importance to compare them at the departmental and subject, as well as institutional, level.

Additionally, social forces may have an impact on the massification of higher education. According to Trow (2005), aspiration to higher social (and economic) status is a common motivation for a student to pursue higher education in China. Chinese families traditionally attach great importance to their children's education, and families tend to concentrate their financial capacity on sending their children to higher education. The large number of one-child families has further reinforced this situation. These features have accelerated the expansion of higher education and students also prefer to study at elite, rather than mass, institutions.

In summary, there are diversities at the programmatic, systematic, reputation, and financial levels in Chinese higher education. On the one hand, the creation of the 211 and 985 projects has reinforced the importance of diversity of reputation, and they, in turn, have promoted financial diversity. On the other hand, institutional mergers, and the aspiration for institutions to expand into new subject areas have resulted in higher education institutions becoming more comprehensive over time, often beyond their original programmatic mission. The establishment of private and independent colleges has certainly contributed to systematic diversity, introducing new forces into the higher education system, but these institutions do not necessarily and substantially differ from their public college counterparts in terms of course provision, delivery methods, and student experiences. The expansion of private and independent colleges and newly-created public institutions has served to supplement inadequate existing places. They are expected by the government to enrol more (and this means different) students, but are not expected to be distinctive in the education they provide. In fact, due to governmental regulations and market pressures, even the older universities may not necessarily differ from the newly-created colleges in these respects. The resulting situation, then, has been described by Mohrman (2003) as "a thousand flowers blooming that are nevertheless all of the same species" (p. 31).

The investigation shows relatively low levels of student satisfaction with the course and other institutional provision. In general, the students' overall satisfaction with their institutions and courses is low across institutions, especially at colleges with lower prestige, and students at all institutions have a strong desire for a change of institution.

Implications and Recommendations

Learning Improvement

The National Student Survey in the UK (Surridge, 2008) and the national postgraduate student benchmarking exercise in Australia (Marsh, Rowe, & Martin, 2002) both found that the majority of institutional differences are not statistically significant in terms of student experience, as most of the institutions fall within a narrow range that is covered by sampling error. This study provides further evidence for this contention.

In fact, many academics have long argued that student experience surveys should be used for formative, rather than summative, purposes. For instance, Professor Prosser, Director of Research and Evaluation at the Higher Education Academy from 2005 to 2007, suggests that student surveys of an NSS nature should not be interpreted as satisfaction ratings and should not be used to make comparisons between institutions (Prosser, 2005). Professor Harvey, who held the same position from 2007 to 2008, argues that the NSS should act as an improvement tool, but it is too generalised and too focused on rankings for this to be the case and "… the broad scale scores are no help to an institution in making targeted improvements" (Harvey, 2008, p. 1).

A study conducted for the Higher Education Academy on the use of the National Student Survey Results Dissemination website

(Machell & Saunders, 2007) provides concrete examples of how institutions have used the results of the National Student Survey in the UK. The study summarises that the results have been used by the institutions to: 1) receive information on student experience; 2) serve quality assurance purposes; 3) enhance quality; 4) identify areas with problems; 5) identify good practice; and 6) open up discussions about the quality of teaching and learning. In the UK, a number of institutions have introduced visible changes as a direct result of the National Student Survey, many of which have involved students working with academics and institutional administrators to improve teaching and learning experiences. For instance, the President of the National Union of Students in the UK presented two concrete examples to show that students have used the survey results to argue successfully for educational changes. At one university, students won more guaranteed contact hours and resources and, at the other, students managed to improve library and learning resources, as well as convincing all departments to create action plans in response to students' concerns. Both occurred as a direct result of the survey.

The active participation of students in this study, as well as in other student experience studies in other countries, suggests that students want their opinions to be acted upon by their teachers and institutions. As suggested by the Open University Centre for Higher Education Research and Information, students value being asked their opinions and want to be treated as full partners in the quality improvement process (CHERI, 2004). The students in the current study can also benefit from student experience research. The assessment of their experience provides an opportunity to communicate with their teachers and the institution. By participating in such communication, students may become more actively engaged in academic and social life in higher education.

Introducing and promoting student experience studies can also offer a valuable contribution to the quality agenda of higher education. Although this study has shown that student experience data are not robust at the inter-institutional level, i.e., its application for ranking institutions is limited, discussions of student experience may still constitute a good way to shift the focus of higher education quality discussions away from research, resource, and reputation indicators and towards other factors that matter in terms of the student experience.

Use of Student Experience Questionnaires

Students are well-equipped to judge the quality of certain aspects of higher education, and their experience and judgment of these aspects provide a valuable source of data and should be trusted. Students can be expected to be reasonable arbiters of the impact of the availability of computers, the quality of teaching spaces, the teaching skills of the academic staff, and so on. Students experience these aspects fully and are expected to have straightforward views on them (James, 2002).

However, the students in the current study are not in the best position to judge many other aspects of higher education quality. There are deeper dimensions to higher education, such as the overall coherence of the curriculum, and the impact of higher education on students in the long-run, into which students may have less insight. These aspects of higher education are usually less tangible and less intuitive, and require a longer-term view. Current students do not necessarily recognise or welcome the good practice experiences of higher education that might lead to educationally valuable outcomes in the long-run. Furthermore, assessment of quality also requires comparison, but students usually are not in a position to compare their experiences. Also, because teaching and learning are highly complex cognitive activities, multiple sources of data are required to provide a comprehensive evaluation (Saroyan & Amundsen, 2001). Therefore, student experience data should not be used in isolation for designing intervention practices to teaching; rather, it should be used in conjunction with other indicators and data sources.

Higher education institutions are not only expected to be responsive to the students, but also to other stakeholders, including the faculty, graduate employers, government, and the wider community. Furthermore, the student perspective should not be narrowly defined;

what is considered to be a good quality, satisfactory experience by one student may not necessarily hold true for another student.

While students are clearly key stakeholders who can provide valuable and reliable data to inform teaching and learning improvement decisions, student experience data should be analysed and used with caution. It should not be used alone, but needs to be backed up with other sources of information.

Diversity in Chinese Higher Education

The student experience has been widely utilised and researched as a tool for quality assurance in higher education but, in this study, it has been used to examine institutional diversification in higher education. Given the diversified nature of higher education institutions in this context, it is essential to analyse the access patterns of different groups of students regarding their choice of institution (Hoelscher et al., 2008) and the range of student experiences the different institutions offer.

The results of this study indicate that there are large differences in the student intake at the different institutions. In summary, students from socially and economically disadvantaged backgrounds tend to have lower educational attainment, and are more likely to attend the less prestigious Private College.

This situation can also be observed in other national contexts. In the US, for example, 71% of the lowest-socio-economic status students do not obtain the academic qualifications necessary to support higher education enrolment, compared with only 30% among the highest-socio-economic status students. Of those high school graduates who qualified for higher education, only 65% from the lowest-socio-economic status background actually apply to a four-year institution, which is 22% less than the rate for students from high-socio-economic status background (Cabrera & La Nasa, 2000). In the United Kingdom, the 20% of students who live in the most affluent areas are five to six times more likely to access higher education than the 20%

who live in the poorest areas (HEFCE, 2005), and those attending fee-paying independent schools are almost ten times more likely to get into Oxford or Cambridge Universities than those attending free state schools (Sutton Trust, 2004).

In terms of basic demographics, the Chinese undergraduate population differs from that of many mature higher education systems in the West. Secondary school-leavers who take the standard examinations enter different programmes, and, very often, different institutions, from non-traditional students who take other admission examinations. This means that the *Tongzhao Benke* population in China is mostly composed of traditional students, and non-traditional adult students are rare at *Tongzhao Benke* institutions.

There is no denying that there is considerable diversity in the Chinese higher education system, in terms of the institutions' particular history, particular faculty and students, and particular geographical location (Meek & Wood, 1998). The evidence in this study has shown that the *Benke* sector as represented in the fieldwork base city, is diversified in terms of student body composition, and is stratified in that the newer institutions take up the task of achieving higher education massification, while the traditional university attempts to guard its status and focuses on research. The hierarchy of reputation of *Benke* institutions implies that the sector fits many of the features of Ulrich Teichler's (2007) "vertical" form of diversity with strong differences in the reputation of the institutions, but not many of the features of the "horizontal" form of diversity.

The new institutions face limitations regarding their ability to be distinctive, most notably in ways that the government is not inclined to approve. This has resulted in a paradox: for all the ideological push associated with the distinctiveness of private and independent institutions, much of the practical drive for establishing these institutions is intended to reduce state costs, rather than to promote diversity. Due to the vocational drift in traditional institutions and the "coercive modelling" pressures in new institutions, the "applied *Benke* colleges" may not have achieved successful and true distinctiveness.

Government Regulations

One of the main forces leading *Benke* institutions towards convergence is the government's control and supervision mechanisms, which aim mainly to assure the quality of the system. The government conducts evaluations of higher education institutions before approving the establishment (or upgrading) of the institution, and on a regular basis after the establishment. The pre-establishment evaluation is certainly crucial, as failure to pass will result in rejection of the application by the establishment. The influences of regular evaluations are also profound, not only because failure to pass can result in penalties, such as warnings, programme closures, enrolment suspensions, or even institutional closure, but also because the results are published and therefore have a huge impact on the institution's reputation. The evaluation criteria act as guidelines for institutional operation in practice.

Almost all newly established institutions have called themselves "applied *Benke* institutions", and the elite universities have publicly claimed to be or claimed to strive to be "world-class research universities", while other universities often claim to be or strive to become "research teaching universities" or "teaching research universities". However, none of these voluntary classifications is officially recognised, and none of them is acknowledged in the evaluation criteria, which treat all institutions offering *Benke* education the same way and evaluates every institution against exactly the same standards. As noted by Liu and Rosa (2008), there is also a problem with the composition of the expert evaluation teams. Members of the expert pool are chosen based on their reputation within their academic field, not on their undergraduate teaching and learning experience. Additionally, no evaluators come from outside the academic world; employers, alumni, and students are not invited to participate in the evaluations.

When it comes to the quality of faculty, the percentage of full professors and associate professors is sometimes used as an indicator for quality. However, since professorship in China are granted by a provincial labour authority based on provincial standards, which emphasise the importance of research outcomes, faculty at new colleges with fewer research opportunities will find it more difficult to obtain promotions. This not only introduces difficulties for new colleges attempting to increase the quality of their faculty through internal growth, but it may also hinder colleges' recruitment of faculty with higher levels of qualifications.

It could be argued that the newly established colleges, especially private colleges, face at least a threefold disadvantage in competing with the established universities. Firstly, quality of student intake, is itself perceived as an indicator of quality that contributes to the institution's place in league tables and state evaluation. Secondly, the state's evaluation system and public league tables do not consider the differences involved in teaching students who begin their higher education with lower qualifications and less familiarity with the higher education environment. Thirdly, "applied education" programmes need more facilities, but there is no special funding to accommodate these needs, and research-intensive universities are usually much better funded through research, business and donation activities.

In summary, the current government's managerial philosophy and practice for higher education institutions in China appears to hinder change at the institutional level. The current incentives tend to encourage homogeneity and conformism rather than diversity and flexibility. While not always perceived positively by institutional leaders and supporters for a "free market", appropriate policy levers could foster diversity among institutions. These could include: incentives to promote alternative priorities, revised definitions of quality and a reduction in the conformist policies.

There are various ways to acknowledge and even encourage differences between institutions. One example is defining quality as the "value added" to students' development, rather than the outcome *per se*, but this requires sophisticated assessment methodologies that are potentially very difficult to implement. A further example is to classify institutions into different categories, possibly with different evaluation standards for each category, and compare institutions only within their category. This would acknowledge the differences between institutions and provide incentives encouraging institutions to differentiate.

Diversity and Quality

In order to meet the needs of students, and therefore compete successfully in the market place, higher education institutions have become more customer-driven by planning their educational product along the lines envisaged by students and their parents. Since the primary relevance of higher education to students and parents is employability, and students demand to acquire the skills and knowledge valued by potential employers, there are incentives and pressures for higher education institutions to make the shift towards vocational and professional education. The demand for vocational and professional degrees in China is indicative of this trend. For example, from 2002 to 2006, the percentage of *Benke* students admitted to engineering programmes increased from 31.5% to 33.8%, and the percentage of *Benke* business enrolments increased from 12.4% to 16.2%, while the proportion of philosophy enrolments decreased from 0.15% to 0.08%, and the proportion of history enrolments went down from 1% to 0.5% (Ministry of Education, 1978–2009).

Many of the newly-created *Benke* colleges, including private and independent colleges, and the new public colleges have embraced the concept of "applied *Benke* education", strengthening the relevance of the course programme to students' future careers, and wishing to capture this market niche by providing a different product than older institutions. However, this study has shown that, in fact, the older and more established Public University also has to respond to the students' and the labour market needs by increasing the relevance of course programmes to employment and therefore becoming more vocational.

The adoption of vocational aims by higher education institutions has met with a great deal of criticism. Critics view vocationalism and the emphasis on notions of skill, competence, and outcomes in higher education as a threat to the traditional higher education merits of critical thinking, reflection and understanding (Barnett, 1994). The new focus of institutions and programmes on professional and practical training is considered to be overly pragmatic, and to encourage students to adopt a utilitarian and materialistic stance which, in turn, prevents them from appreciating the intrinsic value of higher education (Niblett, 1990). Higher education institutions are also considered to neglect their role as social critics, in favour of the production of useful knowledge and training (Wielemans, 1988).

While the above-mentioned criticisms point to serious weaknesses in the increasingly utilitarian character of higher education institutions and programmes, the shift towards vocationalism is likely to continue as long as it is supported by the choices and expectations of higher education students and their parents, who bear a significant proportion of educational costs. Higher education institutions have no option but to adapt to this trend. If they do not, they risk being replaced by other institutions that are willing to meet the demands of the market (Cross, 2000).

Internationally, private higher education is characterised by a large degree of diversity. Some private higher education institutions are research universities that are among the most prestigious in the higher education system, with some examples being Harvard and Yale in the US, and Waseda and Keio in Japan. According to Altbach (1999), these institutions serve as leaders in their own countries. Yet, most private higher education institutions are found to be relatively specialised institutions that offer a smaller range of academic subjects compared with the more comprehensive institutions. In most cases, these private institutions are vocationally-oriented, offering programmes in highly applied fields like management or information technology. In the public perception, the quality of these private institutions is often regarded as low or average, and their main function is perceived to be to cater to an otherwise unmet demand for higher education.

The rapid expansion of higher education and the emergence of hundreds of independent colleges, and a number of private colleges in China naturally gave rise to concerns about the quality of the programmes offered at these institutions. Some critics have portrayed the new private colleges as compromising the overall quality of higher education. The public perceives that there is a lack of quality among private and independent institutions mainly because these new institutions, when compared to the more established traditional universities, have lower admission standards, a narrower focus on teaching in applied or commercial fields, are more vocationally-oriented, conduct little or no research, and their teaching forces are populated by individuals with lower academic credentials or those who work part-time (Pan, 2005; Zhongguo Zhiliang Wanlixing, 2007). The fact that all private colleges were previously vocational institutes strengthens this perception.

The three colleges in the study were promoted to the *Benke* level at similar points. There is no evidence to show that the perceived quality at the Public College is significantly higher to the quality at the other two colleges. However, students are more inclined to apply to public institutions, provided that the actual teaching quality is similar at other institutions, or is unknown to that student. This seems to suggest that ownership type is an important factor in the reputation of institutions and determines students' willingness to apply.

The older universities normally offer a more comprehensive range of academic subjects, but it is not surprising that the percentage of students studying in applied fields in these universities is on the increase due to the strong demand from students. With this more comprehensive range of subjects, older universities have the ability to increase inter-disciplinary interactions, which may benefit student development and offer them more options for educational experiences outside of their chosen subject areas. But, since the pressure from the labour market is still strong, it appears that many older universities may choose to increase the applicability and depth of knowledge, rather than the breadth of knowledge. There are, however, a few exceptions. A few of the elite universities in China have reformed their course organisation, allowing students to apply to a broad field at admission, and choose their specific subject during year three, an innovation that is comparable to general education in the US (Chen,

2006; Huang, 2006). This reform would certainly help undecided students to explore a variety of fields and develop their interests. However, it must be emphasised that it appears that only a few elite universities have the luxury of delaying the teaching of specific subject knowledge, while most other higher education institutions are attempting to increase the relevance of knowledge to employment.

At present in China, it appears that most employers do not have established vocational training schemes for employees, and they have become accustomed to relying on higher education institutions to train skilled students for them (Yang, Ding, & Xi, 2004). The current over-abundance of graduates in relation to the sluggish growth of the labour market demands reinforces the weight of employers in employment negotiations.

In his paper *The Structure of Higher Education: A World View*, Eric Ashby (1973), then Master of Clare College at University of Cambridge, and later Vice-Chancellor of the university, acknowledged that the boundaries between vocational and non-vocational higher education were already blurred. He suggested that a significant distinction between vocational and non-vocational education is that vocational higher education qualifies a person to pursue a specific vocation or profession, and non-vocational higher education does not. However, by these standards, according to the *Higher Education Law of 1998,* which mandates *Benke* education to equip students with the "ability to conduct practical work", all *Benke* education, as well as *Zhuanke* education, should be classified as vocational. As observed by Ashby in 1973, "Universities have always mixed vocational and non-vocational studies, and polytechnics are already doing the same" (p. 145). Furthermore, Professor Wang, former Deputy Vice President of Peking University, argues that the difference between general and vocational is only the different balance between the breadth and depth of knowledge, and that there are no "good" or "bad" qualities associated with them (Wang, 2008).

As well as the seemingly homogeneous curriculum in general and vocational training across the institutions, the evidence in this study also suggests that, different types of institutions may have developed different philosophies and strategies towards student management. Older institutions that have greater prestige, and recruit better students, tend to apply a "light touch" to managing students. Newer institutions that have no established reputation, and recruit less prepared students, may devote more attention to the education of their students, tending to impose more rigid structures of student management. The newer institutions that have invested heavily in student management have already achieved positive results. Although their students were less academically competitive at the point of entry to higher education, they put more effort into studying after entering the institution. However, it should be noted that the study provides no strong evidence for the generalisibility of this finding, and it is expected that institutional strategies may vary on an institution-to-institution basis.

There are reasons for the inferior image of private institutions in China. Public institutions still dominate many aspects of people's lives. Since public organisations have a longer history of serving the society, consumers and students tend to feel a stronger sense of security with publicly-owned organisations. The private higher education institutions started later and, to date, have all focused on undergraduate education; none has provided postgraduate education (of course, one of the reasons for this is they are unlikely to obtain state approval to offer postgraduate education) and most have conducted relatively little research; these are two important aspects of traditional and established rankings and views of higher education quality. In the absence of state subsidies, private institutions also charge higher tuition fees and this can create an image of these institutions as being profit-oriented rather than education-oriented. Furthermore, there have been quite a few scandals at private higher education institutions, including the misleading of prospective students. Although most of these scandals occurred at vocational colleges, and the more established and self-regulated private *Benke* colleges were not involved, the brand damage extended to all institutions labelled "private". All of these factors potentially lead prospective students and the general public to be concerned about the quality of private institutions.

It seems that private institutions are disadvantaged in comparison to public institutions with regard to the public perception of quality. The observations from the Private College in this study suggest that, if private institutions continue to operate legally and effectively, they have the potential to achieve recognition in society. Furthermore, the public sector should be subject to the same rigorous checks as the private sector (Brock, 2002).

Institutional efforts to attract additional resources and enhance their institutional reputation may have little effect on educational quality. As Pike (2004) notes, leaders of higher education institutions who strive for reputation and capacity-based research rankings may be short-changing their students by focusing their efforts on institutional characteristics that are largely irrelevant to high quality education. Prospective students and their parents should also be aware that institutional research capacity, selectivity, and reputation (which is based on the former two factors) may be easily quantifiable, and for which the data are convenient to gather, but they do not automatically translate into good educational experiences and the "top" institutions are not necessarily the *right* choice for individual students. Furthermore, subject diversity is important and rankings that do not take subject diversity into account may be misleading.

Because they largely tend to favour traditional academic performance, particularly in research, university rankings, in fact, have the effect of leading to an increase in mimicking behaviour on the part of institutions imitating institutions with a strong reputation, and therefore, they lead to greater homogeneity, rather than diversity. If the desire is to maintain, and even increase, the diversity of higher education systems, different rankings that assess different institutional performance could be developed to encourage diversity. The classification of institutions could be a first step in this direction. Developing institutional typologies that recognise the diversity of institutional missions and profiles could offer stakeholders a better understanding of the specific ambitions and performances of the various types of higher education institutions (Bartelse & van Vught, 2007).

This study is partly concerned with the issue of quality in higher education in the context of diversification. The literature has concluded that there can be no single indicator of quality; that quality must be considered in terms of each of the functions of an institution, each of the needs of its stakeholders, and, finally, in terms of the many reasonable and acceptable definitions of quality. It should be recognised that different institutions embody different student circumstances and aspirations, that different types of education are needed to meet the needs of different students, and that greater diversity in the *Benke* segment of higher education requires radical changes to the system. Each sector or institution in the diversified higher education system must clearly define what quality means to them. Only then can it be measured, assessed and assured. Increased governmental influence or intervention can help create a working climate of confidence and stability and a culture of mutual respect between institutions.

However, the fundamental question should not be overlooked of whether there should be diversity in the *Benke* sector at all. Regarding homogeneity and diversity in higher education, as argued by Brennan and Osborne (2008), it is always tempting to ask, though difficult to answer, "Which is better"? Should the higher education system conform to and safeguard the traditional view of quality, as seen in the *Benke* sector in China, or acknowledge differentiated standards and encourage diversity between institutions? There seems to be a consensus in the literature that structural diversity is a condition of long-term viability (Clark 1996), as differential treatment in institutional funding and evaluation does not only promote the viability of the new institutions, but also provides a positive environment for the research universities. As suggested by Ashby (1973), the way to eliminate the traditional elitist view of higher education is not to lower standards, but to offer a wide range of standards and not to accentuate the status gap between those with different kinds of education. However, as claimed by Teichler (2008), the public debate and expert discourse on the patterns of the higher education system are strongly shaped by *a priori* value judgments. The discourse is biased by a widespread belief that a high degree of vertical diversity is desirable and, as a consequence, the mainstream discourse does not raise the question of whether this judgment is supported by evidence.

Diversity and Equity

In China, while the higher education sector as a whole has been successful in increasing participation, there is an apparent polarisation of the types of institutions students attend. At one level, it seems that the enrolment expansion policies have opened up higher education to more students, but, at another level, inequalities continue to exist, in the proportion of students of lower socio-economic status attending higher education and those attending leading institutions.

In terms of socio-economic status, the Public University and the Public College had very similar student profiles, with the Public University having slightly more students from large and medium-sized cities, but also slightly more students from rural areas, and the Public College having more students from smaller cities. In comparison, the Independent College students had much higher socio-economic status than the two public institutions, while the Private College students had much lower socio-economic status than the public institution's students.

Since tuition fees are lower at public institutions and higher at Independent and Private Colleges, it seems inequitable and almost paradoxical that the tuition fees are higher at the Private College, but the students there are generally from lower socio-economic backgrounds.

There is also a regional inequity between provinces. The most prestigious universities are concentrated in economically developed cities. For example, of the 39 universities listed in the 985 project, seven are in Beijing, four are in Shanghai, and all the others, except one, are located in very large cities – usually the provincial capitals of the more affluent provinces. Therefore, students from the poorer regions of the country not only receive inferior secondary education

(K. Yu, 2008), since the top universities in affluent regions are inclined to give preference to local students, they are further disadvantaged and face many more difficulties in competing for admission to prestigious universities.

The theories of cultural and social capital presented by Bourdieu (1976, 1977) and Coleman (1988) suggest that students from better off families with parents with higher levels of education have a distinct advantage over their peers who are the first generation in their families to attend higher education, in terms of their understanding of the culture of higher education and its role in personal development and socio-economic attainment after graduation. Those with better-paid and better-educated parents usually have better access to human and cultural capital through family relationships. Consequently, compared to their peers from higher-income and higher-education families, the educationally and economically disadvantaged students are more likely to struggle in accessing and understanding information that facilitates decisions about such matters as the importance of attaining a degree, choosing a higher education institution, and the kinds of academic and social choices to make in higher education. The cultural and social capital theories go on to argue that students not only bring certain levels of cultural and social capital to higher education, but that the higher education experience itself provides a vehicle for acquiring additional cultural and social capital. Therefore, in turn, the disadvantage in social and cultural capitals may translate into a comparatively less influential higher education experience for these students, and perhaps even lower levels of growth in the cognitive and status attainment-oriented outcomes of higher education (Pascarella et al., 2004).

The socio-economically disadvantaged students who achieve lower scores in *Gaokao* and end up paying higher tuition fees at less prestigious institutions attest to the statement that diversity '[...] is elided with "choice" in the context of institutions' (Archer, 2007, p. 636) and, in reality, the ability to exercise choice depends on the possession of economic, social, and cultural capital which is disproportionately held by higher socio-economic groups (see Reay et al.,

2005). In this situation, the establishment of new, low-prestige public and private institutions could be viewed as serving primarily the closing of access to established institutions for the less privileged sections of the population (Teichler, 2008).

The finding that students who pay less to attend the Public University are much better off than students who pay more to attend less reputable Private College is alarming in terms of social equity. The availability of subsidised places in public higher education institutions clearly benefits a more select, privileged group of students, a great many of whom come from better-paid and, better-educated families. This finding suggests that a change in the funding mechanism is necessary; more resources should be allocated to the students who really need them. It also raises the question of whether access to public subsidies should remain the exclusive domain of public institutions. A possible option is to provide students with public funds for higher education, regardless of where the student decides to study. If such funds can flow to the accredited private institutions, as well as to public institutions, public institutions will operate in a competitive environment similar to that of the private institutions and, therefore, the equity of access and the efficiency of subsidies will improve. However, an investigation of this issue is beyond the scope of this study.

Expansion of higher education provision in China does not seem to devote special focus to disadvantaged students, and these students are still much less likely to advance to higher education. The establishment of new, lower-status institutions while traditional universities continue to comprise the elite sector has meant that these disadvantaged students are more likely to attend the lower-status institutions if they have the opportunity to proceed to higher education.

Support strategies in financial and advice terms, would be required to increase higher education participation rates among socioeconomically disadvantaged secondary school students, as well as their access to leading institutions. At present, the rate of secondary school graduates proceeding to higher education is already high, especially in developed urban centres. Therefore, targeting the acquisition of higher education qualifications will comprise the most fruitful area for policy intervention to increase the overall participation rate of underrepresented groups. To increase their participation in leading institutions, there is also a need to improve the quality of the secondary school they attend. Little change will be achieved if the country's students from lower socio-economic groups attend schools lacking high quality teachers and resources.

Other Areas for Improvement in Chinese Higher Education

Although this study provides only a snapshot of student experience at the four selected institutions, it pinpoints a number of areas for improvement, and the findings have implications for the planning and policy-making of higher education institutions in China.

As industry and employers are increasingly looking for graduates with relevant knowledge and skills, and as the competition in the employment market becomes more intense for graduates, it can be observed that students place great value on job-oriented curriculum design. In the survey, "to gain knowledge and skills for career" was chosen by students as one of the top motivations for entering higher education. In fact, when asked how their higher education experience could be improved, increasing the connection between university teaching and the world of work, and the quantity and quality of practical training, were the most frequent suggestions cited by students. Students' desire for practical knowledge and skills were consistent across the institutions. For instance, "combine theories with practice, and more emphasis on the learning of useful knowledge" and "more practice, less theory" are examples of the suggestions made by students at the relatively research-intensive national key Public University. However, even at the colleges that have always depicted themselves as vocationally-oriented, students do not seem to be completely satisfied with the institutions' input into practical training and would like more. As one student at one of the colleges said, "Don't open unnecessary courses; open courses that are relevant to practice".

However, while students show a strong desire for more practice-relevant training, this does not necessarily indicate that students would like the aims and mission of their institutions to be heavily oriented towards vocationalism. For example, students also chose "to help develop as a person and broaden horizons" as one of the top motivations for entering higher education. This, in turn, suggests that higher education institutions should not neglect personal development in favour of narrow specialisation in job-related knowledge and skills. In fact, narrowly-defined and heavily utilitarian vocationalism is not necessarily valued in the labour market, as employers also seek workers with analytic abilities, problem-solving skills, maturity, adaptability, and creativity, and workers who can deal judiciously with technological, economic, and cultural change, as argued by UNESCO's *Policy Paper for Change and Development in Higher Education* (UNESCO, 1995). As noted by Grubb (1996), the "new vocationalism" in the US is more in line with Dewey's ideal of "education through occupations". Dewey believed that academic and vocational education should be combined in order to allow students to learn through the study of occupational themes. However, he emphasised learning *through* occupations rather than *for* them, thus rejecting narrowly-defined utilitarian vocationalism.

The need to find an appropriate balance between academic and vocational elements signals the importance of relevant institutional research. So far, most student experience studies have been conducted in the form of course and instructor evaluations, which are circulated by institutions to obtain course feedback from their students. However, this type of research only provides information on the course experience. It does not offer students the opportunity to assess the mission and character of higher institutions, and the match between institutional aims, policies, learning practices, and student needs. Although there has been an abundance of theoretical discussions on the balance between academic and vocational orientation in China, there is a lack of empirical research on both students' and employers' views of vocationalism.

Although institutions have constructed new campuses and built new and modern teaching and accommodation buildings to facilitate the rapid expansion of higher education in China, investment in human resources has not kept up with this pace and may even have fallen in terms of the quality of instruction. One issue raised was how the teaching force can be improved. Although students frequently quoted faculty as an area in need of improvement, few students gave specific, detailed suggestions or requirements for this improvement. Many students also call for well-known teachers, but do not explain why.

The investigation also revealed that students' experience of teaching varies greatly within institutions and subjects. The primary reason for this is institutions' unbalanced input into different subjects. For example, the Independent College in this study, which has traditionally emphasised engineering and science studies, has not paid sufficient attention to other humanities subjects. This resulted in a sharp difference between students' experiences of the two disciplines (see the chapter on findings). This clearly signals that improvement and greater investment is urgently needed in the humanities subjects offered by this institution. The finding potentially has important implications for other institutions in China, as many of them are developed from specialised institutions and have added new subjects and disciplines in their rapid expansion. It is vital for institutions to monitor and assure the quality of these newly added subjects.

The study also found that there are different philosophies towards the management of students at different institutions. At the colleges this study reviewed, particularly the Private College, there was tighter management of students, as reflected in the more stringent requirements for class attendance, self-study sessions attendance, closer contact with and monitoring by *Banzhuren*, closer contact with students' parents, and so on. At the Public University, there are fewer institutional demands placed on students and the management of students is much looser.

The tighter student management at less prestigious institutions has received recognition from administrators, teachers, students and parents. This suggests that, because the student body is different, institutions with different study bodies should not adhere to the same management models. Newly-built institutions have their own special circumstances, and they should not simply copy their established and prestigious counterparts in all aspects. Within this context, individual institutions should consider student learning improvement activities that would be appropriate to their own specific circumstances.

In line with the findings of Pascarella et al. (2006) and Kuh (2001), the evidence from this study suggests that good practices in undergraduate education are largely independent of the prior attainment of the enrolled students, and such practices are amenable to the influence of institutional policies and practices. This finding mirrors Bogue and Saunders's (1992) notion that every type of university and college has the potential for quality "within its own mission", whatever its resources or reputation (p. 11). All institutions, regardless of their standing and reputation and the quality of their student intake, have the potential to achieve excellence in student experience and to help their students achieve.

The study has also shown that there are problems with the students' financial situation, especially at the Private College. It will require great commitment from both the institution and the government to remedy this situation. There are certain benefits for institutions to increase their financial aid to students, especially in the form of merit-based scholarships. These merit-based scholarships could lead to increased student involvement in academic and social life through encouraging students to excel, and reducing students' obligation to work. Generous scholarship amounts and awareness of the availability of scholarships can attract talented students to the institution and therefore work as a mechanism to improve the institution's standing. The larger proportion of affluent students at publicly supported institutions suggests that the distribution of public resources is not well-managed: the public subsidies have been enjoyed by many people who do not need them, and the students who really need the aid find that it is inaccessible to them. Outside the realm of higher education, it is important to channel more resources to primary and secondary education provision in rural areas, so that students from these regions have the same chance to enjoy quality primary and secondary education and to excel in higher education entrance exams.

In linking the different areas of teaching and learning to students' overall satisfaction, it is clear that most of the academic scales in the questionnaire do not significantly influence students' overall assessments of their experiences. Of the course characteristics, only course organisation had a significant and strong effect on students' overall experience. With regard to the students' characteristics, students' self-evaluation appears to be strongly associated with their overall satisfaction: students who had better academic performance tended to report better overall experiences. The ranking order of the four institutions in terms of students' overall experiences coincided with the hierarchy of reputation of the institutions.

As confirmed by the qualitative evidence, the findings show that the level of reputation and tuition fees are two important factors that directly and strongly influence students' overall satisfaction with their institution. The two factors are relatively stable over time in that they cannot be changed easily or quickly by the institutions. In the Chinese context, this means that the non-public institutions, which lack public recognition and subsidies, and the private colleges in particular (since they have lower reputation than independent colleges) face enormous difficulties in improving student satisfaction. As noted earlier, the Chinese public mistrusts in the country's higher education institutions; the sector is considered one of the least satisfactory areas of public life by the Chinese public. One of the major reasons for their dissatisfaction is the supposedly high tuition fees charged at these institutions. The survey shows that current students' satisfaction with their institutions is already very low and, therefore, the government should be cautious about raising the fees or removing the current limits on fees, as this would further intensify the public's and students' dissatisfaction with the higher education system.

Suggestions for Future Research

This study serves as a first step in understanding the independent and private institutions in relation to the public institutions, and the colleges in relation to universities. Much more research is required to deepen this understanding. Future studies should also include a longitudinal dimension in order to track the changing impact of diversification on student experiences over time.

The results of this study should be regarded as tentative, indicating the still embryonic nature of the understanding of student experience and diversity in higher education in China. Further work should develop the methods pursued here, particularly extending the study of the student experience to a larger and more diverse random sample of public, independent, and private institutions in China, as well as to a more diverse set of disciplines and subjects; this would help to facilitate a greater understanding of both student experience and diversity.

In the data analysis, it was shown that, for many student experience items, there is still substantial variance to be accounted for by other variables that were not included in this study, such as students' expectations, institutional culture, curriculum elements, and so on. These could be developed and incorporated into the models to determine whether they have any influence on students' experience and if different institutions are different in terms of these aspects.

Considering the nature of this study and the researcher's capacity to collect data, the four institutions and 1,264 students in the sample are considered adequate for this exploratory study. In future studies, if the sample size is sufficiently large – for example, 100 institutions or more – the data should be analysed using multilevel statistical methods.

The present study surveys currently enrolled students to assess their higher education experiences. This is an innovation in itself and has proved to be useful. But as discussed, there are certain limitations on currently enrolled students. Understanding the experience of graduates comprises a significant development in student experience research and is suggested for future research.

This study has used a mixed-method approach to answer the research questions. Most other student experience surveys in the field rely on the sole instrument of the student experience questionnaire and on quantitative analysis. As a result, despite the vast and extensive amount of quantitative data, their capacity to generate contextually meaningful information and explanations is limited. By collecting and using qualitative data alongside the survey results, the present study has developed a better understanding of the quantitative results generated. This approach is therefore recommended for future student experience studies.

In future research, it will be necessary to examine students' perceptions of the importance of each experience item, not just its performance. It is much more justified and efficient to invest scarce development resources in items that are perceived to have high importance and low performance than areas with low importance and low performance. This can assist institutions in setting more valid improvement priorities.

References

21st Century Education Development Research Institute. (2005). *China Report on Survey of Satisfaction with Education 2005*. Beijing: 21st Century Education Development Research Institute.

Abbas, A., & McLean, M. (2007). Qualitative Research as a Method for Making Just Comparisons of Pedagogic Quality in Higher Education: A Pilot Study. *British Journal of Sociology of Education,* 28(6), 723–737.

Adamson, G., O'Kane, D., & Shevlin, M. (2005). Students' Ratings of Teaching Effectiveness: A Laughing Matter? *Psychological Reports,* 96, 225–226.

Aguignier, P. (1988). Regional Disparities since 1978. In S. Feuchtwang, A. Hussain & T. P. Boulder (Eds.), *Transforming China's Economy in the Eighties; Volume II: Management, Industry and the Urban Economy*. CO: Westview.

Ainley, J., & Long, M. (1994). *The Course Experience Survey: The 1992 Graduates.* Canberra: Graduate Careers Council of Australia, Department of Employment, Education and Training.

Aldrich, H. E. (1979). *Organizations and Environments*. Englewood Cliffs, NJ: Prentice-Hall.

Altbach, P. (1999). Comparative Perspectives on Private Higher Education. In P. Altbach (Ed.), *Private Prometheus: Private Higher Education and Development in the 21st Century* (pp. 283–292). West Port, Conn.: Greenwood.

Archer, L. (2007). Diversity, equality and higher education: A critical reflection on the ab/uses of equity discourse within widening participation. *Teaching in Higher Education*, 12(5), 635–53.

Ashby, E. (1973). The Structure of Higher Education: A World View. *Higher Education*, 2(2), 142–151.

Astin, A. (1970). The Methodology of Research on College Impact, Part Two. *Sociology of Education*, 43, 437–450.

Astin, A. (1985). *Achieving Educational Excellence: A Critical Assessment of Priorities and Practices in Higher Education*. San Francisco: Jossey-Bass.

Astin, A. (1993). *What Matters in College? Four Critical Years Revisited.* San Francisco: Jossey-Bass.

Attwood, R. (2008, 28 February). Probe Ordered into 'Manipulation'. *Times Higher Education.*

Australian Vice-Chancellors' Committee and Graduate Careers Council of Australia. (2005). *Standard Recommended Methodology for the Graduate Destination Survey, Course Experience Questionnaire and Postgraduate Research Experience Questionnaire*. Melbourne: Graduate Careers Australia.

Australian Vice-Chancellors' Committee. (1995). *Australian Vice-Chancellors' Committee – Code of Practice*. Canberra: Australian Vice-Chancellors' Committee.

Axinn, W. G., & Pearce, L. D. (2006). *Mixed Method Data Collection Strategies*. Cambridge: Cambridge University Press.

Bai, L. (1998). The Metamorphosis of China's Higher Education in the 1990s. In K. Sullivan (Ed.), *Education and Change in the Pacific Rim, Meeting the Challenges* (pp. 241–265). Wallingford: Triangle Books.

Bai, L. (2006). Graduate Unemployment: Dilemmas and Challenges in China's Move to Mass Higher Education. *China Quarterly*, 185, 128.

Bailey, T., Badway, N., & Gumport, P. J. (2001). For-Profit Higher Education and Community Colleges. Palo Alto, CA: National Center for Postsecondary Improvement, Stanford University.

Barnett, R. (1994). The Idea of Quality: Voicing the Educational. In G. D. Doherty (Ed.), *Developing Quality Systems in Higher Education*. London: Routledge.

Bartelse, J., & van Vught, F. (2007). Institutional Profiles: Toward a Typology of Higher Education Institutions in Europe. *IAU Horizons*, 12(2–3), 9–11.

Basow, S. A. (1996). Student Evaluations of College Professors: When Gender Matters. *Journal of Educational Psychology*, 87(4), 656–665.

Basow, S. A., & Silberg, N. T. (1987). Student Evaluations of College Professors: Are Female and Male Professors Rated Differently? *Journal of Educational Psychology*, 79(3), 308–314.

Bastid, M. (Ed.). (1987). *Servitude or Liberation? The Introduction of Foreign Educational Practices and Systems to China from 1840 to the Present*. New York: M. E. Sharpe.

Bian, Y. (1994). *Work and Inequality in Urban China*. Albany: State University of New York Press.

Biggs, J. (1985). The Role of Metalearning in Study Processes. *British Journal of Educational Psychology*, 55, 185–212.

Biggs, J. (1987). *Student Approaches to Learning and Studying*. Melbourne: Australian Council for Educational Research.

Biggs, J. (1989). Approaches to the Enhancement of Tertiary Teaching. *Higher Education Research and Development, 8* (7–25).

Biggs, J. (1993). What Do Inventories of Students' Learning Processes Really Measure? A Theoretical Review and Clarification. *British Journal of Educational Psychology*, 63, 3–19.

Biggs, J. (1999). *Teaching for Quality Learning at University*. Buckingham: Open University Press.

Biggs, J., Kember, D., & Leung, D. Y. P. (2001). The Revised Two-Factor Study Process Questionnaire: R-SPQ-2F. *British Journal of Educational Psychology*, 71.

Birnbaum, R. (1983). *Maintaining Diversity in Higher Education*. San Francisco: Jossey-Bass.

Bogue, E. G., & Sanders, R. L. (1992). *The Evidence of Quality*. San Francisco: Jossey-Bass.

Bourdieu, P. (1976). The School as a Conservative Force. In R. Dale, G. Esland & M. Macdonald (Eds.), *Schooling and Capitalism*. London: Routledge and Kegan Paul.

Bourdieu, P. (1977). Cultural Reproduction and Social Reproduction. In J. Karabel & H. A. Halsey (Eds.), *Power and Ideology in Education* (pp. 56–68). New York: Oxford University Press.

Bradburn, N. M., & Sudman, S. (1988). *Polls and Surveys: Understanding What They Tell Us*. San Francisco: Jossey-Bass.

Bradley, D., & Bradley, M. (1984). *Problems of Asian Students in Australia: Language, Culture and Education*. Canberra: Australian Government Printing Service.

Brandt, R. M. (1958). The Accuracy of Self Estimates. *Genetic Psychology Monographs*, 58, 55–99.

Braskamp, L. A., & Ory, J. C. (1994). *Assessing Faculty Work: Enhancing Individual and Institutional Performance*. San Francisco, CA: Jossey-Bass.

Braxton, J. M., Milem, J. F., & Sullivan, A. S. (2000). The Influence of Active Learning on the College Student Departure Process. *The Journal of Higher Education*, 71, 569–590.

Brennan, J., Brighton, R., Moon, N., Richardson, J., Rindl, J., & Williams, R. (2003). *Collecting and Using Student Feedback on Quality and Standards of Learning and Teaching in He. A Report to Hefce by the Centre for Higher Education Research and Information, Nop Research Group, and Sqw Ltd.* Bristol: Higher Education Funding Council for England.

Brennan, J., & Osborne, M. (2008). Higher Education's Many Diversities: Of Students, Institutions and Experiences; and Outcomes? *Research Papers in Education*, 23(2), 179–190.

Brewer, D. J., Gates, S. M., & Goldman, C. A. (2002). *In Pursuit of Prestige: Strategy and Competition in Us Higher Education*. New Brunswick, NJ: Transaction Publishers.

British Educational Research Association. (2004). *Revised Ethical Guidelines for Educational Research*. Southwell: British Educational Research Association.

Brock, C. (2002, 17–18 October). *First Global Forum on International Quality Assurance, Accreditation and the Recognition of Qualifications in Higher Education: A Review.* Paper presented at the First Global Forum on International Quality Assurance, Accreditation and the Recognition of Qualifications in Higher Education, Paris.

Brown, R. (1999). Diversity in Higher Education: Has It Been and Gone? *Higher Education Review*, 31(3), 3–16.

Bryman, A. (2004). *Social Research Methods* (2 ed.). Oxford: Oxford University Press.

Bryman, A. (Ed.). (2006). *Mixed Methods*. London: Sage.

Byrd, K.L., & Macdonald, G. (2005). Defining College Readiness from the Inside Out: First-Generation College Student Perspectives. *Community College Review*, 33(1), 22–37.
Byrne, M., & Flood, B. (2003). Assessing the Teaching Quality of Accounting Programmes: An Evaluation of the Course Experience Questionnaire. *Assessment & Evaluation in Higher Education*, 28(2).
Cabrera, A.F., & La Nasa, S.M. (2000). Three Critical Tasks America's Disadvantaged Face on Their Path to College. *New Directions for Institutional Research*, 27(3), 23–29.
Carey, K. (2006). *College Rankings Reformed.* Washington: Education Sector.
Carnegie Commission on Higher Education. (1973). *A Classification of Institutions of Higher Education; a Technical Report.* Berkeley, CA: Carnegie Commission on Higher Education.
Cashin, W. (1988). Student Ratings of Teaching: A Summary of Research, *IDEA paper NO. 20.* Manhattan: Kansas Sate University, Center for Faculty Evaluation and Development.
Cashin, W. (1995). *Student Ratings of Teaching: The Research Revisited.* Manhattan, KS: Kansas State University Center for Faculty Evaluation and Development.
Cashin, W., & Downey, R.G. (1992). Using Global Student Rating Items for Summative Evaluation. *Journal of Educational Psychology*, 84, 563–572.
Center for Postsecondary Research at Indiana University Bloomington. (2007). Using Nsse Data. Retrieved 1 October, 2007, from http://nsse.iub.edu/pdf/Using_NSSE_Data.pdf.
Centra, J.A. (1973). Effectiveness of Student Feedback in Improving College Instruction. *Journal of Educational Psychology, 65*, 395–401.
Chan, D., & Mok, K.H. (2001). Educational Reforms and Coping Strategies under the Tidal Wave of Marketization: A Comparative Study of Hong Kong and Mainland. *Comparative Education*, 37(1), 21–41.
Chaney, B., Muraskin, L.D., Cahalan, M.W., & Goodwin, D. (1998). Helping the Progress of Disadvantaged Students in Higher Education: The Federal Student Support Services Program. *Educational Evaluation and Policy Analysis*, 20(3), 197–215.
Chen, D.Y. (2004). China's Mass Higher Education: Problem, Analysis, and Solutions. *Asia Pacific Education Review, 5*(1), 23–33.
Chen, P. (2005, 21 Sep). College Girl's Mother Committed Suicide. *Xinhua News Agency (China).*
Chen, X. (2006). On the Relationship between General Education and Specialty Education Based on a Case Analysis of Yuanpei Program of Peking University. *Peking University Education Review (China)*, 3.
Chenery & Company. (2006, 2–4 March). *State of Higher Education in Mainland China.* Paper presented at the Conference on States of Mind: Creating and Transcending Borders through Education, New York University.

Cheng, K. M. (1998). The Education System. In G. A. Postiglione & W. O. Lee (Eds.), *Schooling in Hong Kong: Organization, Teaching and Social Context* (pp. 25–41). Hong Kong: Hong Kong University Press.

CHERI. (2004). Enhancement Themes: Responding to Student Needs. Retrieved 17 August, 2007, from http://www.enhancementthemes.ac.uk/documents/studentneeds/CHERIREPORT.doc.

Chickering, A. W., & Gamson, Z. F. (1987). Seven Principles for Good Practice in Undergraduate Education. *American Association of Higher Education Bulletin*, 39(3–7).

China Education Online. (2005, 26 June). Clearing up the Self-Determination Admission Policy (China), from http://gaokao.eol.cn/article/20051110/3159871.shtml.

Clark, B. R. (1978). Academic Differentiation in National Systems of Higher Education. *Comparative Education Review*, 33, 242–258.

Clark, B. R. (1983). *The Higher Education System*. Berkeley and Los Angeles: University of California Press.

Codling, A., & Meek, V. L. (2006). Twelve Propositions on Diversity in Higher Education. *Higher Education Management and Policy*, 18(3).

Cohen, P. A. (1990). *Bringing Research into Practice*. San Francisco: Jossey-Bass.

Coleman, J. S. (1988). Social Capital in the Creation of Human Capital. *American Journal of Sociology*, 94, 95–120.

Cooke, R. (2002). Information on Quality and Standards in Higher Education; Final Report of the Task Group. Hefce Report 02/15. Retrieved 20 February, 2007, from http://www.hefce.ac.uk/Pubs/hefce/2002/02_15.htm.

Crawford, K., Gordon, S., Nicholas, J., & Prosser, M. (1998). Qualitatively Different Experiences of Learning Mathematics at University. *Learning and Instruction*, 4(5).

Cronbach, L. J. (1951). Coefficient Alpha and the Internal Structure of Tests. *Psychometrika*, 16(3), 297–334.

Cross, K. P. (2000). *Portraits of Students: A Retrospective*. Paper presented at the AAHE National Conference on Higher Education, Anaheim, California.

Deng, Z., & Treiman, D. (1997). The Impact of the Cultural Revolution on Trends in Educational Attainment in the People's Republic of China. *The American Journal of Sociology*, 103, 391–428.

Department for Education and Skills. (2003). *The Future of Higher Education: White Paper.* London: HMSO.

Donald, J. G., & Denison, D. B. (2001). Quality Assessment of University Students: Student Perceptions of Quality Criteria. *Journal of Higher Education*, 72(4).

Drucker, A., & Remmers, H. (1951). Do Alumni and Students Differ in Their Attitudes toward Instructors? *Journal of Educational Psychology, 70*, 129–143.

Duan, X.-R. (2003). Chinese Higher Education Enters a New Era. *Academe, 89*(6).

Eley, M. (2001). The Course Experience Questionnaire: Altering Question Format and Phrasing Could Improve the CEQ's Effectiveness. *Higher Education Research & Development*, 20(3), 293–312.

Entwistle, N. (2003a). *Concepts and Conceptual Frameworks Underpinning the ETL Project. ETL Project Occasional Report 3.* Edinburgh: University of Edinburgh School of Education.

Entwistle, N. (2003b). University Teaching-Learning Environments and Their Influences on Student Learning: An Introduction to the ETL Project, *Enhancing University Teaching-Learning Environments to Improve Student Learning*. Padova, Italy.

Entwistle, N., & Ramsden, E. (1983). *Understanding Student Learning*. London: Croom Helm.

Entwistle, N., & Tait, H. (1990). Approaches to Learning, Evaluation of Teaching, and Preferences for Contrasting Academic Environments. *Higher Education*, 19, 169–194.

Ertl, H., Hayward, G., Wright, S., Edwards, A., Lunt, I., Mills, D., & Yu, K. (2008). *The Student Learning Experience in Higher Education: Literature Review Report for the Higher Education Academy*. York: Higher Education Academy.

Fairbank, J., & Reischauer, E. (1978). *China: Transition and Transformation*. Boston: Houghton Mifflin.

Fan, J., & Wu, T. (2004). Research on the Cultivating Strategy of Practical Undergraduate Personnel. *Higher Education Forum (China)*, 5.

Feldman, K. (1978). Course Characteristics and College Students' Ratings of Their Teachers and Courses: What We Know and What We Don't. *Research in Higher Education*, 9, 199–242.

Feldman, K. (1986). The Perceived Instructional Effectiveness of College Teachers as Related to Their Personality and Attitudinal Characteristics: A Review and Synthesis. *Research in Higher Education*, 24.

Feldman, K. (1988). Effective College Teaching from the Students and Faculty's View: Matched or Mismatched Priorities? *Research in Higher Education*, 28(4).

Feng, Y. (1994, November). *From the Imperial Examination to the National College Entrance Examination: The Dynamics of Political Centralism in China's Educational Enterprise.* Paper presented at the Annual Meeting of the Association for the Study of Higher Education, Tucson, AZ.

Fleming, N. (1992). *Why Don't They Attend?*: Education Unit, Lincoln University.

Fleming, N. (1995). *Attendance: Why Don't They Attend?*: Education Unit, Lincoln University.

Fraser, B.J. (1998). The Birth of a New Journal: Editor's Introduction. *Learning Environments Research*, 1.

Fulton, O. (1996). Differentiation and Diversity in a Newly Unitary System: The Case of the UK. In V.L. Meek, L. Goedegebuure, O. Kivinen & R. Rinne (Eds.), *The Mockers and Mocked: Comparative Perspectives on Differentiation, Convergence, and Diversity in Higher Education* (pp. 163–187). Oxford: Pergamon.

Geiger, R. (1986). *Private Sectors in Higher Education: Structure, Function, and Change in Eight Countries*. Ann Arbor, Michigan: University of Michigan Press.

Geiger, R. (1996). Diversification in U.S. Higher Education: Historical Patterns and Current Trends. In V. L. Meek, L. C. J. Goedegebuure, O. Kivinen & R. Rinne (Eds.), *The Mockers and Mocked: Comparative Perspectives on Differentiation, Convergence, and Diversity in Higher Education* (pp. 188–203). Oxford: Pergamon.

Gibbs, G., & Lucas, L. (1996). Using Research to Improve Student Learning in Large Classes. In G. Gibbs (Ed.), *Improving Student Learning: Using Research to Improve Student Learning* (pp. 33–49). Oxford: Oxford Centre for Staff Development.

Ginns, P., Prosser, M., & Barrie, S. (2007). Students' Perceptions of Teaching Quality in Higher Education: The Perspective of Currently Enrolled Students. *Studies in Higher Education*, 32(5).

Goldstein, H. (1995). *Multilevel Statistical Models*. London: Edward Arnold.

Goldstein, H. (2003). Multilevel Modelling of Educational Data. In D. Courgeau (Ed.), *Methodology and Epistemology of Multilevel Analysis*. London: Kluwer.

Grubb, N. (1996). The 'New Vocationalism' in the United States: Returning to John Dewey. *Educational Philosophy and Theory*, 28, 1–23.

Guangdong Prices Bureau. (2003). Higher Education Institutions Charging Policy. Guangzhou: Guangdong Prices Bureau.

Guo, Q. (1994). *Ancient Examination Systems of China*. Taipei: Taiwan Commercial Publishers.

Guo, S. (2008, 27 April). 教育部: 部属高校属地招生比例应限制在30%以内 ['Ministry of Education: Ministry-Affiliated Institutions Should Limit the Percentage of Local Students to 30% in Their Total Enrolment']. *The Beijing News (China).*

Guo, W., Qiao, X., & Fu, Y. (2005). 民办二级学院专业设置的现状与未来 ['The Programme Offerings at Independent Colleges: The Present and the Future']. *Jiangsu Higher Education (China)*, 6.

Guri-Rosenblit, S., Sebková, H., & Teichler, U. (2007). Massification and Diversity of Higher Education Systems: Interplay of Complex Dimensions. *Higher Education Policy*, 20, 373–389.

Hai, H. (2005, 31 Mar). Tuitions: Burden That Peasants Cannot Stand. *Chinese Business View (China).*

Hammersley, M. (1996). The Relationship between Qualitative and Quantitative Research: Paradigm Loyalty Versus Methodological Eclecticism. In J. Richardson (Ed.), *Handbook of Qualitative Research Methods for Psychology and the Social Sciences*. Oxford: Blackwell.

Hanbury, A. (2007). *Comparative Review of British, American and Australian National Surveys of Undergraduate Students*. York: Higher Education Academy.

Hand, T., Trembath, K., & Elsworthy, P. (1998). *Enhancing and Customising the Analysis of the Course Experience Questionnaire*. Canberra: Evaluations and Investigations Program, Higher Education Division, Department of Education, Training and Youth Affairs, Commonwealth of Australia.

Hannan, M. T., & Freeman, J. (1977). The Population Ecology of Organizations. *American Journal of Sociology*, 82, 929–964.
Harris, K.-L., & James, R. (2006). *The Course Experience Questionnaire, Graduate Destinations Survey and Learning and Teaching Performance Fund in Australian Higher Education*. Chapel Hill: Department of Public Policy, The University of North Carolina at Chapel Hill.
Hartmann, R. (2006, Dec 21). Chinese Higher Education Fails the Test. *Asia Times*.
Harvey, L. (2001). *Student Feedback: A Report to the Higher Education Funding Council for England*. Bristol: Higher Education Funding Council for England.
Harvey, L. (2003). Student Feedback: Editorial. *Quality in Higher Education*, 9(1), 3–20.
Harvey, L. (2008). Jumping through Hoops on a White Elephant: A Survey Signifying Nothing. *Times Higher Education, 12 June 2008*.
Harvey, L., & Green, D. (1993). Defining Quality. *Assessment & Evaluation in Higher Education*, 18(1).
He, J. (2000). *China Gaokao Report*. Beijing: Huaxia Publishing House.
HEFCE. (2000). *Diversity in Higher Education*. Bristol: HEFCE.
HEFCE. (2003). *Collecting and Using Student Feedback on Quality and Standards of Learning and Teaching in Higher Education: A Report to the Higher Education Funding Council for England*. Bristol: HEFCE.
HEFCE. (2005). *Young Participation in Higher Education*. Bristol: HEFCE.
HEFCE. (2006). Students Continue to Be Very Satisfied with Teaching and Give Higher Rating to Learning Resources, from http://www.hefce.ac.uk/NEWS/HEFCE/2006/survey.htm.
HEFCE. (2007). National Student Survey. Retrieved 20 February, 2007, from http://www.hefce.ac.uk/learning/nss/.
HEFCE. (2008). *HEFCE Strategic Plan 2006–11*. Bristol: HEFCE.
Henderson, B.B., & Kane, W.D. (1991). Caught in the Middle: Faculty and Institutional Status and Quality in State Comprehensive Universities. *Higher Education*, 22, 339–350.
Higher Education Academy. (2005). Strategic Plan 2005–2010. York: Higher Education Academy.
Higher Education Academy. (2007). *National Student Survey (Nss) Institutional Case Studies*. York: Higher Education Academy.
Higher Education Evaluation Center. (2008). Higher Education Evaluation Center's Website. Retrieved 12 December 2008, from http://www.pgzx.edu.cn.
Higher Education Research Institute. (2004). *The American Freshman: National Norms for Fall 2004*. Los Angeles, CA: University of California.
Hills, L. (2005). Evaluating the Evaluation Tools: Methodological Issues in the Fast Project, *British Educational Research Association Annual Conference*. University of Glamorgan: British Educational Research Association.

Hoelscher, M., Hayward, G., Ertl, H., & Dunbar-Goddet, H. (2008). The Transition from Vocational Education and Training to Higher Education: A Successful Pathway? *Research Papers in Education*, 23(2), 139–151.

Hofstede, G. (1986). Cultural Differences in Teaching and Learning. *International Journal of Intercultural Relations*, 10, 301–320.

Hong, Z. (2007). 高校评估 亦喜亦忧-访我国高等教育专家潘懋元教授 ['Evaluation of Higher Education Institutions: The Sorrows and the Happiness – an Interview with Higher Education Expert Professor Pan Maoyuan']. *Education and Vocation (China)*, 537.

Hu, A., & Shi, Z. (1999a). 加快发展加速变革我国高等教育 ['Accelerate the Development and Reform of Higher Education in China']. *Science Times (China)*, 1999.03.26.

Hu, A., & Shi, Z. (1999b). 改革力度还应加大 ['The Reforms Shall Be Further Strengthened']. *Outlook (China)*, 7–8, 80–81.

Hu, J. (2003). Tactful Analysis of Enrolling New Students of Private College and Universities. *Higher Education Forum*, 2.

Huang, F. (2006). From Liberal Education to General Education: A Historical and Comparative Perspective. *Fudan Education Forum (China)*, 4.

Huang, M., & Feng, H. (2003). General Education: A New Orientation of Chinese Higher Education Reform. *Journal of Higher Education (China)*, 4.

Huisman, J. (1995). *Differentiation, Diversity and Dependency in Higher Education*. Utrecht: Lemma.

Huisman, J. (2000). Higher Education Institutions: As Different as Chalk and Cheese? *Higher Education Policy*, 13(1).

Huisman, J., & Morphew, C.C. (1998). Centralization and Diversity: Evaluating the Effects of Government Policies in the USA and Dutch Higher Education. *Higher Education Policy*, 11(1), 3–13.

Hurtado, S., & Dey, E.L. (1997). Achieving the Goals of Multiculturalism and Diversity. In M.W. Peterson, D.D. Dill & L.A. Mets (Eds.), *Planning and Management for a Changing Environment: A Handbook on Redesigning Postsecondary Institutions* (pp. 405–431). San Francisco: Jossey Bass.

Ince, M. (2005, 28 October 2005). Beijing Leads Asia's March to the Forefront. *The Times Higher Education Supplement*.

James, R. (2002). Students' Changing Expectations of Higher Education and the Consequences of Mismatches with the Reality. In P. Coaldrake & L. Stedman (Eds.), *Responding to Student Expectations* (pp. 71–83). Paris: OECD.

Jenniskens, I. (1997). *Governmental Steering and Curriculum Innovations: A Comparative Study of the Relation between Governmental Steering Instruments and Innovations in Higher Education Curricula*. Utrecht: Lemma.

Jin, Y. (2003, 17 Nov). "Ablactating" Independent Colleges. *Business Daily (China)*.

Johnson, T. (1997). *The 1996 Course Experience Questionnaire*. Parkville, Victoria: Graduate Careers Council of Australia.

Johnson, T., Ainley, J., & Long, M. (1996). *The 1995 Course Experience Questionnaire*. Parkville, Victoria: Graduate Careers Council of Australia.

Kang, N. (2000). 论教育决策与制度创新 ['Discussing the Educational Decision-Making and System Innovation']. *Higher Education Research (China)*, 21(2).

Kember, D. (1996). The Intention to Both Memorise and Understand: Another Approach to Learning. *Higher Education*, 31, 341–354.

Kember, D., & Gow, L. (1990). Cultural Specificity of Approaches to Study. *British Journal of Educational Psychology*, 60, 356–363.

Kember, D., & Leung, D. Y. P. (forthcoming). Development of a Questionnaire for Assessing Students' Perceptions of the Teaching and Learning Environment and Its Use in Quality Assurance. *Learning Environments Research*.

Kember, D., Leung, D. Y. P., & Kwan, K. P. (2002). Does the Use of Student Feedback Questionnaires Improve the Overall Quality of Teaching? *Assessment & Evaluation in Higher Education*, 27(5).

Kember, D., Leung, D. Y. P., & Ma, R. S. F. (2007). Characterizing Learning Environments Capable of Nurturing Generic Capabilities in Higher Education. *Research in Higher Education*, 48(5).

Kogan, M. (1993). The End of the Dual System? The Blurring of Boundaries in the British Tertiary Education System. In C. Gellert (Ed.), *Higher Education in Europe* (pp. 48–58). London: Jessica Kingsley Publishers.

Kogan, M. (1997). Diversification in Higher Education: Differences and Commonalities. *Minerva*, 35, 47–62.

Krause, K.-L., Hartley, R., James, R., & McInnis, C. (2005). *The First Year Experience in Australian Universities: Findings from a Decade of National Studies*. Canberra: Department of Education, Science and Training.

Kuh, G., Pace, C. R., & Vesper, N. (1997). The Development of Process Indicators to Estimate Student Gains Associated with Good Practices in Undergraduate Education. *Research in Higher Education*, 38(4), 435–453.

Kuh, G. (2001). Assessing What Really Matters to Student Learning: Inside the National Survey of Student Engagement. *Change, 33*(3), 10–17.

Kuh, G. (2002). *The College Student Report*. Indiana University, National Survey of Student Engagement, Center for Postsecondary Research and Planning.

Kuh, G. (2007). *The National Survey of Student Engagement: Conceptual Framework and Overview of Psychometric Properties*. Bloomington, IN: Indiana University, Center for Postsecondary Research.

Kuh, G., Kinzie, J., Schuh, J. H., & Whitt, E. J. (2005). *Student Success in College: Creating Conditions That Matter*. San Francisco: Jossey-Bass.

Kyvik, S. (2004). Structural Changes in Higher Education Systems in Western Europe. *Higher Education in Europe*, 24(3), 393–409.

Lai, Z., & Wu, Z. (2003). Analysis of the Examination Immigrants Phenomenon. *Contemporary Youth Research (China)*, 4.

Lawless, C., & Richardson, J. (2002). Approaches to Studying and Perceptions of Academic Quality in Distance Education. *Higher Education*, 44(2), 257–282.

Layne, B.H., DeCristoforo, J.R., & McGinty, D. (1999). Electronic Versus Traditional Student Ratings of Instruction. *Research in Higher Education*, 40(2), 221–232.

Lee, H.C. (2000). *Education in Traditional China, a History*. The Netherlands: Drill.

Levy, D.C. (1986). Private and Public: Analysis Amid Ambiguity in Higher Education. In D.C. Levy (Ed.), *Private Education: Studies in Choice and Public Policy*. Oxford: New College.

Levy, D.C. (1999). When Private Higher Education Does Not Bring Organizational Diversity. In P.G. Altbach (Ed.), *Private Prometheus: Private Higher Education and Development in the 21st Century*. Westport CT: Greenwood Press.

Lewin, K., & Wang, L. (1991). Access to University Education in the People's Republic of China: A Longitudinal Analysis of the Structure and Content of the University Entrance Examinations 1984–1988. *International Journal of Educational Development*, 11 (231–244).

Li, K. (2004). Examination Immigration and Equity of Citizens' Right of Receiving Education, *People's Daily (China)*. Beijing.

Li, L. (2004). China's Higher Education Reform 1998–2003: A Summary. *Asia Pacific Education Review*, 5(1), 14–22.

Li, L. (2006, 21 July). Result of 2006 Survey on Employment of Graduates, from http://www.chinanews.com.cn/kj/zczx/news/2006/07-16/758769.shtml.

Li, L. (2006). Several Measures to Improve Our Country's Students' Loans. *Business Economy (China)*, 1.

Li, P. S., Li, L., & Zong, L. (2007). Postgraduate Educational Aspirations and Policy Implications: A Case Study of University Students in Western China. *Journal of Higher Education Policy and Management*, 29(2), 143–158.

Li, R. (1991). A Preliminary Investigation of the Issue of Increasing Cross-Regional Differences in Personal Income. *Social Sciences (China)*, 3(41–44).

Liu, S., & Rosa, M.J. (2008). Quality Assessment of Undergraduate Education in China: A Policy Analysis. *Higher Education Management and Policy*, 20(3).

Liu, Y. (1998). Educational Utilitarianism: Where Goes Higher Education? In M. Agelasto & B. Adamson (Eds.), *Higher Education in Post-Mao China*. Hong Kong: Hong Kong University Press.

Lizzio, A., Wilson, K., & Simons, R. (2002). University Students' Perceptions of the Learning Environment and Academic Outcomes: Implications for Theory and Practice. *Studies in Higher Education*, 27(1), 27–52.

Long, M., & Hillman, K. (2000). *Course Experience Questionnaire 1999: A Report Prepared for the Graduate Careers Council of Australia*. Parkville, Victoria: Graduate Careers Council of Australia.

Long, Y. (2003). *The Conceptions About Colleges and Universities' Admissions System Reform*. Central China Normal University, Wuhan.

Longhurst, R.J. (1999). Why Aren't They Here? Student Absenteeism in a Further Education College. *Journal of Further and Higher Education*, 23(1), 61–80.

Lu, G. (2003). Cost Recovery for Higher Education: A Study of the Undergraduate Students' Ability and Willingness to Pay in the Chinese Mainland. *International Journal of Educational Development*, 23(1), 121.

Lu, X. (Ed.). (2002). *Research Report of Social Classes in Contemporary China*. Beijing: Social Sciences Documentation Publishing House.

Lu, X. (Ed.). (2004). *Social Mobility in Contemporary China*. Beijing: Social Sciences Documentation Publishing House.

Lucas, L., Gibbs, G., Hughes, S., Jones, O., & Wisker, G. (1997). A Study of the Effects of Course Design Features on Student Learning in Large Classes at Three Institutions: A Comparative Study. In C. Rust & G. Gibbs (Eds.), *Improving Student Learning: Improving Student Learning through Course Design* (pp. 10–24). Oxford: Oxford Centre for Staff and Learning Development.

Luo Qi, Witte, H. d., Pasture, P., & Gyes, G. v. (2001). *China's Industrial Reform and Open-Door Policy 1980–1997: A Case Study from Xiamen*. Burlington: Ashgate Publishing.

Maas, C.J.M., & Hox, J.J. (2005). Sufficient Sample Sizes for Multilevel Modeling. *Methodology: European Journal of Research Methods for the Behavioral and Social Sciences*, 1, 85–91.

Machell, J., & Saunders, M. (2007). *An Exploratory Evaluation of the Use of the National Student Survey (NSS) Results Dissemination Website*. York: Higher Education Academy.

MacWilliams, B. (2001). Russia to Try Standardized Exam. *The Chronicle of Higher Education*, 47.

Mao, J.-Q. (2006). A Study on the Main Subjects of Current Higher Education in China: Current Situation, Causes and Policy Suggestions – from the Comparative View of the Public and Private Universities. *Heilongjiang Researches on Higher Education (China)*, 7.

Marginson, S., & Considine, M. (2000). *The Enterprise University. Power, Governance and Reinvention in Australia*. Cambridge: Cambridge University Press.

Marsh, H.W. (1984). Students' Evaluations of University Teaching: Dimensionality, Reliability, Validity, Potential Biases, and Utility. *Journal of Educational Psychology*, 76, 707–754.

Marsh, H.W. (1987). Students' Evaluations of University Teaching: Research Findings, Methodological Issues, and Directions for Future Research. *International Journal of Educational Research*, 11, 253–388.

Marsh, H.W. (2007). Students' Evaluations of University Teaching: Dimensionality, Reliability, Validity, Potential Biases and Usefulness. In R.P. Perry & J.C. Smart (Eds.), *The Scholarship of Teaching and Learning in Higher Education: An Evidence-Based Perspective*. Dordrecht: Springer.

Marsh, H.W., & Overall, J.U. (1979). Validity of Students' Evaluations of Instructional Effectiveness: A Comparison of Faculty Self-Evaluation and Evaluation by Their Students. *Journal of Educational Psychology*, 71(2), 149–160.

Marsh, H. W., & Overall, J. U. (1980). The Validity of Students' Evaluation of Teaching Effectiveness: Cognitive and Affective Criteria. *Journal of Educational Psychology*, 72(4), 468–475.

Marsh, H.W., & Roche, L. (1993). The Use of Students' Evaluations and an Individually Structured Intervention to Enhance University Teaching Effectiveness. *American Educational Research Journal*, 30, 217–251.

Marsh, H.W., & Roche, L.A. (1997). Making Students' Evaluations of Teaching Effectiveness Effective: The Critical Issues of Validity, Bias, and Utility. *American Psychologist*, 51(11), 1187–1197.

Marsh, H.W., & Roche, L.A. (1999). Rely Upon Set Research. *American Psychologist*, 54(7), 517–518.

Marsh, H.W., Rowe, K.J., & Martin, A. (2002). Phd Students' Evaluation of Research Supervision: Issues, Complexities, and Challenges in a Nationwide Australian Experiment in Benchmarking Universities. *Journal of Higher Education*, 73(3), 313–348.

Marton, F., Dall'Alba, G., & Tse, L.K. (1993). *The Paradox of the Chinese Learner. Educational Research and Development Unit (Rmit) Occasional Paper 93.* Melbourne: Educational Research and Development Unit, RMIT.

Marton, F., Hounsell, D.J., & Entwistle, N.J. (Eds.). (1984). *The Experience of Learning*. Edinburgh: Scottish Academic Press.

Marton, F., & Saljo, R. (1976). On Qualitative Differences in Learning. I-Outcome and Process. *British Journal of Educational Psychology*, 46, 4–11.

Marton, F., Wen, Q., & Wong, K.C. (2005). 'Read a Hundred Times and the Meaning Will Appear …' Changes in Chinese University Students' Views of the Temporal Structure of Learning. *Higher Education*, 49(3).

Maslow, A. H. (1943). A Theory of Human Motivation. *Psychological Review*, 50, 370–396.

McNaught, C., Leung, D.Y.P., & Kember, D. (2006). *Report on the Student Engagement Project*. Hong Kong: Centre for Learning Enhancement and Research, Chinese University of Hong Kong.

Meek, V.L. (1991). The Transformation of Australian Higher Education from Binary to Unitary System. *Higher Education*, 21, 464–494.

Meek, V.L., Goedegebuure, L., Kivinen, O., & Rinne, R. (Eds.). (1996). *The Mockers and Mocked. Comparative Perspectives on Differentiation, Convergence and Diversity in Higher Education*. Oxford & New York: Pergamon.

Meek, V.L., & Wood, F.Q. (1998). *Managing Higher Education Diversity in a Climate of Public Sector Reform*. Canberra: Department of Employment, Education, Training and Youth Affairs.

Min, W. (2002). *Economic Transition and Higher Education Reform in China.* Paper presented at the Higher Education Seminar at the Center on Chinese Higher Education at Columbia University, New York.

Min, W. (2004). *Historical Perspectives and Contemporary Challenges: The Case of Chinese Universities.* New York: Columbia University Teachers College.

Ministry of Education. (1978–2009). *National Statistics on Educational Development.* Beijing, China: People's Education Press.

Ministry of Education. (1999). *Third National Conference on Education (China).*

Ministry of Education. (2003). *教育部关于进一步深化教育改革，促进高校毕业生就业工作的若干意见 ['Views of the Ministry of Education on Further Deepening the Educational Reform and Promoting Higher Education Graduates Entering Labour Market'].* Beijing: Ministry of Education.

Ministry of Education. (2004). *Higher Education in China.* Beijing, China: Ministry of Education.

Ministry of Education. (2005). *教育部批准的独立学院名单 ['List of Independent Colleges Approved by the Ministry of Education'].* Beijing: Ministry of Education.

Miyazaki, I. (1976). *China's Examination Hell: The Civil Service Examinations of Imperial China.* New York: Weatherhill.

Mohrman, K. (2003). Higher Education Reform in Mainland Chinese Universities: An American's Perspective. Retrieved July 2005, from http://www.cuhk.edu.hk.

Mok, K. H. (2001). Academic Capitalisation in the New Millennium: The Marketisation and Corporatisation of Higher Education in Hong Kong. *Policy & Politics*, 29(3), 299–316.

Morphew, C. C. (2000). Institutional Diversity, Program Acquisition and Faculty Members: Examining Academic Drift at a New Level *Higher Education Policy*, 13, 55–77.

Murray, H. G., Rushton, J. P., & Paunonen, S. V. (1990). Teacher Personality Traits and Student Instructional Ratings in Six Types of University Courses. *Journal of Educational Psychology*, 82(2), 250–261.

Narasimhan, K. (2001). Improving the Climate of Teaching Sessions: The Use of Evaluations by Students and Instructors. *Quality in Higher Education, 7.*

National Bureau of Statistics of China. (2005). *China Statistical Yearbook 2005.* Beijing: China Statistics Press.

National Bureau of Statistics of China. (2008). *China Statistical Yearbook 2008.* Beijing: China Statistics Press.

National Center for Educational Statistics. (1991). *Education Counts: An Indicator System to Monitor the Nation's Educational Health.* Washington, DC: U. S. Government Printing Office.

National Committee of Inquiry into Higher Education. (1997). Higher Education in the Learning Society: Report of the National Committee of Inquiry into Higher Education. In. London: HMSO.

Neave, G. (1979). Academic Drift: Some Views from Europe. *Studies in Higher Education*, 4(2), 143–159.

Neave, G. (1996). Homogenization, Integration and Convergence: The Cheshire Cats of Higher Education Analysis. In V.L. Meek, L. Goedegebuure, O. Kivinen & R. Rinne (Eds.), *The Mockers and Mocked. Comparative Perspectives on Differentiation, Convergence and Diversity in Higher Education*. Oxford & New York: Pergamon.

Newman-Ford, L., Fitzgibbon, K., Lloyd, S., & Thomas, S. (2008). A Large-Scale Investigation into the Relationship between Attendance and Attainment: A Study Using an Innovative, Electronic Attendance Monitoring System. *Studies in Higher Education*, 33(6), 699–717.

Newman, M. (2008a). Students More Satisfied Than Ever Before. *Times Higher Education, 11 September 2008*.

Newman, M. (2008b). Students Urged to Inflate National Survey Marks to Improve Job Options. *Times Higher Education, 15 May 2008*.

Niblett, W.R. (1990). An Absence of Outrage: Cultural Change and Values in British Higher Education 1930–1990. *Higher Education Policy*, 3, 20–24.

Nielsen, H.D., Moos, R.H., & Lee, E.A. (1978). Response Bias in Follow-up Studies of College Students. *Research in Higher Education*, 9, 97–113.

Niland, J. (1999). *The CEQ and Accountability a System-Wide Perspective and the UNSW Approach*. Paper presented at the Course Experience Questionnaire Symposium 1998, Sydney.

NSSE. (2006). *Engaged Learning: Fostering Success for All Students. Annual Report 2006*. Bloomington, IN: Indiana University, Center for Postsecondary Research.

NSSE Institute. (2009). NSSE Regional Accreditation Toolkits. Retrieved 6 April, 2009, from http://nsse.iub.edu/institute/?view=tools/accred.

Nunnaly, J. (1978). *Psychometric Theory*. New York: McGraw-Hill.

OECD. (2003a). *Education at a Glance – Oecd Indicators*. Paris: OECD.

OECD. (2003b). *OECD Review of Financing and Quality Assurance Reforms in Higher Education in the People's Republic of China*. Paris: OECD.

OECD. (2007). Online Education Database. Retrieved 10 April 2007, from http://www.oecd.org/document/54/0,3343,en_2825_495609_38082166_1_1_1_1,00.html.

Overall, J.U., & Marsh, H.W. (1980). Students' Evaluations of Instruction: A Longitudinal Study of Their Stability. *Journal of Educational Psychology*, 72, 321–325.

Pace, C.R. (1984). *Measuring the Quality of College Student Experiences*. Los Angeles, CA: The Center for the Study of Evaluation, Graduate School of Education, University of California, Los Angeles.

Pace, C.R. (1985). *The Credibility of Student Self-Reports*. Los Angeles, California: University of California, The Center for the Study of Evaluation, Graduate School of Education.

Pan, M. (2005). 中国大陆民办高等教育基本情况与发展中的若干问题 ['The Basic Situation and a Few Issues of Private Higher Education on Mainland China']. *Private Education Research (China)*, 2.

Parsons, T., & Platt, G.M. (1973). *The American University*. Cambridge: Harvard University Press.

Pascarella, E.T., Cruce, T., Umbach, P.D., Wolniak, G.C., Kuh, G.D., Carini, R.M., Hayek, J.C., et al. (2006). Institutional Selectivity and Good Practices in Undergraduate Education: How Strong Is the Link? *Journal of Higher Education* 77(2), 251–285.

Pascarella, E.T., Pierson, C.T., Wolniak, G.C., & Terenzini, P.T. (2004). First-Generation College Students: Additional Evidence on College Experiences and Outcomes. *Journal of Higher Education* 75(3), 249–284.

Pascarella, E.T., & Terenzini, P.T. (1991). *How College Affects Students: Findings and Insights from Twenty Years of Research*. San Francisco, CA: Jossey-Bass.

Pascarella, E.T., & Terenzini, P.T. (2006). *How College Affects Students: A Third Decade of Research*. San Francisco: Jossey-Bass.

Perellon, J.-F. (2003). The Creation of a Vocational Sector in Swiss Higher Education: Balancing Trends of System Differentiation and Integration. *European Journal of Education*, 38(4).

Phillips, D., & Zhong, Z. (2006). Comparative Education and Policy Borrowing. *Tsinghua Journal of Education (China)*, 2.

Pike, G.R. (1995). The Relationships between Self Reports of College Experiences and Achievement Test Scores. *Research in Higher Education*, 46, 1–22.

Pike, G.R. (2004). Measuring Quality: A Comparison of U.S. News Rankings and Nsse Benchmarks, 45, 2.

Pintrich, P.R., McKeachie, W.J., & Smith, D. (1989). *The Motivated Strategies for Learning Questionnaire*. Ann Arbor, MI: National Center for Research to Improve Teaching and Learning, University of Michigan.

Porter, M. (1980). *Competitive Strategy*. New York: Free Press.

Porter, M. (1985). *Competitive Advantage*. New York: Free Press.

Prebble, T., Hargraves, H., Leach, L., Naidoo, K., Suddaby, G., & Zepke, N. (2005). *Impact of Student Support Services and Academic Development Programes on Student Outcomes in Undergraduate Tertiary Study: A Synthesis of the Research*. New Zealand: Research Division, Ministry of Education.

Prosser, M. (2005). Why We Shouldn't Use Student Surveys of Teaching as Satisfaction Ratings. Retrieved 10 February, 2007, from http://www.heacademy.ac.uk/research/Interpretingstudentsurveys.doc.

Prosser, M., & Trigwell, K. (1999). *Understanding Teaching and Learning*. Buckingham: The Society for Research into Higher Education and Open University press.

Prosser, M., Trigwell, K., Hazel, E., & Gallagher, P. (1994). Students' Experiences of Teaching and Learning at the Topic Level. *Research and Development in Higher Education*, 16, 305–310.

Qing, M. (2005, 2 June 2005). Decision That Changed the Nation. *Shanghai Star (China).*

Ramsden, P. (1983). Institutional Variations in British Students' Approaches to Learning and Experiences of Teaching. *Higher Education*, 12, 671–705.

Ramsden, P. (1986). Students and Quality. In G.C. Moodie (Ed.), *Standards and Criteria in Higher Education.* Surrey: Society for Research into Higher Education and NFER-NELSON.

Ramsden, P. (1991). A Performance Indicator of Teaching Quality in Higher Education: The Course Experience Questionnaire. *Studies in Higher Education*, 16.

Ramsden, P. (1999). *The CEQ-Looking Back and Forward.* Paper presented at the Course Experience Questionnaire Symposium, Sydney.

Ramsden, P. (2003). *Learning to Teach in Higher Education. (2nd Edition).* London: Routledge Falmer.

Ramsden, P., & Entwistle, N. (1981). Effects of Academic Departments on Students' Approaches to Studying. *British Journal of Educational Psychology*, 51, 368–383.

Reay, D., David, M., & Ball., S. (2005). *Degrees of Choice. Social Class, Gender and Race in Higher Education.* Stoke-on-Trent: Trentham.

Remmers, H. (1963). Rating Methods in Research on Teaching. In N.L. Gage (Ed.), *Handbook of Research on Teaching.* Chicago, IL: Rand McNally.

Rhoades, G. (1990). Political Competition and Differentiation in Higher Education. In J.C. Alexander & P. Colomy (Eds.), *Differentiation Theory and Social Change.* New York: Columbia University Press.

Richardson, J.T.E. (1994). A British Evaluation of the Course Experience Questionnaire. *Studies in Higher Education*, 19.

Richardson, J.T.E. (2000). *Researching Student Learning: Approaches to Studying in Campus-Based and Distance Education.* Buckingham: SRHE/Open University Press.

Richardson, J.T.E. (2005a). Instruments for Obtaining Student Feedback: A Review of the Literature. *Assessment & Evaluation in Higher Education* 2005(4).

Richardson, J.T.E. (2005b). *National Student Survey: Interim Assessment of the 2005 Questionnaire.* Bristol: Higher Education Funding Council for England.

Richardson, J.T.E. (2005c). Students' Perceptions of Academic Quality and Approaches to Studying in Distance Education. *British Educational Research Journal*, 31(1), 7–27.

Riesman, D. (1956). *Constraint and Variety in American Education.* Lincoln: University of Nebraska Press.

Salili, F. (1996). Accepting Personal Responsibility for Learning. In J. Biggs & D. Watkins (Eds.), *The Chinese Learner: Culture, Psychological, and Contextual Influences.* Hong Kong: Comparative Centre, Faculty of Education, University of Hong Kong.

Samuelowicz, K. (1987). Learning Problems of Overseas Students: Two Sides of a Story. *Higher Education in Research and Development*, 6, 121–133.
Saroyan, A., & Amundsen, C. (2001). Evaluating University Teaching: Time to Take Stock. *Assessment and Evaluation in Higher Education*, 26(4), 337–349.
Sastry, T., & Bekhradnia, B. (2007). *The Academic Experience of Students in English Universities*. Oxford: Higher Education Policy Institute.
Schmitt, M. (1996). Uses and Abuses of Coefficient Alpha. *Psychological Assessment*, 8(4), 350–353.
Scott, P. (1996). Unified and Binary Systems of Higher Education in Europe. In A. Burgen (Ed.), *Goals and Purposes of Higher Education in the 21st Century* (pp. 37–54). London: Jessica Kingsley.
Shanghai Education Commission. (2005). *The Past, Present and Future of Education in Shanghai*. Paper presented at the Shanghai Education Forum.
Shi, Q., & Wang, A. (2008). On the Basic Characteristics of Applied Undergraduate Education. *Research in Educational Development (China)*, 21.
Skolnik, M.L. (1986). Diversity in Higher Education: The Canadian Case. *Higher Education in Europe*, 11, 19–32.
Smith, D. (Ed.). (1991). *The Confucian Continuum: Educational Modernization in Taiwan*. New York: Praeger Publishers.
Smith, P.J., & Smith, S.N. (1999). Differences between Chinese and Australian Students: Some Implications for Distance Educators. *Distance Education*, 20(1).
Society of Research in Higher Education. (2009). Student Experience Network Retrieved 6 April, 2009, from http://www.srhe.ac.uk/networks.sen.asp.
Spencer, K., & Schmelkin, L. (2002). Student Perspectives on Teaching and Its Evaluation. *Assessment and Evaluation in Higher Education*, 27(5), 397–409.
State Education Commission. (1986). *普通高等学校设置暂行条例 ['Provisions on Establishment of Higher Education Institutions']*. Beijing: State Education Commission.
Stenhouse, L. (1975). *An Introduction to Curriculum Research and Development*. London: Heinemann.
Su, Y., & Zhang, C. (2006). The Current Situation and Way-out of Our Country's Students' Loans. *China Market Retail Today (China)*, 14.
Sue, S., & Okazaki, S. (1990). Asian-American Educational Achievements: A Phenomenon in Search of an Explanation. *American Psychologist*, 45(8), 913–920
Sun, J. (2005). Pros and Cons of Examinations Self-Compiling. *Journal of Teaching and Management (China)*, 10.
Surridge, P. (2006). *The National Student Survey 2005: Findings*. Bristol: Higher Education Funding Council for England.
Surridge, P. (2008). *The National Student Survey 2005–2007: Findings and Trends: A Report to the Higher Education Funding Council for England*. Bristol: HEFCE.
Sutton Trust. (2004). *The Missing 3000: State School Students under-Represented at Leading Universities*. London: Sutton Trust.

Svensson, L. (1977). On Qualitative Differences in Learning: Study Skill and Learning. *British Journal of Educational Psychology*, 47, 233–243.

Tang, K. (1991). *Effects of Different Assessment Procedures on Tertiary Students' Approaches to Learning*. University of Hong Kong, Hong Kong.

Tang, M. (1999). 教育启动消费呼之欲出 ['Educational Spending Is Boosting']. *Jing Ji Xue Xiao Xi Bao (China)*, 1999.02.09.

Tang, M., & Zuo, X. (1998). 关于启动中国经济有效途径的思考-扩大高校招生一倍的建议 ['On the Effective Ways of Boosting the Chinese Economy – a Suggestion to Double Higher Education Enrolment']. *Can Kao Qing Yang (China)*, 1998.11.

Tang, M., & Zuo, X. (1999). 换个思路，大学扩招才能既有供给又有需求-与北大课题组商权 ['A Change of Mind- Higher Education Enrolment Expansion Boosts Supply and Demands – Discuss with the Project Team at Peking University']. *Jing Ji Xue Xiao Xi Bao (China)*, 1999.9.

Tashakkori, A., & Teddlie, C. (1998). *Mixed Methodology: Combining Qualitative and Quantitative Approaches*. Thousand Oaks, CA: Sage.

Taylor, J. (2003). Institutional Diversity in Uk Higher Education: Policy and Outcomes since the End of the Binary Divide. *Higher Education Quarterly*, 57(3), 266–293.

Teichler, U. (1998). The Changing Roles of the University and the Non-University Sectors. *European Review*, 6(4), 475–487.

Teichler, U. (2007). *Higher Education Systems: Conceptual Frameworks, Comparative Perspectives, Empirical Findings*. Rotterdam and Taipei: Sense Publishers.

Teichler, U. (2008). Diversification? Trends and Explanations of the Shape and Size of Higher Education. *Higher Education*, 56, 349–479.

Teixeira, P., & Amaral, A. (2001). Private Higher Education and Diversity: An Exploratory Survey. *Higher Education Quarterly*, 55(4), 359–395.

Terenzini, P. T., Springer, L., Pascarella, E. T., & Nora, A. (1995). Influences Affecting the Development of Students' Critical Thinking Skills. *Research in Higher Education*, 36(1).

The Economist. (2006). Chaos in the Classrooms: An Education Policy Torn between the Market and the State. *The Economist*, 10 August 2006.

Theall, M., & Franklin, J. (1990a). Student Ratings in the Context of Complex Evaluation Systems. In M. Theall & J. Franklin (Eds.), *Student Ratings of Instruction Tissues for Improving Practice. New Directions for Teaching and Learning*, No. 43. San Francisco: Jossey-Bass.

Theall, M., & Franklin, J. (Eds.). (1990b). *Student Ratings of Instruction: Issues for Improving Practice (Pp. 97–111). New Directions for Teaching and Learning, No. 43*. San Francisco: Jossey-Bass.

Thomas, S. L. (2000). The Ties That Bind: A Social Network Approach to Understanding Student Integration and Persistence. *The Journal of Higher Education*, 71, 591–615.

Times Higher Education. (2008). *The Top 200 World Universities*. London: Times Higher Education.

Tinto, V. (1993). *Leaving College: Rethinking the Causes and Cures of Student Attrition* (2 ed.). Chicago: University of Chicago Press.

Trigwell, K., & Ashwin, P. (2003). *Undergraduate Students' Experience of Learning at the University of Oxford*. Oxford: Institute for the Advancement of University Learning, University of Oxford.

Trigwell, K., & Prosser, M. (1991). Improving the Quality of Student Learning: The Influence of Learning Context and Student Approaches to Learning Outcomes. *Higher Education*, 22(3), 251–266.

Trow, M. (1973). *Problems in the Transition from Elite to Mass Higher Education*. Berkeley, California: Carnegie Commission on Higher Education.

Trow, M. (1979). *Elite and Mass Higher Education: American Models and European Realities*. Stockholm: National Board of Universities.

Trow, M. (2000). *From Mass Higher Education to Universal Access: The American Advantage*. Center for Studies in Higher Education: UC Berkeley.

Trow, M. (2005). *Reflections on the Transition from Elite to Mass to Universal Access: Forms and Phases of Higher Education in Modern Societies since WWII*. Berkeley, CA: University of California, Berkeley.

Tsinghua Admission Office. (2005). Information of Tsinghua University Admission. Retrieved 31 Jan, 2006, from http://www.tsinghua.edu.cn/chn/zsxx/.

UKCOSA. (2004). *International Students in UK Universities and Colleges: Broadening Our Horizons*. London: UKCOSA.

UNESCO. (1995). *Policy Paper for Change and Development in Higher Education*. Paris: UNESCO.

UNITE. (2005). *The Student Experience Report 2005*. Bristol: UNITE.

University of Buckingham. (2006). News: Buckingham's Success in National Student Survey 2006. Retrieved 19 February, 2007, from http://www.buckingham.ac.uk/news/newsarchive2006/nss-results.html.

University of Buckingham. (2008). The 2-Year Degree from http://www.buckingham.ac.uk/standingout/twoyear/.

van Vught, F. (1996). Isomorphism in Higher Education? Toward a Theory of Differentiation, Diversity in Higher Education Systems. In V.L. Meek, L. Goedegebuure, O. Kivinen & R. Rinne (Eds.), (pp. 42–58). Oxford: Pergamon/IAU Press.

van Vught, F. (2008). Mission Diversity and Reputation in Higher Education. *Higher Education Policy* 21, 151–174.

van Vught, F. (2009). Diversity and Differentiation in Higher Education In F. van Vught (Ed.), *Mapping the Higher Education Landscape: Towards a European Classification of Higher Education* (pp. 1–16). Dordrecht: Springer.

Vavra, T.G. (1997). *Improving Your Measurement of Customer Satisfaction: A Guide to Creating, Conducting, Analyzing, and Reporting Customer Satisfaction Measurement Programs*. Milwaukee, WI American Society for Quality.

Wang, S. (2006). To Pursue Essential Values of University Education – Trials and Practices of General Education Conducted in Fudan University. *Fudan Education Forum (China)*, 6.

Wang, Y. (2008). Generalist or Specialist: Two Different Aims of Higher Education. *Journal of Peking University (Philosophy and Social Sciences)*, 45(3), 5–15.

Watkins, D. (2001). Correlates of Approaches to Learning: A Cross-Cultural Meta-Analysis. In R. Sternberg & L. Zhang (Eds.), *Perspectives on Thinking, Learning, and Cognitive Styles*. Mahwah, NJ: Lawrence Erlbaum.

Watkins, D., & Biggs, J. (Eds.). (2001). *Teaching the Chinese Learner: Psychological and Pedagogical Perspectives*. Hong Kong: Comparative Education Research Centre.

Watkins, D., & Biggs, J.B. (Eds.). (1996). *The Chinese Learner: Cultural, Psychological and Contextual Influences*. Hong Kong: Comparative Education Research Centre.

Watkins, D., & Hattie, J. (1985). A Longitudinal Study of the Approaches to Learning of Australian Tertiary Students. *Human Learning*, 4, 127–141.

Weathersby, G.B. (1983). State Colleges in Transition. In J. Froomkin (Ed.), *The Crisis in Higher Education* New York: Academy of Political Science.

Weber, R.P. (1990). *Basic Content Analysis*. Newbury Park, CA: Sage Publications.

Whitman, N., & Weiss, E. (1982). *Faculty Evaluation: The Use of Explicit Criteria for Promotion, Retention and Tenure (Higher Education Report No. 2)*. Washington, DC: AAHE-ERIC.

Wielemans, W. (1988). The Labour Market as the Driving Force of Belgian Higher Education. *European Journal of Education*, 23, 77–90.

Wilson, K.L., Lizzio, A., & Ramsden, P. (1997). The Development, Validation and Application of the Course Experience Questionnaire. *Studies in Higher Education*, 22(1), 33–52.

Winn, S. (2002). Student Motivation: A Socio-Economic Perspective. *Studies in Higher Education*, 27(4), 445–457.

Xie, Y., & Goyette, K. (2003). Social Mobility and the Educational Choices of Asian Americans. *Social Science Research*, 32(3), 467–498.

Xinhuanet. (2005). Peking University "First in Asia". Is Times Kidding Chinese? Retrieved 6 Mar, 2007, from http://news.xinhuanet.com/school/2005-11/04/content_3729565_1.htm.

Xu, D. (2004, 9 Jun). Father Committed Suicide before Son's Exam. *Yanzhao Daily (China)*.

Xu, X. (2008). Applied Undergraduate Education – Diversification Strategy in Practical Background. *Journal of Jiangsu Higher Education (China)*, 4.

Yan, F., Zhuo, X., & Yu, J. (2006). System Changes in China's Massification of Higher Education. *Peking University Economics of Education Research (China)*, 4(3).

Yang, H., Ding, X., & Xi, G. (2004). Literature Review on the Studies of Training Management Conditions in Chinese Enterprises. *Scientific Management Research (China)*, 1.

Yang, M. (2005). On the Historical Transformation of Teacher's Authority in China. *Education Science Forum (China)*, 5.

Yang, Q. (2006). Survey Shows Demand of Graduates Falls. Retrieved 21 July, 2006, from http://news.sina.com.cn/c/2006-07-21/014510488177.shtml.

Ye, F., Zhong, Z., & Li, Y. (2006). An Critical Analysis of the World University Rankings by the Times Higher Education Supplement. *Tsinghua Journal of Education (China)*, 1.

Yin, Q., & Gordon, W. (1994). The 'Marketisation' of Chinese Higher Education: A Critical Assessment. *Comparative Education*, 30(3).

Yorke, M. (1996). *Indicators of Programme Quality*. London: Higher Education Quality Council.

Yu, K. (2005). *An Investigation of Students' Choice of Higher Education Institutions in China (Unpublished MSc dissertation)*. University of Oxford, Oxford.

Yu, K. (2008). Equity of Access to Higher Education: Lessons from Britain. *Fudan Education Forum (China)*, 3.

Yu, L. (2008). *Reform and Internationalization in the Move to Mass Higher Education*. Paper presented at the 5th International Workshop on Higher Education Reforms, East China Normal University, Shanghai.

Yu, L., & Suen, H. K. (2005). Historical and Contemporary Exam-Driven Education Fever in China. *KEDI Journal of Educational Policy*, 2(1), 17–33.

Yue, C., Wen, D., & Ding, X. (2004). An Empirical Study on the Employment Competition of Graduates. *Economics of Education Research (Beida)*, 2(2), 1–18.

Zemsky, R., Wegner, G., & Innozzi, M. (Eds.). (1997). *A Perspective on Privatization*. Phoenix: American Council on Education and the Oryx Press.

Zhang, D. (2000). Personal Disposable Income Is the Main Basis Determining Tuition Levels. *Education and Economics (China)*, 4.

Zhang, W. (2000). *Transforming China: Economic Reform and Its Political Implications*. New York: Macmillan Press.

Zhao, B., & Yao, W. (2004). General Education: An Inevitable Trend in University and College Education in Our Country. *Journal of Educational Science of Hunan Normal University (China)*, 3.

Zhao, C., & Zhu, M. (2007). Teacher Authority's Dispelling and Rebuilding on the Background of New Curriculum. *Forum on Contemporary Education*, 4.

Zhong, Z. (2005). *A Critical Analysis of Chinese Higher Education in the Context of Its Contribution to China's Development (Unpublished DPhil thesis)*. University of Oxford, Oxford.

Zhong, Z. (2006). A Critical Analysis of Chinese Higher Education in the Context of Its Contribution to China's Development. *Tsinghua Journal of Education (China)*, 4.

Zhongguo Zhiliang Wanlixing. (2007). 民办教育问题多 ['Problematic Private Education']. *Zhongguo Zhiliang Wanlixing (China)*, 7.
Zhou, J. (2003, 8 Jul). *Speak in Conference on Operation of Independent Colleges.* Paper presented at the Conference on operation of independent colleges (China), Beijing.
Zhou, J. (2006). *China's Journey to Mass Higher Education: A Historical Sketch.* Singapore: Thomson Learning.
Zong, L., Sun, S., Luo, Y., & Cao, W. (2007). Present Situation and Causes of the Repetition in Undergraduate Major Programs and Its Countermeasures. *Research in Educational Development (China)*, 23.
Zumeta, W. (1992). State Policies and Private Higher Education: Policies, Correlates, and Linkages. *Journal of Higher Education*, 63(4), 363–417.

Appendix A

Questionnaire – English Version

Unless otherwise specified, questions relating to the learning experiences refer to the modules of the degree programme of study, including *Zhuanye Ke* and *Gonggong Ke*, but do not include *Xuanxiu Ke*. Please mark the appropriate boxes with √ or answer the questions in words as instructed. Only one answer is allowed for each question.

Section One: Personal Information

1. The name of your subject is ______________________________
2. Your gender is 1 □ Male 2 □ Female
3. You come from _______ province. The place you come from is a
   1 □ *Shenghui Chengshi/Zhixiashi*; 2 □ *Dijishi*;
   3 □ *Xianjish;* 4 □ *Xiangzhen*; 5 □ *Nongcun*
4. Your National Exam grade was ____________, and you majored in 1 □ Arts 2 □ Science

Section Two: Expectations of the Experience of Higher Education

Motivations for Studying in Higher Education (Items)

5. I want to develop knowledge and skills I can use in a career
6. I hope the things I learn will help me to develop as a person and broaden my horizons.
7. I'm focused on the opportunities here for an active social life and/or sport

8. I hope the whole experience here will make me more independent and selfconfident.
9. I'm mainly here because I did well academically in the past.
10. I want to learn things which might let me help people, and make a difference in the world.
11. I want to study the subject in depth
12. I mainly need the qualification to enable me to get a good job when I finish
13. I want an opportunity to prove to myself or to other people what I can do
14. I am preparing to continue to postgraduate study after graduation

Section Three: Perceptions of Teaching

Course organisation and structure (Scale)

15. I understand the teaching goals in my subject
16. The actual teaching matches the goals of teaching
17. The overall teaching structure of the degree course (including *Zhuanye Ke* and *Gonggong Ke*) is well-designed.
18. The teaching activities (including theoretical classes, experiments classes, and practical classes) are closely related and support each other

Class Teaching (Scale)

19. The teaching staff is always well prepared for classes
20. The teaching staff always explain the contents of modules
21. The teaching staff always make the teaching interesting
22. The teaching staff always use examples and illustrations
23. The teaching staff always use technologies to support teaching
24. The teaching staff is always prepared to answer students' questions after class
25. The teaching staff always value students' thoughts and suggestions

Learning environment (Scale)

26. Teachers and course directors have high demands on students' studies
27. My classmates study very hard
28. My classmates often discuss academic problems with each other
29. My classmates are co-operative and companionate

Learning resources (Scale)

30. The textbooks or teaching materials of my courses are very helpful to my learning
31. The teaching equipment (e.g. computers, labs) is helpful to my learning
32. The library resources and services are helpful to my learning
33. Online resources (e.g. teacher's website, subject's website, department's website) are helpful to my learning
34. The institution provides convenient and ample learning resources (public computers, information resources, etc.)

Xuanxiu Ke (Scale)

35. I think the learning in *Xuanxiu Ke* is very significant
36. The teaching staff of *Xuanxiu Ke* take the teaching very seriously
37. My classmates take the *Xuanxiu Ke* very seriously

Section Four: Orientations of Teaching

Emphasis of Teaching

38. The subject teaching emphasises *memorising* knowledge
39. The subject teaching emphasises *analysing* knowledge
40. The subject teaching emphasises *making judgements* of information
41. The subject teaching emphasises *applying* knowledge

Teaching – Academic Orientation

42. The foundational and subject teaching of *Gonggong Ke* and *Zhuanye Ke* can help me establish an understanding of the theoretical system of my subject
43. We are offered the opportunities to see the current development and advanced knowledge of my subject

Teaching – Practical Orientation

44. The subject teaching contains practical elements and stresses the formation of practical skills of students
45. The practical elements form an important part of the student assessment
46. The teaching stresses foreign language and information (like Internet and Computer) skills that are relevant to the subject

Teaching – General Orientation

47. The teaching is organised in a manner that encourages interaction between different subjects
48. Teachers do not only teach subject knowledge, but also stress the development of learning to learn skills
49. The teaching aims to develop students' values and ethics

Section Five: Learning Approaches

50. I feel a sense of satisfaction and achieving when gaining new knowledge and skills
51. I feel learning subject knowledge or skills is like reading an interesting novel or watching an interesting film
52. I use my spare time to look for subject information I am interested in on my own initiativc
53. I find that I can connect the knowledge and skills I learned in class with real life situations or use the knowledge and skills to deal with practical problems

54. I think doing coursework is not only finishing the teacher's tasks, it is more about deepening understanding of knowledge
55. I often answer or ask questions in class or group discussion
56. I am not interested in the subject I am studying at all
57. My goal is to pass the examination with minimum efforts
58. I think it is meaningless to spend time studying knowledge that is not to be examined
59. I think it is unnecessary to go too deep into studying, as it wastes time and makes people more confused
60. I think it is more important to memorise the knowledge rather than understanding it

Section Six: Others

Self-Evaluation (Items)

61. I always complete the coursework assignments on time
62. I always complete the coursework assignments to a high level of quality
63. I master the knowledge and skills taught by teachers and books
64. I am fully confident that my studies will provide me with good career prospects

Overall Experience (Items)

65. I think the educational and social experience at this institution is excellent.
66. If I could start all over again, I definitely would go to the same institution I am now attending.

Time on Studying

67. How many hours of time-tabled sessions do you have scheduled by your institution in an average week during term-time? ____Hours
    Please include time spent in lectures, tutorials, seminars, supervised practical work. Don't worry if you can't be precise, just try to give a reasonable average.

68. About how many hours of these do you attend in the average week? ____ Hours

69. In an average week during term-time, roughly how many hours do you spend on private study? ____ Hours
Please include time spent reading, researching, writing essays and reports, etc.

70. Are you currently a committee member of an extracurricular organisation at the institution? 1 □ No; 2 □ Yes

Section Seven: Family Background

71. Your father's highest formal educational qualification is ________, your mother's highest formal educational qualification is ________.
    (1) Did not graduate from Primary School
    (2) Graduated from Primary School
    (3) Graduated from Junior Secondary School
    (4) Graduated from Senior Secondary School
    (5) Graduated from *Zhuanke*
    (6) Graduated from *Benke*
    (7) Postgraduate Graduate

72. Your father's current occupation is ___________, your mother's current occupation is ___________.
    (1) Official Administrative Personnel
    (2) Managerial
    (3) Public Authority Clerk
    (4) Professional
    (5) Home/Small Business Owner
    (6) Staff in Business/Service Industry
    (7) Private Business Owner
    (8) Industrial Worker
    (9) Off-farm worker
    (10) Farmer
    (11) Retired

(12) Unemployed
(13) Other ________________

73. How concerned are you about your or your family's ability to finance your current education
1☐Not concerned 2☐Somewhat concerned 3☐Very concerned

Section Eight: Open-ended Questions (Optional)

74. What do you like most about your institution?
75. In your opinion, what could your institution do to improve your learning experience?

Appendix B

Interview Schedules

Interview Instrument for Presidents/Provosts/Directors of Study

1. What is the profile of *Benke* teachers at your institution?
   a) What academic qualifications and professional title do they have?
   b) How many of them work part-time? Where else do they work at?
   c) Is there any preference for recruiting teachers from certain groups? Like gender, age, professional qualifications? What is the justification for this preference?

2. What is the profile of *Benke* course directors at your institution?
   a) Are they full-time course directors or do they also have teaching responsibility?
   b) Does your institution "manage" students? e.g. set formal requirements for class attendance

3. How would you describe your *Benke* programmes?
   a) How would you describe the teaching contents and methodology of your *Benke* programmes?
   b) Are there any special characteristics of your *Benke* programmes that make them distinct?
   c) What kind of courses this institution would like to offer? Is there any role model/target institution for this institution?

4. How would you describe the teaching facilities and learning resources of your institution?

5. How does your institution regard students' employment after graduation?
   a) How is this reflected in the teaching of *Benke* students?
   b) How is this reflected in the career office's work?
   c) Do you think it is the institution's responsibility to get graduates employed?

6. What is the balance between general/moral education and application/practice education in *Benke* teaching at your institution?
   a) What is the philosophy behind this?
   b) Do you have sufficient software and hardware resources to successfully implement this philosophy?
   c) How is this philosophy regarded by your teachers, students and students' employers?

7. How is the performance of *Benke* teachers evaluated?
   a) Is there student input in the evaluation process? How do you respond to the students' voice?
   b) Is there employer input in the evaluation process? How do you respond to the market's needs?

Interview Instrument for *Benke* Teachers

1. What module and course do you teach?

2. Have you taught at other institutions? Which one?
   a) Can you tell any difference in your experience at different institutions? e.g. teaching philosophy, management, students

3. Do you set formal requirements for students' class attendance? Why?

4. Does your module include lab/experiment/practical elements?
   a) How important are these elements?
   b) How are these element taught and assessed?

c) Do you take the market needs into consideration in determining the contents of these elements?
d) How often do you review or update the contents of these elements?
e) Do you think it is important to have these practical elements alongside class/theoretical teaching? Why?

5. What is the balance between general/moral education and application/practice education in *Benke* teaching at your institution?
   a) Does your institution have a philosophy or strategy behind this?
   b) Can you successfully implement this philosophy in your teaching?
   c) How is this philosophy regarded by your colleagues, students and students' employers?

6. Do you have sufficient support for your teaching? e.g. teaching facilities, library resources, training

7. How would you describe your *Benke* teaching?
   a) How would you describe the teaching contents and methodology of you teaching?
   b) Are there any special characteristics of your *Benke* teaching that make them distinct?
   c) What kind of teaching do you want to offer? Do you have any role model/target course or teacher outside this institution?

8. How is your teaching evaluated?

Zhijian Tao

Drawing the Dragon

Western European Reinvention of China

Bern, Berlin, Bruxelles, Frankfurt am Main, New York, Oxford, Wien, 2009.
233 pp., 4 ill.
Euro-Sinica. Bd. 12
Herausgegeben von Adrian Hsia
ISBN 978-3-03911-812-0 pb.
sFr. 65.– / €* 44.80 / €** 46.10 / € 41.90 / £ 31.40 / US-$ 64.95
* includes VAT – valid for Germany ** includes VAT – valid for Austria

The Western reinvention of China can be found in various discourses ranging from French Enlightenment philosophes, German political economists, to British writers through centuries. It covers all aspects of Chinese culture, and varies from zealous idealization to blatant demonization.

But do those divergent and even contradictory accounts offer an alternative to «Orientalism?» Or are they artifacts with inherent and even dangerous limitations? More fundamentally, does the cultural theory of Orientalism provide an adequate basis for cross-cultural studies? This study examines conflicting 18th- and 19th-century European presentations of China and the inherent consistency in them. It also critiques contending positions on major cultural theories and contributes distinct and dynamic perspectives in the field of cross-cultural studies.

Contents: The Long and the Dragon – Contending Positions on «Orientalism» – Sir John Mandeville and His Exotic Desires – Scope of Study – Enlightenment: The Problem of Civility and Government: Leibniz's Hallucinations - Montesquieu: An Opposite View – Imperialism. Theoretical Foundations: Hegel: China and World History - Tragic Contradiction: China and Political Economy - The Encyclopaedic Vision – Practical Imperialism and the Literary Culture: Goldsmith: Portrait of a Citizen - Coleridge's Reveries - Landor's Caricatures - De Quincey: Opium and Power - Cartoons in Punch – Picturing the Dao. «Other» than Logocentrism?: Derrida's Use of the Pictographic Poetics - The Mist around the Chinese Script - The Dao and the Logos - Dao and Différance – Toward a Cultural Dialogue.

PETER LANG
Bern · Berlin · Bruxelles · Frankfurt am Main · New York · Oxford · Wien